SARAH JOHNSON'S MOUNT VERNON

Sarah Johnson's

THE FORGOTTEN HISTORY

Mount Vernon

OF AN AMERICAN SHRINE

Scott E. Casper

ⓦ HILL AND WANG

A DIVISION OF FARRAR, STRAUS AND GIROUX

NEW YORK

Hill and Wang
A division of Farrar, Straus and Giroux
18 West 18th Street, New York 10011

The Library of Congress has cataloged the hardcover edition as follows:
Casper, Scott E.
    Sarah Johnson's Mount Vernon : the forgotten history of an American
shrine / Scott E. Casper.—1st ed.
        p.   cm.
    Includes bibliographical references and index.
    ISBN-13: 978-0-8090-8414-2 (hardcover : alk. paper)
    ISBN-10: 0-8090-8414-7 (hardcover : alk. paper)
        1. African Americans—Virginia—Mount Vernon (Estate)—History—
19th century. 2. African Americans—Virginia—Mount Vernon (Estate)—
Biography. 3. African American families—Virginia—Mount Vernon (Estate)—
History—19th century. 4. Mount Vernon (Va. : Estate)—History—19th century.
5. Mount Vernon (Va. : Estate)—Biography. 6. Plantation life—Virginia—
Mount Vernon—History—19th century. 7. Mount Vernon (Va.)—Social life and
customs—19th century. 8. Mount Vernon (Va.)—Race relations—History—
19th century.   I. Title.

E312.5.C37   2008
973.4'1092—dc22

                                                              2007009348

Paperback ISBN-13: 978-0-8090-8415-9
Paperback ISBN-10: 0-8090-8415-5

Designed by Jonathan D. Lippincott

www.fsgbooks.com

1   3   5   7   9   10   8   6   4   2

for Tracy and Andrew

CONTENTS

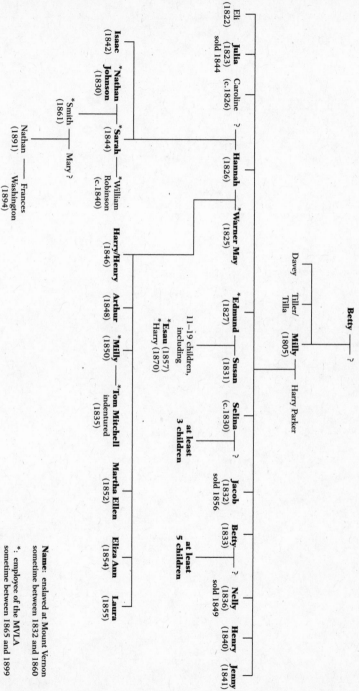

Sarah Johnson's Family

Name: enslaved at Mount Vernon
sometime between 1832 and 1860

*: employee of the MVLA
sometime between 1865 and 1899

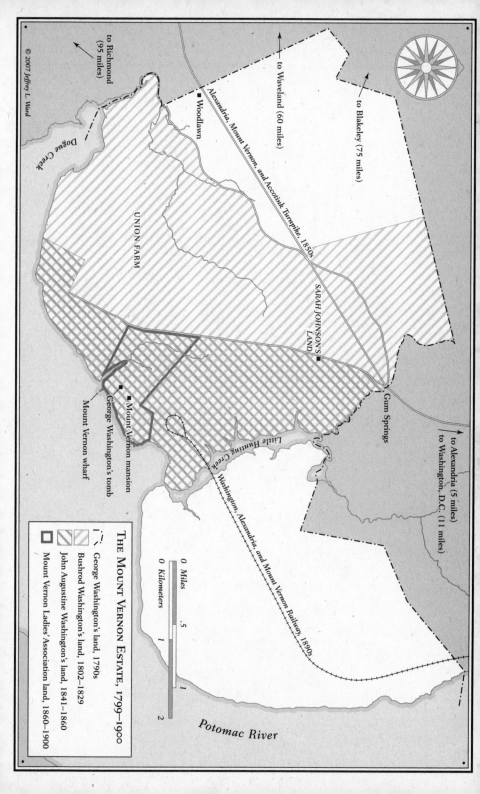

© 2007 Jeffrey L. Ward

to Richmond (95 miles)

to Waveland (60 miles)

to Blakeley (75 miles)

Dogue Creek

Woodlawn

Alexandria, Mount Vernon, and Accotink Turnpike, 1850s

UNION FARM

SARAH JOHNSON'S LAND

Gum Springs

to Alexandria (5 miles)
to Washington, D.C. (11 miles)

George Washington's tomb

Mount Vernon mansion

Mount Vernon wharf

Little Hunting Creek

Washington, Alexandria, and Mount Vernon Railway, 1890s

Potomac River

THE MOUNT VERNON ESTATE, 1799–1900

George Washington's land, 1790s
Bushrod Washington's land, 1802–1829
John Augustine Washington's land, 1841–1860
Mount Vernon Ladies' Association land, 1860–1900

0 Miles   .5   1

0 Kilometers   1   2

SARAH JOHNSON'S MOUNT VERNON

Forever Old, Forever New

On January 27, 1920, the American flag at Mount Vernon flew at half-mast, in memory of a black woman. Visitors that Tuesday would never have guessed whom it honored: a former slave, who had lived long ago in one of the little whitewashed houses to the right of George Washington's mansion. They could easily mistake the lowered Stars and Stripes for a perpetual tribute to the Father of His Country, entombed a few hundred yards away. The superintendent who ordered the gesture that day meant no statement about racial equality. In his words, the flag commemorated a "faithful ex-servant of M.V.," a woman who had earned respect by knowing her place.[1]

Thirty years earlier nobody knew Mount Vernon better than Sarah Johnson. She had lived there almost half a century by then, longer than even Martha Washington had. Born to a teenage mother in 1844, Sarah grew up surrounded by kin, celebrated the births of new siblings and cousins, grieved for relatives sold away. She trained from childhood for a lifetime of domestic service, but not the one she got. After the Civil War she returned to Mount Vernon as a wife, a mother, and an employee of America's pioneer association for historic preservation. Washing, cooking, and tending the chickens, she drew upon lessons from slavery days, now for a monthly wage and a public audience. Sarah Johnson played a featured role in the Mount Vernon that visitors saw, as she courteously sold them milk for five cents a glass. Behind the scenes she won the confidence and the friendship of the wealthy white women who owned the place and were restoring its eighteenth-century appearance. Neither the visitors nor the Mount Vernon Ladies' Association knew much about Sarah's other world, a community off the historic site's two hundred acres. Sarah attended church, sent her son to school, and enjoyed a network of friends and kinfolk in the black neighborhood beyond Mount Vernon's fences. After she resigned her position in 1892, she did not go far. She used her earnings to buy a farm, four acres of the seventy-six hundred that had once belonged to George Washington.

Mount Vernon's flag remained at half-mast until noon on Wednesday, January 28, the day Sarah's black neighbors laid her to rest in their cemetery four miles away. Only one Mount Vernon employee, a black gardener in his mideighties, took time off to attend her funeral. By 1920 almost everyone else working there was white. Few of them had known Sarah, whose final residence was a segregated nursing home for the indigent in Washington, D.C. Nobody then at Mount Vernon could have told visitors about the odyssey of Sarah's seventy-five years, but visitors did not come to hear that story anyway. They had come for George Washington's Mount Vernon, which evoked the Father of His Country and his eighteenth-century world. Sarah Johnson's Mount Vernon was being obliterated, a nineteenth-century place erased by Jim Crow and historic preservation.

One hundred and twenty winters earlier an entire nation had mourned for George Washington. America's founding father died in his bed on December 14, 1799, surrounded by his wife, three doctors, and several slaves. His funeral procession at Mount Vernon numbered more than two hundred people, beginning with military companies and ending with a multitude that included his farm manager, his overseers, and some of his slaves. Cities and towns across the United States staged their own reenactments of Washington's funeral. Their ministers preached sermons on the life and character of America's departed hero. Their citizens marched in processions of riderless horses, local dignitaries, somber musicians, and pallbearers, everything except a corpse. Homage to Washington endured long after the official mourning period ended on what would have been his sixty-eighth birthday in February 1800. His remains, interred in the family tomb overlooking the Potomac

River, became a pilgrimage shrine, an American Mecca or Westminster Abbey. Americans' tears moistened "the sod that presses upon his bosom," one writer rhapsodized. Wandering the grounds and floorboards that Washington once trod, visitors imagined a world where time stood still.[2]

Time had not stopped for the people who still lived there, especially the 316 slaves Washington had counted a few months before he died. The people he owned outright, 123 in all, would soon win freedom. By Washington's last will and testament, they were to be emancipated upon Martha's death, the old and infirm among them clothed and fed for as long as they lived, and the children without parents taught to read and write and educated in "some useful occupation." Martha felt great affection for many of these slaves but, Abigail Adams reported, "did not feel as tho her Life was safe in their hands." Would people destined for freedom upon her death seize a chance to hasten that event? After rumors of an attempted fire, Martha emancipated them early, on New Year's Day 1801. Some of them remained at or near Mount Vernon as paid workers or pensioners. Washington's revolutionary-era body servant William Lee, singled out in the will for immediate freedom, became a minor celebrity, garrulous in his reminiscences of the general. In 1835, after Washington's remains had been moved from their original resting place to a new tomb uphill, eleven black men were seen leveling the ground for a brick mausoleum at the new site, while a black woman brought them food and water. All of them owed their freedom to George Washington, either directly or because he had freed their mothers. They said that they volunteered their services on "this last melancholy occasion." They labored that day for their liberator's memory, not for his kin.[3]

The rest of George Washington's slaves were less fortunate, because they were not legally his. Most of them, or their forebears, had belonged to Martha Washington's first husband. After she died in May 1802, they were divided among her four grandchildren. Some of these "dower slaves" remained on Mount Vernon land. Martha's granddaughter Nelly Custis had married George's nephew Lawrence Lewis, who inherited one of Washington's five Mount Vernon farms just two miles from the mansion house. Her grandson George Washington Parke Custis built a mansion outside Alexandria, nine miles from Mount

Vernon, and his share of the dower slaves formed the basis of a black community that persisted for generations at Arlington House, better known today as the home of Custis's son-in-law Robert E. Lee. The other dower slaves were taken farther away, to Washington, D.C., and some were sold.[4]

Over the next sixty years an entirely new community of African Americans peopled Mount Vernon. This book tells their story. The term "Mount Vernon" referred to a diminishing estate because Washington heirs to the mansion and tomb received successively less of the surrounding acreage with each generation. George Washington bequeathed about half his Mount Vernon land to his nephew Bushrod, but nobody to work the farm or serve the household. Bushrod Washington brought to Mount Vernon black families he had inherited from his own parents' estate, along with others he had purchased himself. After he died and his estate was divided, fewer than a dozen of those slaves remained at Mount Vernon. So the subsequent Washington heirs transplanted more people there, including the teenage girl who became Sarah Johnson's mother. Over two decades the community multiplied to more than seventy-five men, women, and children.[5] The Mount Vernon Ladies' Association, which bought two hundred acres in 1860, hired some of these people when the Civil War ended. They returned as free people to the place that had become their home, and the site of their enslavement, only after George Washington died.

These African Americans made history at Mount Vernon, in two senses. For the thousands of people, overwhelmingly white, who sojourned there every year, they evoked and preserved George Washington's world—a past that neither they nor their ancestors had known in that place. Visitors imagined Mount Vernon as an oasis of constancy amid disquieting national change. Whether they came overland through forests and across unbridged brooks or took the steamboat down the Potomac, travelers put metaphorical as well as physical distance between their ordinary lives and their hallowed destination. Mount Vernon was a national shrine, site of reverent pilgrimage. It seemed also a self-contained universe, a microcosm of a mythic harmonious, preindustrial America where Washington's guiding hand benevolently governed the domestic and agricultural spheres. By their words and by their very presence, black slaves before the Civil War and black employees after it contributed to the impression that Mount Vernon belonged to the past. Rather than challenge visitors' most common misconception, that they or their parents had belonged to George Washington, they became the keepers of his tomb and memory and earned coins and accolades for their borrowed reminiscences.[6]

Paradoxically, Sarah Johnson and her community also made history by forging distinctly nineteenth-century lives at this supposedly eighteenth-century place. The kin networks transplanted there in the early 1800s persisted for three generations on the hallowed grounds and in the surrounding black neighborhood, a local world of social and economic relations that travelers rarely saw. Mount Vernon's African Americans were thoroughly immersed in the same contemporary issues that visitors came to escape: commercial speculation; labor unrest; the conflict over slavery; black people's quest for equality and opportunity. Their Mount Vernon was no island, enclosed by the fences around the historic area. To people who had grown up on the Washingtons' plantation, even the term "Mount Vernon" denoted something different from the diminished area the visitors and the Mount Vernon Ladies' Association knew. African Americans' neighborhood stretched across the surrounding countryside, on and off the main roads, all the way to Alexandria. Their Mount Vernon was embedded at once in a fabled national geography and a local terrain of everyday life, in an imagined, fixed past and an all-too-real changeable present. In the words of an 1879 travel book, Mount Vernon was "forever new, yet forever old."[7]

The flag that flew for Sarah Johnson in 1920 marked the end of an era that had taken a century to forge and a few decades to dismantle. At the same time, the star-spangled banner, like Mount Vernon itself, symbolized an enduring mythic national identity, a set of stories about national origins and heroes, rooted in the eighteenth-century past even if the stars had multiplied from thirteen to forty-eight. The history of Sarah Johnson's Mount Vernon belies the national imagination, but it is a story no less American. It is a story not just of Washingtons but also of black people named Parker and Smith, Johnson and Ford. It is the sort of story Sarah and her contemporaries might have told their friends and their children, not the one the tourists usually heard.

ONE

Oliver Smith's Memories

To most visitors, Oliver Smith was the slave who had seen George Washington die. Again and again, pilgrims to Washington's tomb in the 1830s described this "venerable colored man" in his seventies, whose gray hair alone suggested an authentic connection to the past. One writer claimed to repeat Smith's own words: he was "as familiar with the General as with the palms of his own hands." Oliver Smith told of Washington's character and habits, so methodical and exacting that the slaves respected him better than they liked him. On the piazza of the mansion, overlooking the Potomac, Smith reminded visitors that Washington had walked the same floorboards. Most compellingly, he described George Washington's last day on earth. He was there when the general breathed his last, Smith explained. Tears in his eyes, he told of his own "deserted and desolate" present condition, and he "hobbled onwards . . . talking continually of time gone by."[1] There was only one problem with his story: Oliver Smith had come to Mount Vernon in 1802, three years after George Washington's death, with Washington's nephew Bushrod. He got his knowledge secondhand, from one of the slaves present at the deathbed.

Oliver Smith told an utterly different story to an abolitionist traveler in 1834. He had been Bushrod Washington's pet, he explained, and now belonged to Bushrod's niece Jane Washington, the new owner of Mount Vernon. He had had nine children, one of them now Mount Vernon's gardener and two dead. Where were the other six? inquired the writer. "Sold into Georgia." Wasn't it hard to part with them? "O, it was like cutting off my own limbs," Smith replied, almost in tears. Smith's sense of desertion and desolation had another cause entirely. His own children were gone, sold by Bushrod Washington's heirs. In the day of judgment, he opined, all of America's slaves would appear before the bar, and slaveholders would have to answer for their sins.[2]

It is fair to take Oliver Smith at his word—his family's dispersal felt akin to dismemberment in every sense. At the same time, Smith was an expert in fulfilling visitors' fantasies of Mount Vernon. No other recorded encounter with him suggests such a protest against the institution of slavery or even discloses his family's story. Nor was he telling the abolitionist writer everything. Like thousands of other slaves across the South who learned early to assume different faces for different listeners, Oliver Smith had alternate scripts for encounters with Mount Vernon's visitors. He calibrated those versions of the past to the scripts that visitors brought with them. No matter what he said, however, Smith's very presence belied the fundamental incongruity of his standard script. If George Washington had famously freed his slaves, why were people still enslaved at Mount Vernon?

The story of Oliver Smith's family begins to reveal the answer. When he was born around 1760, Oliver belonged not to George Washington but to his brother John Augustine, commonly called Jack. Jack Washington and his wife, Hannah Bushrod, lived at Bushfield plantation in Westmoreland County, ninety-five miles southeast of Mount Vernon in Virginia's tidewater. They owned more than 130 slaves by the early 1780s, when their eldest son, Bushrod, approached adulthood and Oliver and his wife, Doll, became his personal servants. As a "waiting man" Oliver Smith was Bushrod's closest attendant, seeing to his master's needs and running errands near and far. After Jack died in 1787, Bushrod Washington legally inherited Oliver and Doll and thus any children they would have, beginning with a son named Phil in 1790. Bushrod brought the Smiths to live with him when he inherited Mount Vernon from his uncle George. He also brought another family, its anchors a woman named Sinah (born in 1761) and her brother Ham (1773), also inherited from Jack and Hannah Washington's estate. Sinah and her husband, Joe, another Bushfield house servant, had eight children, two sons-in-law, and eleven grandchildren at Mount Vernon by 1815. Ham and his wife, Pat, started their family there with a son in 1807 and three more children in the next eight years. Sinah, Ham, and their family lived at Union Farm, one of the outlying Mount Vernon farms that Bushrod inherited along with the "mansion house" property. About half of his slaves, seventy-nine in all in 1815, including people he had purchased from relatives and neighbors, lived and worked there.[3]

In the two decades between 1815 and the abolitionist's visit, three dramatic events reshaped the contours of Oliver Smith's family and community: a massive, traumatic slave sale; an apparent crime and its grueling aftermath; and finally the dismantling of Bushrod Washington's estate. By the 1830s, when he guided visitors around Mount Vernon, Oliver had become the place's foremost living, speaking link to two pasts: George Washington's world and the saga of his own broken family.

Bushrod Washington was bound to suffer by comparison with his uncle. An 1823 visitor estimated Bushrod "as unlike the General, as any man in the United States." He was short, slight, pale-faced, and blind in one eye, the result of overwork. One observer thought he looked "nervous and feeble." Another called him "a little dryed up Virginian." In two deeper ways, though, he resembled George Washington. Both men devoted enormous care to raising children not their own. Much as George had superintended and loved Martha's children Jacky and Patsy Custis and then Jacky's children Nelly and Wash, Bushrod made Mount Vernon a home for at least a half dozen orphaned nieces and nephews. George Washington and Bushrod Washington also shared a commitment to public service. After enlisting in the Revolutionary War, Bushrod studied law with James Wilson, one of the new nation's foremost legal minds and a leader at the 1787 Constitutional Convention. Bushrod was elected to the Virginia General Assembly in 1787 and to the state's ratifying convention for the Constitution a year later. His legal work in the 1790s earned wide admiration, and in 1798 President John Adams offered him Wilson's seat on the Supreme Court after John Marshall declined it. Washington and Marshall, who became chief justice three years later, had been friends since their college days at William and Mary. Together they formed the bulwark of the Federalist Supreme Court that affirmed a strong national government in the nation's fledgling years. Appointed at thirty-six, Bushrod Washington was one of the youngest justices in American history, and he served one of the longest tenures, thirty-one years.[4]

In two other ways, uncle and nephew differed significantly. First, Bushrod was a lawyer, not a farmer. When he died, his books and pamphlets were appraised at $5,553.75, more than double the value of all the work animals, livestock, crops, and farm equipment at Mount Vernon combined. He lived away from home most of the year because justices of the Supreme Court were required to sit with the federal circuit courts and Bushrod made his circuit in Philadelphia and New Jersey. Judicial duties, his work as an executor of his uncle's will, and guardianship of nieces and nephews all crowded agricultural management from Bushrod's attention.[5] George Washington, by contrast, had known every detail of the farms: when to accomplish any task; how to make best use of slave labor; how many bricks it would take to build a sixteen-sided barn. George Washington's care saved Mount Vernon from the fate of so many other Virginia estates (notably Thomas Jefferson's Monticello), deep indebtedness and ultimately sale.

Even if Bushrod had been a farmer, his hand would have been far weaker than his uncle's. Northern Virginia had entered an agricultural decline years before George Washington died. Tobacco farming had exhausted the soil. Washington and other planters began shifting to grain production as early as the 1760s, but the land still worsened with each passing year. Moreover, planters divided their estates among multiple heirs, creating ever-smaller holdings. If a planter failed to leave a will, his land was divided anyway because Virginia in 1785 had abolished primogeniture, the ancient custom that kept estates whole by passing them to the eldest son. Bushrod Washington, who inherited about four thousand acres of his uncle's seventy-six hundred, found it nearly impossible to make ends meet at Mount Vernon. Some years he even sold land to buy corn to feed the slaves, reversing the normal economy in which slaves produced their essential foodstuffs along with cash crops. In such circumstances, slaves themselves could become a plantation's most valuable, marketable commodity. As the cotton frontier grew to the southwest, slaves became eastern Virginia's greatest export from early in the nineteenth century.[6]

With the division of old fortunes and the new generation's economic travails, the lifestyle of the Old Dominion's gentry was changing. These transformations help account for the second major difference between Bushrod Washington and his uncle: George Washington's religious belief was largely a private matter, while Bushrod remained deeply religious in private and public. Bushrod preferred domestic life to his worldly career. He led family prayers at Mount Vernon, morning and evening, and that "family" included household slaves. Librarian of Congress George Watterston in 1818 described Judge Washington in these terms: "He appears to be one of those men to whom the pleasures of the domestic circle are more seducing than the fitful tho' captivating splendor which surround the temples of the statesman or the warrior, and he prefers what the world would term the inglorious repose of domestic felicity to the fevorish [sic] agitation and sickly turmoil of public life."[7]

Living at Mount Vernon inevitably subjected Judge Washington to another kind of public life, the endless scrutiny of visitors. George Washington had made his own private life into "a perpetual performance for the touring public." The Father of His Country courteously entertained scores of strangers, creating a routine that included tours conducted by family members or aides and meals at which he presided. Bushrod Washington had neither political reason nor personal inclination nor money enough to follow his uncle's lead. Still, the travelers came, as a pilgrimage to Mount Vernon became part of any visit to Washington, D.C. If admitted to the mansion, they admired the few possessions of George Washington's that remained once the Custis grandchildren had taken most of the furnishings: the key to the Bastille prison in Paris, which was a gift from Lafayette, and an ornately carved marble mantelpiece in the large dining room. All visitors saw Washington's tomb, an old family vault built into the side of a hill. Shaded by cedars, it looked like an icehouse to some, an oven to others, and a dog kennel to still others. No matter: it was sacred space, Mount Vernon's Holy Grail. Americans and foreigners alike experienced reverie and reverence there, imagining Washington's spirit and paying homage to his memory. Taking relics was part of any pilgrimage. One traveler had to reach high to pluck a cedar branch because others had already stripped all the low-hanging boughs and leaves. Until Bushrod had the tomb padlocked in the 1810s, visitors commonly tore pieces from the cloth over Washington's coffin. The expense and maintenance of the entire pilgrimage site fell to Judge Washington.[8]

Bushrod received undue blame for Mount Vernon's unkempt state. Few travelers blamed themselves for tramping over the grounds and picking relics at will. Fewer acknowledged the underlying difficulties that plagued Judge Washington and his neighbors. Thomas Cope, a Quaker merchant, blamed slavery, "that pest to improvement," and believed that smaller, single-family farms would produce richer crops despite the sterile soil. Other travelers lumped slaves into their descriptions of Mount Vernon's ruined state. "Negroes of all ages" milled about, and they seemed "miserable looking objects living in dirty houses," the "dirty, homely, and tattered children" worst of all. Over time Bushrod set boundaries that his uncle had not. Above all, he attempted to ban Sunday visitation, even turning away a party of congressmen. One Sunday traveler, an Englishman, wrote that the judge "received us coldly and reluctantly" and said, "I do not like to see people on this day, but you may walk round."[9]

Religious belief fueled Bushrod Washington's public commitments off the bench as well, placing him in the forefront of an emerging cluster of benevolent reform movements. His name became virtually synonymous with the movement to create African colonies of free American blacks. The antislavery fervor of the 1770s and 1780s cooled quickly in the new century, in the wake of slave revolts successful (blacks' overthrow of slavery in St. Domingue) and not (Gabriel's Rebellion in Richmond in 1800). Advocates of colonization were a mixed lot. Some opposed slavery on moral or religious grounds. Others, including Bushrod's godson Charles Fenton Mercer, argued that a slave labor economy stunted the growth of a more productive capitalist system. Many of them coalesced in the American Colonization Society, founded in 1816 with the support of such leading slaveowner-statesmen as Henry Clay and James Madison. Bushrod Washington became its founding president, served until he died, and afforded the society immediate national legitimacy.[10]

Judge Washington's name became attached to republican and religious arguments for colonization. An 1817 memorial to Congress suggested that free people of color were becoming a separate caste in a nation built on the ideal of equality. Free blacks were deprived of the social and political rights that fostered human betterment, especially as state after state evicted newly manumitted African Americans. In Africa, however, free black people would gain ample sphere for their "pursuit of happiness and independence" and diffuse the blessings of Christianity "through the vast regions and unnumbered tribes, yet obscured in primeval darkness." When a Liverpool merchant and abolitionist visited Mount Vernon in January 1820, Judge Washington explained the movement primarily as an "instrument in the conversion of Africans to Christianity," a step toward establishing "the kingdom of the Messiah in every quarter of the globe."[11]

The Liverpool visitor was not so sure, and neither were Bushrod's slaves. Removing free blacks, the Englishman replied to his host, would merely "rivet more strongly the chains of those who are in bondage." Many African Americans considered colonization a "decoy," at least to defer emancipation and at worst to sell them into African slavery. While the distinguished visitor enjoyed the comforts of Mount Vernon's study, his servant fielded questions from the judge's slaves. Did Bushrod, or colonizationists generally, plan "to compel them to go"? Such talk could be dangerous. Visitors asked slaves whether Bushrod Washington planned to free them, as George Washington had freed his people. Mount Vernon's black people possessed an unusual, perhaps unique proximity to white people talking politics, the travelers from around the United States and Europe who came there from Washington, D.C.[12]

Bushrod's slaves had other access to political conversation as well. The free blacks whom so many white people feared, and whom colonizationists targeted for emigration to Liberia, were no abstraction at Mount Vernon. People manumitted by George Washington still lived there as tenants and pensioners. Some of Bushrod Washington's slaves joined the Alexandria Baptist Society, a church of white people, free blacks, and urban slaves founded in 1803, within which developed the Colored Baptist Society. Prominent free black men, including a shipwright and a substantial Alexandria landowner, joined this church, as did some free black women. Between 1810 and 1824 nine Mount Vernon slaves appeared on the Alexandria Baptist Society's membership rolls, including Ham, Pat, and their niece Dinah.[13] George Washington had foreseen "disagreeable consequences" from Martha's dower slaves left in bondage when his own people became free. He might have fore-told the next generation of incendiary potential. A new enslaved popu-lation at Mount Vernon mingled with nearby free blacks just as the dower slaves had.

By early 1821 rumors of freedom were roiling the slave quarters. Sally, a twenty-five-year-old "dark mulatto" with a speech impediment, ran away on February 24; Bushrod figured she was nearby or hiding in Alexandria. To stem the talk, Bushrod called his slaves together in March. He planned never to free anyone, he assured them, now or in his will. As Mount Vernon's memory and legacy of emancipation came face-to-face with its social and economic reality, insubordination ensued. Wearing a field hand's clothes, a man named Fielding escaped late that month. Three men escaped in the spring, while the judge was in Philadelphia. Two were recaptured en route to Pennsylvania, but catching them cost Bushrod $250. The third, Emanuel, had been trained as a cook in Mount Vernon's kitchen and had learned his pro-fession well. Even though he stammered and appeared deferential, he was smart, resourceful, and probably literate. He had undoubtedly procured or forged free papers before he fled northward on June 10, Bushrod advertised: all the better to pass for a free man. Bushrod never caught him. By that summer the judge believed all his laboring men contemplated escape.[14]

So "compel them to go" he did, but not to Africa. In August 1821 Bushrod Washington sold fifty-four of his slaves to Horatio S. Sprigg and Archibald P. Williams, Louisiana plantation owners from Bayou Robert on the Red River. Once the bargain was struck, he gave his slaves another speech, explaining the financial struggles that occa-sioned the sale. Then the men, women, and children who had been sold—nearly two-thirds of the eighty-three enslaved people counted in the previous year's census—were taken to the slave jail in Alexandria. After two days there they passed through Leesburg, Virginia, in "a *drove* of negroes" numbering about a hundred. Though precise names cannot be determined, Bushrod appears to have sold the families that lived and worked at Union Farm, including Sinah and Joe, Ham and Pat, and all their children and grandchildren, about thirty in all. Gone, too, were several mansion house slaves, including Emanuel's parents, Ben and Suck, and the rest of their children. Oliver Smith and his family stayed, probably because Oliver had been Bushrod's most trusted servant for four decades.[15]

A Leesburg paper broke the news on August 21: "*Judge Washington, of Mount Vernon, president of the mother colonization society*," had sold fifty-four slaves southward. Baltimore's *Morning Chronicle* picked up the story three days later. A letter to its editor painted a portrait of grief. The writer had visited Mount Vernon and seen the remaining slaves' despondent, dejected faces. They told him that Washington had sold their compatriots for ten thousand dollars. "One would have thought that the poor creatures who were left, the aged and blind, had lost every friend on earth." Families had been sundered, the slaves reported. The visitor asked one old man whether he had been at Mount Vernon when George Washington died. No, the man replied, "not so lucky—I should not be a slave *now* if I had." The story became national news on September 1, when *Niles' Weekly Register*, a widely circulated Baltimore paper, republished this article. To abolitionist critics, the episode became exhibit A in the colonizationists' hypocrisy, for it gave the lie to any pretense that African colonization would doom American slavery. One piece of anonymous hate mail called Bushrod a "stinking cur," worse than a Spanish pirate and unfit to administer American justice.[16]

Bushrod Washington needed to answer the charges, for the movement's sake if not for his own. His reply, published in the *Baltimore Federal Republican* and circulated nationwide, mixed equal parts defiance, morality, and self-justification. How dare anyone question his or any southerner's moral and legal right to sell his property? How dare the writer visit Mount Vernon in his absence and "hold conversations with my negroes"? Not only had the writer given all credence to the slaves' version, but he had not even asked Judge Washington or his neighbors for their side of the story. Exasperated, Washington wondered why people were so sensitive about the division of slave families. Americans were accustomed to migration. Parents had immigrated to the United States leaving children behind, and children, including some of his own slaves, routinely left parents and lit out for new territories. He did not comprehend, or could not admit, that witnessing one's relations sold deeper into slavery was a far cry from watching them escape to freedom.[17]

Had the visitor asked, Washington claimed, he would have learned that the judge had tried *not* to separate families. The buyers had assured him that they would keep families together. To secure that promise, he had accepted twenty-five hundred dollars less than he wanted. Naturally those left behind would appear dejected, Washington wrote. However, the people sold "carried with them no feelings of despondency or regret" because they understood the exigencies that forced his hand. Of course these were the slaves no visitor could now ask to corroborate his version. Furthermore, Bushrod's definition of families may not have been the slaves' own. Kin networks of grandparents and uncles and aunts and cousins, not merely husbands and wives and their children, defined African American slave communities.[18]

Washington offered three reasons for his action. First, for twenty years Mount Vernon had hemorrhaged money. Many years it ran at a loss of five hundred to a thousand dollars. Matters had reached a crisis the previous May, when he had to buy corn for ninety slaves the entire month. Second, insubordination made the slaves "worse than useless." They had become more intractable than those on neighboring plantations, he argued, because this was Mount Vernon. Visitors raised slaves' hopes and stoked their desires for freedom. Specifically, the slaves had come to believe that "they would be free at *my death*." Like Martha Washington two decades earlier, Bushrod suspected plots against his life. But unlike Martha, he was bound by nobody else's will to free anyone. Third, when he told the slaves so, escape attempts followed.

The way Bushrod Washington explained it, the problem lay where Mount Vernon's identities intersected. As private property, this unproductive farm and its restive slaves were his to dispose of. For the most part, the people he sold lived at Union Farm, not in the mansion house quarters. Situated west of the mansion area, Union Farm was a working plantation, not part of Mount Vernon's "sacred" space. Few travelers by land or water visited it, so visitors were unlikely to incite insubordination there. A conversational spark ignited near the mansion could have erupted into conflagration at Union Farm, because familial and communal ties linked the separate slave quarters. More likely, though, Judge Washington's problems stemmed from Union Farm itself, with its hundreds of unprofitable acres. After he had sold the people who worked there, he must have scaled back its agricultural production. In an instant he was no longer Fairfax County's third-largest slaveowner.[19] He no longer possessed a workforce sufficient to maintain its earlier dimensions, even if he transferred some slaves from mansion house families to keep it going. All the rumors and unrest may have clinched an economic decision Bushrod would have made anyway.

But Mount Vernon could never be Bushrod's alone. Often called the American Mecca, it bore the weight of visitors' expectations. Having addressed the problem of insubordinate slaves, he turned the following year to thoughtless visitors. In the summer of 1822 he advertised that "the feelings of Mrs. Washington and myself . . . so much wounded by some late occurrences at this place," parties arriving by steamboat would no longer be welcome, nor would "eating, drinking and dancing parties."[20] This edict stood for nearly three decades, forcing most visitors to take the boat to Alexandria and make a difficult overland journey the nine miles from there to Mount Vernon. Once more, Bushrod Washington could not measure up to his uncle.

Spared from the traders' shackles, consigned to watch their compatriots taken away forever, Oliver Smith and his family had more troubled times ahead. Oliver and Doll's daughter Hannah, twenty-four years old, worked as a house slave at Union Farm, serving Bushrod Washington's resident manager, Leland Seal, and his family there. On August 27, 1821, less than a week after the newspapers had broken the story of the slave sale, Seal's wife, Mary, prepared the morning coffee and left it in Hannah's care. When the young woman brought the pot from the kitchen to the breakfast table, Mary Seal served her husband, then their little child, then herself. Leland Seal felt "strangely sick," suspected the coffee had been poisoned, and called Hannah to the table. He commanded her to drink a cup, then another. After the first cup, Hannah refused to have any more unless the coffee was sweetened, so Seal added some sugar and made her drink again. He ordered her to take another cup, but she resisted. Seal never knew if she followed that command because he was seized with vomiting. He instructed his wife to pour the coffee out, so that they could observe what else was in the pot. "Something of a white colour" remained in the bottom. When Hannah claimed not to know what it was, Seal demanded that she eat it. "I will not eat it for anybody," she replied. Hannah went out to the fields to take breakfast to the slaves who remained at work there. They brought her back to the house within fifteen minutes, too sick to return on her own feet.[21]

· Seal summoned a doctor from Alexandria, who pronounced the whitish substance to be arsenic. Poisoning by African slaves had long numbered among white Virginians' gravest fears. Medicine generally and poison specifically belonged to the arts of African conjure, or obeah, but in Virginian slave society those same arts could become weapons in the hands of the oppressed. Like other forms of insurrection, poisoning required forethought. It attacked its victim and the slave system itself from the inside out, beginning with the central nervous system and the household. And its chances of success were far greater than those of armed insurrection. The colonial assembly had legislated against slaves practicing medicine, more than a hundred eighteenth-century Virginia slaves had been tried for "illegal use of medicine," and thirty-five had been sentenced to hang for the offense before 1800. Virginia prosecutions and convictions for poisoning declined in the early nineteenth century (only eight slaves were convicted for poisoning whites in the 1810s), but isolated examples continued to furnish whispered reminders of the potential danger within. Arsenic was a substance native to Virginia, available to the slave conjurer or cook. In late September, when Bushrod Washington defended his slave sale against the newspaper onslaught and alluded to threats against his life, he clearly had this incident in mind.[22]

None of those who pilloried him, it seems, ever learned of the poisoning, which made an offhanded appearance in the local paper only after the controversy had begun to subside. Hannah's brothers George and Ned ran away in early October, apparently confirming the spirit of insubordination that coursed through Oliver Smith's family. George was twenty-seven, Ned seventeen; both stood about five feet five. Dressed in field hands' clothing and possibly carrying other garments, they seized an opportunity while Judge Washington was on his circuit in Philadelphia. The newspaper advertisement described George as "very black, with small ears, and a scar on the upper joint of the last finger, on his right hand," and Ned as "black with broad teeth far apart." Both men, it said, had been "refractory" for some time, "defying all dis-

cipline and control, particularly since their sister attempted to poison
the manager." George and Ned were recaptured and returned to
Mount Vernon, where Bushrod chose not to sell them, perhaps owing
to Oliver Smith's pleading.[23]

On December 3, Lawrence Lewis, a Fairfax County justice of the
peace, ordered Bushrod Washington's property Hannah brought into
custody to stand trial. George Washington's nephew and the master of
adjacent Woodlawn plantation, Lewis knew Bushrod better than most
fellow planters did because both served as executors of their uncle's
will. Lewis surely knew many of Bushrod's slaves as well, for as Nelly
Custis's husband he was also master of the dower slaves she had inherited on Martha Washington's death, slaves who mixed with Bushrod's
people in the neighborhood. Why did it take more than three months
for him to order Hannah imprisoned for the alleged crime? Apparently
someone else had been accused first: Hannah's husband, a man
named Hezekiah Scott, who was released when Leland and Mary Seal
failed to appear as witnesses against him. Now it was Hannah's turn.
In county court on December 17, the prosecutor requested a post-
ponement until the next court date. So Oliver Smith's daughter remained in jail, making a joyless, apprehensive Christmas for her family
at Mount Vernon.[24]

Not guilty, Hannah pleaded when five "gentlemen justices" convened on January 21, 1822, to hear her case. A lawyer was appointed
to represent her, and the prosecution called its witnesses. First Leland
Seal recounted the events of August 27, from his first taste of the coffee to Hannah's own sickness from the poison. Next his wife took the
stand. No other servants, male or female, had been around the house
that morning, Mary Seal testified. As soon as her husband drank his
coffee and said something was wrong with it, she tried a bit, enough to
be "partly afflicted in the same manner" but not enough to produce the
vomiting Leland had suffered. As the final witness, the doctor attested
that he had found the farm manager ill, examined the coffee grounds
in the pot, and identified arsenic in the residue. The physician concluded that he had also treated Hannah, whom the poison had left
"dangerously ill."[25]

Guilty, pronounced the justices. Their language bespoke the larger
fears associated with poisoning: Hannah was convicted of plotting the

deaths of Leland and Mary Seal and administering the arsenic to them and their child. She was ordered to be taken back to jail until Friday, March 1. On that day, between ten in the morning and four in the afternoon, she was to be taken to the place of execution, "to be hung by the neck . . . until she is dead." Because she would be executed under the laws of the commonwealth of Virginia, the Old Dominion was to pay Bushrod Washington fifty dollars, the appraised value of the enslaved property he would lose that day.[26]

Eleven days before Hannah's scheduled execution, Governor Thomas Mann Randolph received a petition signed by twenty white men of Fairfax County. Hannah had powerful supporters: Fairfax County's clerk and his deputy, two deputy sheriffs, the commissioner of revenue, and the jailer who held her prisoner. Most of them were slaveholders. Only five lived in Truro Parish, which contained Mount Vernon; Bushrod Washington's neighbors apparently did not rally to Hannah's defense. Another five signers lived in Providence District, site of the county courthouse and jail. There people were most likely to encounter Hannah during her trial and incarceration, and there her words and demeanor may have persuaded them of her innocence. Hannah was "a wretched and miserable victim," the petitioners argued. She had been wrongly accused and convicted only after the prosecutors' case against her husband had collapsed. She was also still suffering the aftereffects of arsenic poisoning. The petitioners asked Governor Randolph and his council of state to review the trial records, overturn her conviction, and spare her life.[27]

Rather than void the conviction, the governor and council reprieved Hannah for a year, after which she was to be moved to the state penitentiary "for sale & transportation." Sale to a slave trader, who promised to transport the convict away from Virginia forever, was a typical sentence for women convicted of violent crimes like poisoning or arson. After 1801, when the legislature authorized the governor and council to sell condemned slaves for deportation from the state, it became a common choice for convicts male or female. To those officials, transportation was a reprieve akin to commutation. It salved their consciences about the treatment of slaves in Virginia's legal system. To women and men sold to the lower South, to Cuba, or to the Dry Tortugas islands off the Florida coast—anywhere a trader could unload a convicted felon—the sentence seemed little more appealing than the gallows.[28] ·

As Hannah's reprieve neared its end in January 1823, the clerk of Fairfax County wrote to the governor again: Hannah was pregnant. No evidence survives to identify the child's father, but Hannah and her advocates imagined that a baby would cause the governor and council to reconsider exiling her from Virginia. Those hopes, and any stratagem that suggested the notion of a pregnancy in the first place, were dashed when the council upheld its judgment. For now, Hannah could be moved out of the county jail, provided with more comfortable safekeeping, and given all necessary medical attention. On March 11 she gave birth to a healthy baby boy, and her countdown to the state penitentiary began anew. On June 8 the governor ordered Hannah brought to Richmond. The Fairfax County jailer responded that Hannah was now "in a situation to be removed to the penitentiary," but that she should be taken in a "cart or gig" (rather than on foot, presumably), because she still did not possess "good use of herself," owing to "the poison she drank"—possibly what Leland Seal had forced her to swallow two years earlier. The jailer's letter was presented to the governor's council the following week, and at last on June 16 Governor James Pleasants issued his order: "You will deliver to Mr. Jno. P. Lord the slave Hannah (and her child) sentenced by the Court of Fairfax for administering poison to the family of Leland Seal; she having been reprieved by the Executive for sale and transportation, according to law."[29]

Hannah went to the penitentiary, but she never made it out of Virginia. In early August the governor's council heard slave dealers' bids to buy and deport the twenty-one slaves then residing in the penitentiary. Hannah and a Brooke County slave named Letty, convicted of murdering her own child, were the only women. The men were imprisoned for arson, burglary, assault, or murder. The trader William C. McAlister proposed a purchase price for each slave, ranging from $200 to $350. Hannah's was $255, a substantial profit over the state's expenses on her ($50 to Bushrod Washington, medical bills of $20.50, and jailer's fees). Then the governor changed his mind. He and the council believed they had no right to sell Hannah's infant for transportation and thought it "improper" to separate a mother from such a young child. So the council accepted the trader's bid for "all the slaves aforesaid except

Hannah and her child." Nineteen men and Letty were to be taken away, while Hannah remained behind. The next week a fire destroyed the state penitentiary. Alarm spread through the interior of the prison building, the jailers raced to open the convicts' cells, and the prisoners rushed into the central yard amid suffocating smoke. "Where are the convicts? Are they safe?" wondered everyone at the scene. As rumors spread that some had been trapped in the burning building, "shrieks, and groans, and cries for assistance" rang out.[30]

Back at Mount Vernon, Hannah's family could have followed every step of her ordeal. The courthouse was twenty miles distant, Richmond seventy-five miles farther south. But news could spread in many ways. During the early stages of the case, Lawrence Lewis's slaves at Woodlawn would surely have learned about it and taken word to Oliver and Doll Smith and their other children. Bushrod Washington knew about Virginia's judicial and legislative proceedings, and he could share information of Hannah's condition with her worried parents, his long-time household servants. As long as the young woman remained in Fairfax County, there might be occasions for family members to visit her, while conducting the master's business in the county seat or on quiet Saturday night and Sunday journeys, the way slaves across the South visited spouses and loved ones who lived "abroad" on other plantations. Oliver and Doll could take pride that wealthy, well-connected citizens of Fairfax County came to their daughter's defense, even as they lamented Bushrod Washington's failure to join their cause. Once Hannah's advocates exhausted their appeals and she was taken to the penitentiary, her parents and brothers must have felt her slipping away. Hope punctuated the gloom when the governor decided to sell all the convicts but Hannah to the slave trader—and then the *Alexandria Gazette* reported the penitentiary fire on August 9. Within days, good news reached Alexandria. All 244 convicts had survived the fire (although one sick prisoner died afterward), and the 11 women prisoners had been moved under guard to a Richmond barracks. There was once again reason for optimism, however slim.[31]

Hannah's chances and her family's hopes finally ran out when she died on December 10, 1823, still the property of the commonwealth of Virginia. Lingering effects of arsenic poisoning, recovery from childbirth, smoke inhalation, despair: any of these, or all of them, or some illness that went unrecorded ended her twenty-six years. What would become of her baby son? his grandparents and uncles at Mount Vernon surely wondered.[32]

So did Governor James Pleasants. Guided by no precedent, Pleasants asked the legislature if the little boy, like his mother, belonged to Virginia. The question was referred to a committee, which recommended on January 24, 1824, that the child be sold and the proceeds deposited in the state treasury. Robert T. Thompson, a delegate from Fairfax County, objected, and on his motion the committee's report was tabled. When discussion resumed six weeks later, Thompson offered a surprising alternative motion: "that the said child is free" and that he be apprenticed to a "humane tradesman" until he turned twenty-one. The House of Delegates rejected that proposal in favor of a third alternative: that the child belonged to Bushrod Washington, who had owned his mother at the time of her conviction and sentencing. The fate of Oliver Smith's grandson had commanded the attention of Virginia's governor and legislature, and all three potential outcomes had been considered. Robert Thompson may have come to the child's defense out of humanitarian sympathy. More likely, he knew Hannah's case better than his fellow delegates because the men who signed the petition for her innocence were his Fairfax County colleagues and neighbors. In the end, the bedrock principle of the slaveowner's property carried the day, and there the written record ends. Whether the baby was returned to Mount Vernon, whether he survived childhood there, even his given name are all lost to history. But Hannah's story, and the uncertain fate of her child, remained inscribed on the memories of the family at Mount Vernon they left behind.[33]

West Ford and Hannah's brother Phil lived parallel lives. Each was born to parents from Jack Washington's Bushfield. Venus, a teenage house slave, gave birth to West in 1784 or 1785; Oliver and Doll Smith welcomed their first son into the world six years later. West and Phil both came to Mount Vernon with Bushrod Washington, and both became master craftsmen through the process of apprenticeship. West Ford, a carpenter, remained at or near Mount Vernon through the 1850s, plying his trade for a series of Washington heirs. Phil Smith trained under Johann Ehlers, Mount Vernon's highly skilled German gardener, who had worked for two decades in the Hanoverian gardens of King George II and immigrated to America as a bound servant to George Washington. For much of their adult lives, West and Phil enjoyed positions of trust in the eyes of Mount Vernon's proprietors and visitors alike. West sometimes managed accounts and farm operations when Bushrod and his successors were away, and he occasionally guided visitors around the grounds and to Washington's tomb. Phil succeeded Ehlers as the visitors' guide to George Washington's gardens, retelling stories of the general's orange tree or rattling off the Latin names of various flowers and shrubs. Sometimes he presented visitors with a flower or a piece of fruit, a souvenir to embody the connection between past and present.[34]

For all their common experiences, West Ford and Phil Smith had profoundly different fates, thanks to Washington family wills.

Jack Washington had bequeathed West's mother and her parents to his wife, Hannah, to "devise to such of my children as she please." Alone among Jack's slaves, their disposition was not left to simple division based on monetary value. When Hannah Bushrod Washington wrote her own will in the 1790s, Venus had two children, West and Betty. She left Venus and Betty to her grandson Richard Henry Lee Washington (Corbin Washington's son and Bushrod's nephew), but by the time Hannah died in 1801 both Corbin and his wife were dead. Richard and his siblings became wards of Bushrod and his wife and moved to Mount Vernon. Venus and Betty followed. The teenage West went too, but his situation was unusual. Hannah's will explained part of the story. He had been born before Jack wrote his will, but Jack had failed to mention West when he listed Venus and her parents. Thus West became part of the unnamed enslaved property, divided between Bushrod and Corbin, who in turn gave the boy to Hannah when she offered to buy him. Her ownership having been thus established, Hannah Washington's will continued, she wanted West inoculated for smallpox as soon as possible and bound to a "good tradesman" until he turned twenty-one, "after which he is to be free for the rest of his life."[35]

Twenty years earlier Hannah Bushrod Washington could not have done this legally. From 1723 to 1782 Virginia law mandated that an owner who wanted to free a slave had to petition the legislature, specifying the slave's "meritorious service." As the Revolutionary War was ending, several northern states took the first steps toward emancipation, but typically northern abolition was gradual. Instead of outlawing slavery entirely, Pennsylvania, New Jersey, and New York set ages at which yet unborn slaves would become free. In Virginia, Quakers and others petitioned the legislature to permit private manumission, and in 1782 the General Assembly changed the law. Owners could now free their slaves through a will, deed, or other written document. Other states followed suit with similar acts, and manumissions increased. Virginia's free black population multiplied from about 1,800 in 1782 to 12,766 in 1790 and to 30,750 twenty years later. However, few planters released entire enslaved populations; George Washington was unusual in the sweep of his manumission. His provisions for educating those he freed went beyond the letter of the law, as did his sister-in-law Hannah's. But Hannah was more typical in another way. Most commonly, masters who manumitted anyone freed selected people while leaving the majority in slavery.[36]

Hannah's will did not explain why she made such explicit provision for this young man: West's father was almost certainly a Washington. Some of his descendants argue that George Washington was that man, a claim that made national headlines in the 1990s. Their argument relies on family oral history. Likelier suspects lived right at Bushfield: Jack Washington and his unmarried teenage sons Corbin and William (who died in 1785). Even Bushrod himself, who returned from Philadelphia to Bushfield to establish his legal practice in 1784, was more likely to encounter Venus than was his famous uncle.[37]

In any event, Bushrod Washington raised not just his brother's five children and several of his wife's nieces but also an African American man who was a Washington too. West did not call himself one. He took the name Ford, perhaps a family name. He learned to read and write, completed his apprenticeship, became free sometime around 1806, and married Priscilla Bell, a free woman of color, six years later. Their four children grew up at Mount Vernon, where West continued to work. Sources originally intended for surveillance reveal something of the Fords' physical appearance. Concerned about African Americans "going at large"—especially slaves pretending to be free in a society with a fast-growing free black population—the General Assembly required "every free negro or mulatto" to register in his or her home city or county and to reregister every year in cities or every three years in counties. In practice many free blacks apparently never registered. Reregistration was seldom enforced except at extraordinary moments, such as the aftermath of Nat Turner's 1831 revolt in Southampton County. Reregistering on October 17 of that year, West Ford was described as "a yellow man . . . five feet eight and a half inches high" with a "pleasant countenance, a wrinkle resembling a scar on the left cheek, [and] a scar on the left corner of the upper lip." Such language, familiar in advertisements for runaways, enabled free African Americans to prove their identity if mistaken for slaves. Ford took his two younger children to court with him; his older children, William (nineteen) and Jane (sixteen), also reregistered that day.[38]

By then West Ford had succeeded. He had lobbied Bushrod Washington for the care of his mother, Venus, whose fate was uncertain after Richard Henry Lee Washington died in 1817. When Richard's property was divided between his brothers, Venus stayed at Mount Vernon. There she remained, in her early sixties, when Bushrod Washington died in November 1829. The men who took inventory of Bushrod's estate appraised her at just five dollars. When Bushrod's heirs divided his slaves, his nephew John Augustine Washington, who inherited the 1,225 Mount Vernon acres containing George Washington's mansion and tomb, also got Venus. She was to remain with her son, at only token cost to John Augustine's share of the estate settlement. Bushrod Washington's will also acknowledged West Ford's service long after his manumission and perhaps implicitly the "yellow" man's descent from a white Washington. Along with any money still owed for Ford's work at Mount Vernon, the judge bequeathed "West Ford and his heirs" a 160-acre tract of land on Hunting Creek. West Ford parlayed his inheritance into a legacy for his children. He sold the land Bushrod had willed him and purchased 214 acres, at the gum trees and spring adjacent to the Mount Vernon property. For most of the 1830s Fairfax County appraised Ford's land and the buildings on it at $4,280. And from 1837 to 1850, in all but two years, he was taxed for one, two, or three slaves ages sixteen or older. He may at last have purchased his mother or other family members still in bondage.[39]

"Gardner Phil" Smith figured in Bushrod Washington's will too, but as inheritable property. Bushrod, like his father and true to his word, set nobody free. As the keeper of Mount Vernon's horticulture and its lore Phil seemed to belong to the place, not merely to its owner. So John Augustine Washington got first claim to him. Bushrod's wife and her heirs would receive at least eleven other slaves, most of them originally her property. Almost everybody else went unnamed, consigned to the "rest and residue" of Judge Washington's real and personal estate. All that residue was split five ways among Bushrod's nephews and niece after the judge and his wife died two days apart.[40]

The fortunes of Mount Vernon's slave families now depended on negotiations among new owners. The executors held an estate sale to dispose of farm equipment and livestock, then divided the enslaved people on the basis of dollar values, not kin ties. One family, specifically bequeathed to Bushrod's wife and her heirs, exemplified how the system of valuation worked. Louisa, about forty years old, was listed at $150. Her fifteen-year-old daughter, Criss, was worth nearly twice that ($275), but not a younger daughter, Louisa ($75), whose childbearing years lay too far in the future to bank much on her reaching them. Mother Louisa's three sons, ages nineteen to twenty-five, were field hands or skilled tradesmen, "likely" men in owners' parlance. They were assigned values of $400 each, the highest appraisals of any slaves in the estate. Old people like West Ford's mother, Venus, were worth the least. After the specific bequests were honored, the remaining people were sorted into five groups of roughly $1,100 each, a formula certain to split families. Oliver and Doll Smith, both about seventy years old and valued at $50 and $5, respectively, went to John Augustine Washington along with Phil ($400). Their other sons, Jack, George, Davy, and Ned, at least two of whom had attempted escape back in 1821, did not. All four were likely men, and they went to Bushrod's other nephews. Neither emotional nor financial considerations impelled these heirs to respect African American family ties. Jack, George, Davy, and Ned were taken away.[41]

Phil Smith stayed. Perhaps he did not share his brothers' rebelliousness because he believed that his calling for gardening at Mount Vernon transcended his bondage there. He was married, to a woman named Jenny who lived nearby but did not belong to Bushrod Washington or his heirs. Because someone else owned her or, perhaps, because she was a free woman, we know nothing about her other than that John Augustine's son later bought a few chickens from her. Nor is there evidence of any children she and Phil had. Any papers, like the children themselves, would have belonged to her owner.[42]

Mount Vernon's new owners, John Augustine and his wife, Jane Charlotte, both had lived there as young adults. Jane Charlotte was Bushrod's wife's niece, orphaned young, as John Augustine had been. Each of them inherited slaves from their aunt and uncle. Besides Phil, Oliver, Doll, and Venus, John Augustine got a young dairymaid named Sarah and two children ages ten and one (but not their parents). Jane Charlotte received three people Bushrod had left to his wife and her heirs: Jesse Clark (forty-five years old), George Frazier (twenty-one), and a woman called "old Jenny" (approximately fifty-five). In addition, an advocate of the colonization movement, Jane Charlotte received a five-year-old child named Lewis (also without his parents), whom she intended to raise for freedom and possibly emigration to Africa.[43] John Augustine and Jane Charlotte Washington spent much of every year at Blakeley, their Jefferson County plantation seventy-five miles northwest, a welcome retreat from the press of visitors. Situated on nearly nine hundred acres inherited from John Augustine's father, Corbin, Blakeley had been their home for fifteen years before they inherited Mount Vernon.

In the owners' absence, slaves became Mount Vernon's most visible inhabitants. John Augustine and Jane Charlotte hired farm managers but essentially left the place, and the visitors, in the care of the slaves. They quickly learned what Bushrod had known: financially, Mount Vernon was a losing proposition. It was home to a half dozen slaves like Oliver Smith and "old Jenny," people of little economic value who nonetheless had to be clothed, housed, and fed. So in 1831 John Augustine advertised in the *Alexandria Gazette* that Phil was authorized to sell plants from the greenhouse. Jane Charlotte, who inherited Mount Vernon at her husband's untimely death the following year, refined the system. An old woman at the porter's lodges opened the gate to the estate, usually receiving visitors' tokens of appreciation. Other slaves performed small services for visitors around the grounds. Tappan Wentworth, a lawyer from Lowell, Massachusetts, visited in 1833, when Jane Charlotte was away in Alexandria. Wentworth noted that the "art of sponging is so well understood . . . and the division of labor is so well regulated" that he had little choice but to spend $1.25 in gratuities to various slaves. The mansion remained off-limits to those without letters of introduction, but strangers clamored so tirelessly to get in that Jane Charlotte grew weary of being considered "one of the *curiosities* of the place." Still, she appreciated and fostered the significance of Mount Vernon as a national shrine.[44]

The new Washington owners may have established the routine, but slaves like Oliver and Phil Smith wrote the script. Only nine years old when Washington died, Phil was less likely than his father to have had any familiarity with the general. Nevertheless, visitors found in Phil tangible links to the fabled past. The gardener retold old Johann Ehlers's stories, and he conveyed souvenirs while guarding the most precious trees. He would not allow a leaf to be taken from "the Ginnerl's" exotic lemon tree but generously arranged bouquets of roses and other flowers for ladies. For visitors not permitted inside the mansion, the grounds evoked the most stirring images of the great man himself: the statesman striding the piazza; the visionary gazing at the Potomac; the farmer dirtying his hands in the garden; the agricultural general commanding his enslaved army. Phil's stories blended many sets of memories: his father's, Ehlers's, his own, and those of free blacks in the neighborhood whom George Washington had manumitted. By all accounts loquacious, Phil took pride in his association with greatness.[45]

He also took pride in his work preserving the site of that greatness. In 1835 a fire destroyed the old greenhouse containing Washington's remaining exotic plants. Phil saved many of these botanical relics, personally "nursing them through the winter" in another building. For the writer Ann S. Stephens, such associations bestowed nobility on Phil as on Washington or his home. The southern novelist William Gilmore Simms wrote similarly about an "old negro" he met at Mount Vernon, perhaps Oliver Smith: "I regarded him with infinitely more veneration than I am accustomed to pay most white men."[46] But what did their historic associations make African Americans? Did visitors imagine them the equivalent (or even the superior) of white Washington descendants who possessed no such store of memories? Or were these slaves merely speaking equivalents of Mount Vernon's walls and shrubbery?

The fascination with Oliver, Phil, and other Mount Vernon slaves was part of a larger phenomenon. In the fall and winter of 1835 an old black woman named Joice Heth became a national celebrity, a "marvelous relic of antiquity" billed as George Washington's 161-year-old childhood nurse. According to handbills and advertisements, she was the first person ever to diaper and clothe the future Father of His Country. A certificate of authenticity, a bill of sale dated 1727 and signed by George's father, attested that Joice was fifty-three at that time. A hundred and eight years later she was quite a sight. She weighed just forty-six pounds, and the newspapers wrote that she resembled a "mummy just escaped from the sarcophagus." One New York paper said she had "not enough flesh left to make a grease spot, or entice a Jersey mosquitoe." Her left arm was paralyzed. The fingernails of her left hand had grown to about four inches, and her toenails were a quarter inch thick. She was toothless and completely blind. But she was perfectly sociable, enjoyed a good pipe, and talked as long as people wanted. She conversed about "dear little George," sang ancient hymns, and reminisced about life at home with the Washingtons. Audiences all over the Northeast paid 25 cents (12½ cents for children) to see and hear her, a lucrative initial investment for the man who organized her tour, P. T. Barnum. Joice Heth did not live to see her own second act, a celebrated autopsy in 1836 that revealed her to have been about eighty. Real or fake, Joice Heth was a relic in both senses of the word: an object, a withered specimen that people could connect to George Washington, and a human being, sharing memories of days and scenes that nobody in the audience could ever experience.[47]

Why did Mount Vernon, and especially its aged slaves, command so much fascination in the 1830s and 1840s? Interest in the place was not new, but black people's presence and actions there assumed new meanings in the years after George Washington died. The system John Augustine and Jane Charlotte Washington devised—new uses for old people—meant that visitors were more likely to interact with African Americans, but there were other reasons as well. Newspapers carried obituaries for century-old veterans and leaders of the revolutionary generation, notably the former presidents James Monroe, in 1831, and James Madison, five years later. They also ran death notices for old black people who had once belonged to George Washington.[48] An earlier, more heroic time was fast disappearing from firsthand memory. Its replacement seemed less heroic and far more divisive. Jacksonian party politics energized but also split an enormously expanded electorate; Democrats and Whigs alike claimed to inherit the founders' mantle. The ideal of economic independence, embodied in the twin images of the yeoman farmer and the skilled artisan, became harder to achieve. More and more Americans worked for other people, not as a temporary step toward self-employment or landownership but as permanent wage labor.

Most of all, beginning in the early 1830s, slavery roiled America's political and social waters. Debates over slavery had diminished after the emancipationist movements of the 1770s and 1780s. Nat Turner's revolt and the rise of the abolitionist movement reignited the subject. In 1831 William Lloyd Garrison began publishing the *Liberator* by thundering, "I do not wish to think, or speak, or write with moderation . . . I am in earnest—I will not equivocate—I will not excuse—I will not retreat a single inch—AND I WILL BE HEARD." The American Anti-Slavery Society, founded two years later, echoed Garrison's argument for immediate emancipation without compensation to slaveowners. Southern politicians successfully pushed back; the Jackson administration suppressed abolitionist publications from the mails. In the North, abolitionist printers became targets of mob action. In the South, politicians and writers defended slavery as a positive good, a system that treated the lowliest far more humanely than northern capitalism ever would. Legislators rewrote statutes to make enslavement both more humane (for instance, increasing punishments for owners who mistreated slaves) and more restrictive (for instance, making it illegal to teach groups of slaves to read and write). They also imposed tighter controls on free African Americans, in many cases mandating their emigration from a state's borders. In Virginia some legislators advocated gradual emancipation and deportation of African Americans in the aftermath of Turner's revolt. Slavery's defenders won that debate, the last time before the Civil War that Old Dominion politicians seriously questioned the institution. Instead, the legislature in 1832 consolidated its scattered restrictions on slaves and free Negroes into one chapter of the state's code.[49]

In this desert of fractiousness, Mount Vernon seemed like an oasis of patriotism, a world apart. Getting there was a pilgrimage in the ancient sense, especially after Bushrod Washington banned steamboats from landing. The difficult journey through forests and over stumpy, muddy paths gave visitors the sense of entering a landscape utterly separate from their everyday existence. Worshipping at Washington's tomb, Americans of all parties and stripes imagined a land free of turmoil. Politicians seized the occasion of a visit to bemoan the lack of a present-day Washington and to experience the aura of purer motives. Writers who were not politicians lamented contemporary pettiness as they paid homage to the Father of His Country. All contrasted Washington's selfless devotion to country with contemporary politicians' rhetoric and actions. Anything associated with Washington, including the gray-haired African Americans who conducted travelers around his estate, became the object of veneration.[50]

In another sense, Mount Vernon was not so far removed. Visitors who celebrated Washington's patriotism often contrasted it with the actions of politicians they disagreed with. Politicians themselves employed Washington's home as a backdrop for their own ends. In the election year of 1832 John Augustine Washington welcomed the Young Men's National Republican organization at Mount Vernon. Speakers praised the glory of Washington, draped themselves in his mantle, and cataloged the deficiencies of the Jackson administration. When *The New-England Magazine* wrote in 1834 that Oliver Smith was "a sound Whig, and sticks to the principles of his world-revered master," it may have referred to Whigs and Tories of the revolutionary era, but Andrew Jackson's opponents, many in New England, were coalescing under the same name. Eleven years later the Whig writer Theodore Dwight used a visit to Mount Vernon as the occasion for bitter denunciation of the Mexican War.[51]

As a southern plantation Mount Vernon could not escape the clamor of the slavery issue. Some northern travelers frowned on the presence of slaves there. One visitor asked an old man if George Washington had whipped his people. "The answer . . . was stamped on every feature of his withered and wrinkled time-worn face, as he exclaimed, 'Whip me! the General order me to be punished! No, sir!' " *Freedom's Journal*, the nation's first newspaper published by African Americans, revived the old story of Bushrod Washington's slave sale. In March 1834 that entire saga appeared on the front page of the *Liberator*, under the title "Judge Washington, or a Specimen of the Conduct of the First President of the American Colonization Society." Early abolitionists sought to discredit colonization as a sham "antislavery" movement. William Lloyd Garrison furthered that objective by reprinting the thirteen-year-old announcement of Bushrod's sale, his reply, and his advertisement for runaways George and Ned, with its mention of their sister, the poisoner. Eight months later the *Liberator* published "A Tour at the South," featuring an abolitionist's visit to Mount Vernon—and his conversation with Oliver Smith.[52]

Entering one of the slave cabins near George Washington's mansion, the *Liberator*'s reporter asked an old black woman for some water. As she brought him a cup, he asked if Bushrod Washington had treated his slaves well. "So well, that he sold them all in Georgia," she told him. She had borne eleven children, she said. Only two remained. Seeing her children sold could not have been pleasant, the writer remarked. It was pleasant neither to her nor to God, she replied. She never expected to see her children again "this side of the grave."[53]

Left unnamed in the *Liberator*'s pages, this woman was named Hannah, about seventy years old when her words appeared in print. "Old Hannah," as she was known in a community with other Hannahs (including Oliver Smith's doomed daughter), had arrived at Mount Vernon early in the century, after Bushrod Washington purchased her and her husband, James. Six of their children had grown up near the Mount Vernon mansion, but only two daughters remained in 1830, when Bushrod's executors listed his human property. Betty was allotted to a nephew who inherited some Mount Vernon land west of the mansion house farm. Only Sarah, a twenty-one-year-old dairymaid pregnant with her first child, became John Augustine Washington's property. James and Hannah, appraised at five dollars apiece, were assigned to John Augustine's brother Bushrod Corbin, who lived in Jefferson County. This time, however, division was not destiny. Because no economic reason existed for moving the old couple, their new owner allowed them to remain at Mount Vernon and paid his brother annually for their upkeep. Bushrod Corbin Washington, like John Augustine, had grown up at Mount Vernon as his uncle's ward. He knew the relationship between Sarah and her parents. He surely remembered also that Judge Washington had sold James and Hannah's other children.[54]

To the abolitionist reporter, Oliver Smith presented as forlorn an appearance as did Old Hannah. Oliver did not mention that his wife, Doll, had died in the winter of 1832–33. He shared only the barest information about his children: one gardener, six sold away, two dead. He never intimated that one of the dead had perished while a prisoner of the state of Virginia. Implicitly and explicitly, though, Oliver Smith talked politics. "Sold into Georgia," the fate of four sons, described a metaphorical destination rather than a literal one, echoing the wrenching lines of a slave song:

> See these poor souls from Africa,
> Transported to America:
> We are stolen, and sold to Georgia, will you go along with me?
> We are stolen and sold to Georgia, go sound the jubilee.
>
> See wives and husbands sold apart,
> The children's screams!—it breaks my heart;
> There's a better day a coming, will you go along with me?
> There's a better day a coming, go sound the jubilee.[55]

Oliver's words revealed the political acuity, and the extraordinary platform, that Mount Vernon's black people possessed. He could not read, but having lived with the president of the American Colonization Society and among free and enslaved African Americans, some of them literate, he knew the arguments for and against abolition and colonization. When members of Congress visited, he had told them they must abolish slavery, following Great Britain's "noble example." He and most fellow slaves had no desire to emigrate to Africa, as many white Americans wished. The "great horror of slavery," he said, lay in the danger of being sold away, taken by an unknown master into a strange, faraway land. Oliver Smith believed that slavery would someday be abolished. Most slaves, he said, shared his belief that they or their children would someday be free. Lacking that hope, "they would run almost any hazard to obtain their freedom." He remembered: confronted with

Bushrod Washington's determination never to free anyone, his sons had risked their lives for freedom.[56]

In his last years—he died before the 1830s were out—Oliver Smith became a national character. He may not have known the ways his words were disseminated across the United States, but he understood how his utterances and his person embodied America's deepest mythologies and contradictions. Recalling the stories that others had told ever since he came to Mount Vernon, he could conjure up the memory of George Washington the exacting Virginia paternalist or of George Washington the revolutionary liberator. Perhaps too, embracing George Washington's legacy compensated in some small measure for the loss of his own family. Remembering his own three decades there, always listening for the visitor's proclivities and tone, Oliver Smith could present Mount Vernon as the static, idealized pilgrim shrine that most Americans imagined or as the living, changing plantation where human bondage persisted.

TWO

Hannah Parker's Kin

Hannah Parker was fifteen when she became pregnant with her first child, probably sometime in December 1841. By the next April she was working in the fields planting corn, the only girl alongside six men and three teenage boys. George Frazier and Jim Michum hauled out manure, and Hannah loaded it onto carts to spread in the cornfields. Her pregnancy must have been evident by June and July, when Hannah, her brother Edmund, the other teenage boys, and fifty-seven-year-old Jesse Clark wielded hoes in the cornfields while young men drove ox plows. She may have welcomed variations from the routine: planting peas; sowing beet seeds; weeding the sweet potato field. In four spring and summer months Hannah worked with six different crops and spent a rainy May day packing herring and shad harvested from the Potomac. Remarkably, given her condition, she was out sick just twelve days—two each in April and May, one in June, the rest in July. Some Saturdays Hannah left the field workers and joined the women for washing clothes. Carding wool, as she did for a few days well into her seventh month of pregnancy, was also women's work.[1]

Hannah Parker's full initiation into the world of women occurred the first or second week in September. Eliza Smith and Sarah, both in their early thirties and both mothers, probably attended the delivery. A black midwife from the neighborhood would receive a dollar and a half for her work. Hannah must have witnessed similar events before, as childbirth was often a communal event. She had been twelve when Sarah's son West was born four years earlier. Now younger girls, such as fifteen-year-old Sally or even Eliza's nine-year-old daughter, Amanda, watched and wondered when this would be their lot.[2]

Birthing Isaac Parker was women's work, but the news mattered to men too. Augustine Washington (the third John Augustine), who had taken command of Mount Vernon the previous year at the age of twenty-one, was away from home when this newest slave entered the world. On September 12, 1842, he received a letter from West Ford. "Hannah has a son," Augustine summarized the news. Three days later Augustine entered a written agreement with his mother, Jane Charlotte, formally leasing the land and twenty-two slaves from her. Twenty-one he listed by name in his diary. Then, as an afterthought or because he had already drawn up the agreement, he penciled "& her son" above Hannah's name.[3]

Hannah did not return to the fields after giving birth. When Augustine Washington got home and resumed his chart of farmwork in early October, he listed her as "knitting" for most of the month. He left her off entirely when he began a new page on October 28. The first time he named her son in writing was to record a business transaction that would relieve him of the expense of feeding a new mother and child. On the last day of 1842, he wrote, "hired Hannah and her child (whom she calls Izaac Walton) to Chas. A. Washington for $20.00 for the year, food clothing taxes &c." Augustine and his cousin Charles Augustine Washington repeated the arrangement for 1844.[4] Sometime around New Year's 1844 seventeen-year-old Hannah Parker became pregnant again.

Born on April 4, 1826, Hannah had spent her early childhood at Blakeley, John Augustine and Jane Charlotte Washington's Jefferson County plantation. The origins of her father, Harry Parker, are elusive. On her mother Milly's side, her family had once been the property of George Washington's brother Jack, the first John Augustine Washington. Rather than go to Mount Vernon with Bushrod, however, they were inherited by his brother Corbin and then by Corbin's son John Augustine. Between 1822 and 1836 Milly and Harry Parker had at least nine children, three boys and six girls. Hannah grew up surrounded by other children, not just her own brothers and sisters; twenty-five of Blakeley's sixty slaves in 1832 were twelve or younger.[5]

Mount Vernon's workforce—Phil Smith in the garden, Sarah in the dairy, and the other people John Augustine and Jane Charlotte had inherited from their uncle Bushrod—barely sufficed to maintain a farm or a home for the new owners, their three children, and various nieces who came for extended visits. Blakeley offered a solution to their labor shortage. By 1832, when John Augustine died, they had transplanted perhaps five Blakeley slaves. Two were brother and sister, Jim Starks, a twenty-seven-year-old field hand, and Eliza Smith, a house servant six years younger. Another was "Aunt Jenny," Jane Charlotte's trusted housekeeper, who often traveled with her mistress between the two plantations. At other times Aunt Jenny commanded Mount Vernon's mansion and its servants when the Washingtons were away. Probably one of the two "sable dames" a British visitor encountered in 1841, she opened the door after a combination of sweet talk and "quick silver." All of them left relatives at Blakeley. Aunt Jenny, born around 1785, had a husband, Mingo, and five children there. Jim and Eliza left parents, two brothers, and two sisters.[6]

Working at Mount Vernon did not require sundering ties with Blakeley's much larger African American community. Black and white people often moved back and forth. Coordinated work cycles allowed some people to participate in planting, harvesting, and domestic chores in both places, especially because Jane Charlotte apparently maintained only household agriculture at Mount Vernon. She traveled frequently between the two plantations, always accompanied by at least a driver and a maid. On their two-day caravan from Blakeley to Mount Vernon, across the Shenandoah River and over the Blue Ridge Mountains, Jane Charlotte's family rode in a carriage, the baggage and the slaves in wagons. Black people's transplantation to Mount Vernon multiplied in 1841, when Jane Charlotte leased it to her son Augustine for five hundred dollars a year. Because the young master hoped to revive Mount Vernon's commercial agriculture, he brought a cadre of farmhands or potential farmworkers from Blakeley, including Aunt Jenny's son Gabriel (born in 1820) and four of Milly and Harry Parker's children—Hannah, her sisters Julia (1823) and Betty (1833), and her brother Edmund (1827). Milly, Blakeley's skilled cook, stayed there with Harry, while her mother, Betty, went to Mount Vernon.[7]

A new black community was taking shape at Mount Vernon as

émigrés from Blakeley joined the remnants of Bushrod Washington's people, and children were integral to it. Sarah, the dairymaid John Augustine had inherited from Judge Washington, had five sons between 1830 and 1843. At least three of them—Joe (1832), West (1838), and Andrew (1843)—were related to old West Ford, either his children or more likely his grandchildren.[8] Eliza Smith had two sons and a daughter in the 1830s. Youngsters, like old people, played a role in the division of labor that managed visitors. Sarah's eldest son, William, studied gardening with Phil Smith. Little boys secured travelers' horses and pumped water to refresh visitors after the overland journey. Girls who performed household work also monitored the mansion door and took letters of introduction inside. When the British author Harriet Martineau visited, "little negroes peeped at us from behind the pillars of the piazza as we drove up." The last of George Washington's pensioners had died, and Bushrod Washington's remaining slaves were dwindling. But a new generation had begun. In September 1842 Hannah's son Isaac Parker became the first child born at Mount Vernon under Augustine Washington's management.[9]

Who was his father? Isaac's paternity virtually defies resolution. Hannah was unmarried, and she could have been at Mount Vernon or at Blakeley when her son was conceived. On April 6, 1842, Augustine Washington wrote that Hannah and another slave left Blakeley for Mount Vernon with a wagon bearing supplies and pigs. Only on April 11 did Hannah first appear in his work charts. The universe of Isaac's potential fathers therefore includes the men at both plantations: more than a dozen adult slaves at Blakeley and half a dozen at Mount Vernon, the free African Americans in Mount Vernon's vicinity, overseers, and Jane Charlotte Washington's two sons.[10]

Augustine Washington's parents had groomed him from childhood to inherit Mount Vernon. The timetable accelerated when his father died and Jane Charlotte inherited the estate. While Augustine attended the University of Virginia, she kept him apprised of Mount Vernon's activity, whether she was accepting an overseer's resignation or supervising as her little workforce filled the icehouse. On school vacations he returned to Mount Vernon, where one visitor described him as a gracious host who accompanied the guest all over the estate. Augustine left the university in 1841 to take proprietorship of the storied plantation. He soon placed two advertisements in the *Alexandria Gazette*. The first, in January 1842, grandiloquently reiterated the long-standing ban on commercial traffic: "The owners of *Stages and Omnibuses* are positively prohibited from sending *those vehicles* to Mount Vernon," and anyone who arrived in "*such conveyances*" would be treated as a trespasser. (He had similar notices printed, to post at Mount Vernon's gates.) The second, four months later, hung out a shingle: "John A. Washington, Attorney at Law, will attend to any professional business entrusted to his care."[11]

By late summer Augustine was falling in love. Marriage to Eleanor Love Selden would consolidate his standing as a master of means. The Seldens, longtime residents of Exeter plantation in neighboring Loudoun County, gave the couple an elaborate wedding, complete with Philadelphia confections such as "baskets of nougats filled with colored flowers made of sugar" and "bonbons in quaint and curious shapes." An only child, Nelly Selden Washington inherited Exeter when her father died in 1845, and Augustine became one of the commissioners of the estate. Now mistress of Mount Vernon, Nelly succeeded her mother-in-law as manager of the household, dairy, and orchard. She also took over the garden, along with the income from travelers' purchase of flowers and fruit. Beginning in 1844, Nelly bore a child nearly every other year, seven in all. As Jane Charlotte had done, Augustine and Nelly traveled frequently to Blakeley, and Augustine regularly commuted into Alexandria. They also made regular circuits of Selden and Washington relatives' plantations around northeastern Virginia.[12]

Augustine understood early how slaves made the master. He bought his first manservant in December 1842, during his engagement to Nelly. Alfred, who belonged to Augustine's sister, had absconded after exhibiting "rebellious conduct." Augustine paid his brother-in-law five hundred dollars, retrieved Alfred from the Charles Town jail in Jefferson County, and took him to Mount Vernon. The estate and the rest of its slaves still belonged legally to Jane Charlotte Washington, but Alfred was Augustine's alone, a symbol of his independence, however circumscribed. Washington's small expenses suggest the servant's status: a pair of gloves; a tailor's bill for "cutting out Alfred's coat";

twelve and a half cents to buy licorice. Over the next two years Alfred routinely accompanied his owner and represented Augustine in public, conducting household business with merchants in Alexandria. The gloves and the coat revealed Augustine's pretensions—the slave's clothing attested to the master's gentility—while the licorice was a small indulgence. For good or ill, Alfred's appearance served as a public extension of Augustine Washington's own person. In January 1845 Alfred ran off when Augustine was about to punish him for more "rebellious conduct." Augustine found him in the Alexandria jail the next day and left him there. On March 6 Augustine unloaded him on a congressman from Mississippi for $500 plus $18.92 to pay the jailer's fees. Augustine never recorded what led Alfred to run off: a series of small resentments, a specific conflict, or the simple desire for some slight measure of self-determination. The act itself was enough to clinch his sale, however. To the precise extent that Alfred represented Augustine—not as his mother's property, not as one of a dozen field workers—his flight betokened the master's lack of control.[13]

Appearances counted for any master concerned with his standing in the neighborhood, and from the start Augustine conducted business with the surrounding planters and tradesmen. Some was legal. Appointed a justice of the peace for Fairfax County in 1844, Augustine tried, convicted, and sentenced slaves at least twice for trespassing on other masters' land. In 1847 a man named Edward confessed to breaking the 1832 law, passed after Nat Turner's revolt, forbidding free blacks from carrying firearms. Augustine directed the constable to administer the full sentence, thirty-nine lashes. More regularly, however, relations with neighbors were economic, involving slaves. As eastern Virginia developed a labor surplus, hiring slaves out became essential to the Old Dominion's economy. Many tidewater counties such as Fairfax no longer produced staple crops on the scale of eighteenth-century tobacco, while newer western regions were booming. City dwellers and small farmers who could not afford to purchase slaves could still profit from a slave's rented toil, as could industrial establishments. The market for hired slaves helped preserve slavery's sway in Virginia, giving potential hirers as well as slaveowners a stake in the institution. Within Mount Vernon's vicinity, hiring another man's slaves or hiring one's own slaves out smoothed the peaks and valleys of a year's economic activity, provided the labor that made land productive, or allowed owners to reduce expenses on surplus people. So Augustine hired Jim Starks out to a local fishery for the seven-week fishing season in the spring of 1842, and he hired several men from other planters to supplement his own field laborers that year.[14]

Augustine understood the economics: hiring slaves out reaped long-term dividends for owners as long as the price of slaves kept rising. One of his wife's relatives asked his advice in 1844 about selling an enslaved family. Better to wait, Augustine replied; the family would presently command twelve hundred dollars, but the four children's value would likely double in the next five years as they became old enough to work. In the meantime the mother could have more children. For now the owner could hire the father out for perhaps sixty dollars a year, hire the mother and children out "for victuals and clothes," and escape the expense of supporting any of them. The terms of a hire depended on the slave's age and abilities. For people skilled in domestic, agricultural, or industrial work, the hirer generally paid the owner an agreed-upon sum and provided the slave's food and clothing for the year. If a master wanted simply to unload people, particularly small children, he could offer them rent-free. Augustine routinely hired out women and girls whom he could not use in the fields and who would be surplus house servants. In January 1844 he rented out three Parker sisters: nineteen-year-old Julia for twelve dollars for three months' work at the Alexandria Theological Seminary; seventeen-year-old Hannah (and baby Isaac) for twenty dollars for the whole year to his cousin Charles; ten-year-old Betty for just six dollars "& victuals & clothes" for the year in a family friend's household near Blakeley. The system had myriad permutations, but for Augustine personal relationships were the common denominator. He hired laborers from, and hired his own slaves out to, people he knew: neighbors near Mount Vernon, friends in Jefferson County.[15]

Augustine asserted mastery too in his determination to restore Mount Vernon as a working plantation. Following his great-uncle Bushrod's lead, he might have supervised the farms in desultory fashion while focusing on his legal career and his growing family. Instead he chronicled the farms' daily operations, recording his slaves' activity, the amount of crop planted or harvested, and the weather. He partook of the language and spirit of "improvement" that suffused the United States in the 1840s, North and South. He read the *American Farmer* and *The Southern Planter*, a Richmond monthly magazine for enterprising farmers who aimed to increase the productivity of their lands and their slaves. He became vice president of a county agricultural society. He even wrote a letter, published locally and reprinted in a Chicago agricultural periodical, about the best uses and application of guano (a fertilizer of South American bird droppings), testimony to his penchant for scientific farming.[16]

When Augustine Washington took over, 145 of Mount Vernon's acres were in cultivation. He doubled that acreage within five years and tripled it in ten. From June 1849 through May 1850 Mount Vernon's output included six hundred bushels of wheat, two hundred of oats, and a thousand of corn. Thirty-five head of cattle produced beef to sell as well as to consume at home. Hogs were for home consumption, thousands of pounds of pork being salted every winter. Two flocks of sheep, more than 160 head in 1847, made for a business in wool as well as meat for the plantation. By the 1840s spinning had long been abandoned at Mount Vernon; this was an era of intertwined household and factory production. Augustine sent his wool to be exchanged for factory-made cloth in Jefferson County, where cloth manufacturer Colin Porter was among Blakeley's neighbors. Augustine directed not only the sale of the wool but also the precise amounts and varieties of cloth he wanted. His wife visited the factory—days or weeks after giving birth at Blakeley!—to buy finished clothes for male slaves as well as fabrics for the household. It is difficult to discern whether all this work ran a profit. Margins were small. In one case he made just twenty-six cents' (2 percent) profit on a 346-pound cow, but he kept a quarter of the meat, as well as the tallow and other by-products, for home use. Augustine Washington also thought expansively; in 1851 he bought a second plantation. For Marshall Hall, a 377½-acre farm across the Potomac in Maryland, he paid more than seven thousand dollars, income likelier from the sale of Exeter or of other Washington family holdings than from Mount Vernon's farm products.[17]

The first proprietor since George Washington to pour his own energy into Mount Vernon's agricultural operations, Augustine benefited from several trends. A brighter day was dawning for Fairfax County farming. The introduction of lime and especially guano enriched the long-exhausted soil. Lands that once yielded fewer than fifteen bushels of wheat an acre now produced twice as much, Augustine wrote. National agricultural magazines reported that Virginia land could be had cheap, for three to fifteen dollars an acre. The county's population, which had declined by 30 percent from 1800 to 1840, slowly began to increase again. To northerners who might be squeamish about moving to slave territory, one emigrant explained that he had seen none of the abuses associated with the institution. Indeed, he thought Fairfax County masters without exception treated their slaves well, even taking them to church on Sundays. About two hundred northern families, especially Quakers from New Jersey and New York, encouraged by the county's abundant timber, another commercial asset, migrated there. Quakers purchased Woodlawn, formerly George Washington's Dogue Run Farm, after Lawrence and Eleanor Custis Lewis died. There and on the land once called Union Farm, Friends established scores of small farms, generally of 100 to 200 acres, on the outskirts of Mount Vernon's 1,225 acres.[18]

His own slaves' actions and the Quakers' proximity prompted Augustine Washington to question the long-term viability of slavery. In August 1845 his overseer jailed Gabriel, the son of Jane Charlotte's trusted housekeeper Aunt Jenny, for "misconduct." Combined with the desertion of some hired workers (perhaps slaves rented from their owners), Gabriel's absence cost time in harvesting the corn. Augustine considered selling Gabriel but decided instead to have him "punished"—whipped—as a deterrent to other slaves. Describing the situation to his wife, he continued, "If it were possible to do without them, I do not think I would own one, but situated as we are, landed property would be almost valueless without them, and it is a matter of necessity to have their labour." The Quakers' arrival suggested an alternative, he wrote. Industrious free workers would drive out "ignorant" slave labor and "still more degraded" poor whites. Schools would follow, farms would be improved, and land values would double. Thus inspired, Augustine experimented with a new system in 1849. He hired four recent Irish immigrants "to see if I could substitute them in any way for negroes." Three men were to work in the fields; a woman was to assist them and sew clothing for the slaves. The trial failed after two weeks because Augustine and the Irish workers could not reach satisfactory terms. The downside of free labor was the necessity of mutually acceptable contracts.[19]

Slaves continued to fuel Mount Vernon's farm operation. Augustine relied mostly on their natural increase, as the children born in the 1830s grew into field and household laborers. But his purchases and sales also altered the workforce and the black community. Whether or not by design, he bought slaves who were plausible spouses for his single people. Mary, a woman bought from one of Nelly Washington's Selden relatives, married Gabriel. Augustine also made a long-term arrangement with a free black man, Joe Michum. Possibly the son of a Mount Vernon slave who was married to a free woman of color, Michum apprenticed his six-year-old son, Tom, to Augustine, to serve until his twenty-first birthday.[20]

Augustine Washington sold slaves infrequently. More often he elected to punish, not sell, people who got into trouble. "My negroes have a jail fever," he wrote in 1845, after two slaves had run off and landed in jail within two days. Family considerations may have persuaded him to punish rather than sell them. One was Gabriel. Born a year apart, he and Augustine had grown up together at Blakeley. Similarly, when sixteen-year-old Joe Ford ran off a few years later and turned up in the Alexandria jail, Augustine brought him home, perhaps because he was West Ford's kin. Family reasons sometimes occasioned a sale. Julia Parker, Hannah's older sister, had a husband in Jefferson County, and a judge there offered to pay four hundred dollars for her. As Augustine explained to his mother, the transaction benefited everyone. Julia wanted to go, and he wanted to buy a blacksmith in her stead. The circumstances of a sale were not always so congenial. Ben, a nineteen-year-old he had purchased, and Sally, a young Blakeley émigrée with a small child, "misbehaved in such a manner" that Augustine thought it his "duty" to sell them in 1847. Bruin & Hill, a leading Alexandria slave dealer, paid in cash: $750 for Ben, a $123 profit over Augustine's purchase price, and $525 for Sally and her child. Partner Joseph Bruin came to Mount Vernon to take them away.[21]

"Slaves on the estate of Washington!!" The sight horrified Caroline Healey, a twenty-year-old schoolteacher from Boston who visited in

1843, nine months after Isaac Parker was born. Healey's journey began with a cool, delightful boat ride from Washington to Alexandria but then turned arduous. Traveling by coach over muddy roads, Healey and her companions heard locusts chanting in the trees along the nine-mile route. After two hours overland, the party finally arrived around eleven o'clock at two small buildings, the "porter's lodges" that marked the entry to Mount Vernon. An old black woman in a white cap opened the gate, told the visitors that she was "in the family" before General Washington died, and accepted a coin for her service—or perhaps for her connection to the historic past. Once they were within Mount Vernon's grounds, the half-mile road was so bumpy and unkempt that Healey mused, "It seems as if every stone cried out to the patriot pilgrim, 'stay at home.' " The travelers came upon slave quarters within view of George Washington's mansion. A little boy interrupted the visitors refreshing themselves at a water pump. Taking water was against the rules, but paying the child to get them a drink might not be. The sight of a "strange old blind woman, with a crutch in her hand" left Healey too emotional to speak. Passing through a narrow lane, Healey saw "signs of life" in the woman churning butter near the springhouse: Sarah, the dairymaid, was to give birth to her fifth son the following month. To the young teacher, the most interesting of Mount Vernon's slaves was the white-haired gardener. Healey did not learn, or did not record in her diary, that this was Phil Smith. As he had done for countless other travelers, Smith pointed out the orange tree that General Washington had planted and told how he had studied with Washington's original gardener. He too accepted a coin, but not before answering Caroline Healey's question: How many "negroes" were on the place? Thirty, he replied.[22]

Most visitors saw only a few of them, and they tended to misinterpret what they witnessed. Enslaved children especially elicited northerners' critiques of African Americans, of slavery, or of both. Seeing only "females or boys," one abolitionist concluded in horror that the home of Washington had become a "slave breeding pen!" Elizabeth Martin, a Wisconsin congressman's wife, saw the children as products of a squalid, slothful environment, their slave quarters littered with corncobs, fragments of barrels, and "filth of every kind." The "half naked" children she spied running in and out of slave cabins that February day seemed to care nothing about the cold. But Mrs. Martin knew little of

Mount Vernon's geography and work cycle. She came on a Sunday, the slaves' day of rest. Had she visited the previous day, she would not have seen "negroes of all ages." That Saturday Hannah Parker's sister Betty was scraping manure and doing the washing, while black men were shelling two weeks' allowance of corn, hauling firewood, and making stakes for fences—all out of visitors' sight. The corncobs that looked like trash were residue from Saturday's labors. On Monday, the day after Mrs. Martin's visit, the men went out to prepare a new field for corn, a mile or more away from the area travelers saw, separated from the mansion grounds by dense forest. This distance between Mount Vernon's sacred landscape and its agricultural workscape also explains why the abolitionist saw no adult men. Mount Vernon's enslaved people inhabited a different world, a community of growing families connected to people and places, like Blakeley, beyond the patriot pilgrims' view and even the plantation's boundaries.[23]

On September 30, 1844, Augustine Washington wrote these words in his diary: "Hannah had a daughter last night whom she calls Sarah." He paid Rachel, a black midwife, a dollar for "attending Hannah in her confinement" and wrote that he owed the woman another fifty cents to complete the transaction. Perhaps because Hannah did not give birth at Mount Vernon, he did not record another fact: Sarah Parker was a "mulatto." Censuses and visitors' accounts across half a century confirm that she was light-skinned. Hannah was not; census takers in 1850 and 1860 recorded her as "black."[24]

Sarah Parker was conceived when her mother was hired out to Augustine's cousin. Twenty-nine years old, Charles Augustine Washington lived at Wellington, a plantation just across Little Hunting Creek from Mount Vernon that had once been part of George Washington's River Farm. Later described as jovial and impecunious, Charles Washington never married. Still, with Sarah Parker's paternity as with Isaac's, there were multiple possibilities. A "mulatto" could be another mulatto's child, and "yellow" men lived nearby. Moreover, slave hiring contracts usually ran fifty-one weeks. Between Christmas and New Year's, slaves often returned home for a respite while their masters made contracts for the coming year. If Sarah was conceived that week in 1843, precisely nine months before she was born, then other potential fathers lived at Mount Vernon. Speculation inevitably outruns resolution.[25]

The sole surviving evidence of Sarah Parker's first nine years appears in the parish registers of Christ Church, the Episcopal edifice where white Washingtons had worshipped since George and Martha. "July 9, 1847. Baptized at Mount Vernon three colored children, servants of J. A. Washington, Esq., viz. Isaac, Sarah, & Henry." The minister performed the ritual on a Friday, a workday, somewhere at Mount Vernon: the mansion, the slave quarter, or out-of-doors. Hannah Parker was surely there, along with other black people, enslaved and free. So, probably, was Augustine, although Nelly Washington and their daughters Louisa and Jane, who had been baptized in Christ Church on Sundays, were away at Blakeley. The one-sentence notation, part of a list of "Black Baptisms," suggests more than it reveals. Eight-month-old Henry may have been Hannah's first child with Warner May, whom Augustine purchased from a Jefferson County estate in 1846, around the time Henry was conceived. Over the next ten years Hannah and Warner had five more children. But for the church's purposes, as for the law's, the parents of enslaved children were invisible. Masters possessed the power to buy, sell, and discipline slaves of any age and the power to have them baptized. This does not mean that Hannah had no say. Only two other slave children at Mount Vernon appeared in Christ Church's baptismal record between 1842 and 1855; many more did not. Christ Church had a scattering of black communicants throughout this period, but other African Americans at Mount Vernon may have preferred rituals unmediated by the master's church. Hannah may have proposed that her daughter and sons receive the sacrament, even if the minister came at Augustine's behest.[26]

When she was old enough to hold a baby, little Sarah Parker was probably put to work minding her littler brothers, Henry and Arthur (born in 1848). If Mount Vernon was typical of plantations its size, she began her training as a house servant around the age of six or seven. That education included drawing water from a well, picking fruit, collecting eggs, or helping with the cooking and washing. It also meant attending the master's children. Augustine's young daughters could each be assigned a slave attendant under Eliza Smith's watchful care. Several visitors around 1850 reported being admitted to the mansion by a "negro girl" or "little negro," likely Eliza's daughter Amanda, nine years older than Sarah. But Sarah's light skin may have encouraged the decision to place her in the master's house. Eventually she might be assigned the doorkeeper's responsibility.[27]

Six days a week Sarah and other small children like her watched their adult relatives go to work. Twelve or thirteen people labored in the fields: six or seven men ages eighteen to forty-five, one or two "old men," four "boys" fourteen to seventeen, and sometimes a teenage girl. Before daybreak and before breakfast they tended to the horses, cut wood, carried water to the laundry, shelled corn, chopped oats, and put away the previous night's ashes. Age and skill dictated the division of labor and tools. West Ford, who turned sixty around 1845, continued to work in the carpentry shop, helping in the fields only at peak times. Old Jesse Clark mostly tended hogs or worked in the garden after a long illness in spring 1847. As boys grew into men, their tasks required increased skills: a hoe at fifteen, a one-horse plow at nineteen or twenty, a two- or three-ox plow a few years later.[28]

Specific tasks varied from day to day, but barring extremities in the weather, a year's cycle was as predictable as malaria in September. In January and February the farmworkers grubbed (cleared roots and stumps from new land, using hoes and plows) and put up fences to mark off the fields. By early March they had broken new ground for corn, although a late freeze could harden the land and break their plows instead. Planting corn began in mid-April, with field hands dropping seed and covering the new furrows. Plowing and hoeing continued through late spring and summer. Meanwhile winter wheat planted the previous September came ready for harvest in late June. "Borrowed labor"—workers and horses from nearby plantations, to be reciprocated another season—helped thresh the wheat in July. While the corn grew, slaves fired a kiln to make lime from oystershells and created the mix of lime and guano to fertilize the soil for the coming September wheat planting. Mid-September to mid-October was the busiest month: winter wheat was sown, corn harvested, wheat land fertilized. The rest of October younger slaves shucked corn to be stored for the coming year, 430 barrels in all in 1847. Almost everyone participated in killing hogs in December and January, the pork—more than 2,500 pounds of it that year—salted for consumption through the winter and spring. Other tasks filled any lulls in these cycles: packing fish and shearing sheep in May; planting and harvesting oats, clover, potatoes, and vegetables.

Domestic labor at Mount Vernon resembled its counterpart at myriad other plantations. Supervised by the mistress of the mansion, skilled slave women operated the household. The elder Sarah managed the dairy and orchard, churning butter and preserving fruit every fall. Eliza, the plantation seamstress as well as cook and nanny, made most of the slaves' clothes from coarse "negro cloth," especially the weave of linen and wool known as linsey-woolsey. This work had its perils. When a needle became lodged in Eliza's arm and broke off, Augustine Washington feared the worst. His wife reacted with a mixture of caring and selfishness: sorry to hear of "Eliza's accident," but also "distressed on my own account," worried about losing "such a faithful servant." Despite Eliza's considerable pain, the doctor declined to extract the needle, saying that it could be lodged there for years. Within a week she was sewing again. Other enslaved women assisted in the household duties. While they worked, their children came under the questionable care of girls not much older than they themselves, such as little Sarah. Hannah Parker may have superintended the slaves' nursery; alone among the enslaved women, she never appeared in Augustine's diaries or letters as tending the white people's household or working the fields after 1844. Such a practice was not unusual on plantations with numerous children, and by 1853 Mount Vernon had nine enslaved children under eight years old.[29]

The busiest season of the year was also Mount Vernon's unhealthiest. Hell Hole, a low-lying, undrained area of the grounds near the Potomac, bred mosquitoes and malaria in late summer. Visitors were scarce then. Congress typically adjourned by the third week in August so that members could flee the humid capital. Augustine's wife and children usually decamped for Blakeley, and Augustine joined them in years when he trusted an overseer to manage the harvest. Meanwhile the slaves, the only people who could not leave, suffered. Eliza nearly died of congestive fever in 1844, a particularly bad year; only "strong remedies" that induced profuse salivation and sweat saved her. The next year six slaves and the overseer all had bilious fever. Little Sarah Parker caught the malarial chills around her tenth birthday. Virginia's temperate climate made for a healthier environment than many other parts of the South, and the strain of malaria most common in northeastern Virginia, *Plasmodium vivax*, was rarely life-threatening. Still, it weakened resistance to other maladies. "Gardener Phil" Smith's death in September 1846, at the age of fifty-six and after a series of illnesses, probably resulted from such a combination.[30]

He was interred a short walk uphill from Hell Hole, at the only place at Mount Vernon shared by the dead and the living, black and white, resident and visitor. George Washington's tombs—the original one built into the hillside and a new brick mausoleum to which all the family remains were removed in the 1830s—evoked travelers' reverie and awe. The new tomb, where George and Martha's sarcophagi could be seen behind an iron gate, now furnished the symbolic culmination of any pilgrimage. It was also the surviving Washingtons' family plot, with obelisks in front for Mount Vernon's subsequent owners and headstones to the side for other relations. Not fifty yards away lay another small cemetery, neatly marked by visible mounds and well preserved with wood fencing. This was the slaves' graveyard, where black people had buried their own since George Washington's day. Many of Bushrod Washington's older slaves, people like Oliver Smith who had regaled visitors with stories of the general, were interred there. So were children: Betty Parker's infant, just days old; the elder Sarah's third son, Ephraim, dead of dysentery during an unhealthy season; Eliza's son John, perished in a violent snowstorm. An 1846 visitor observed slaves there completing the newly sodden grave of "a favorite servant, an aged colored woman" who had died the previous Sunday. Most visitors never noticed the unmarked mounds that bore meaning only for black people.[31]

When the workday ended, slaves divided into two sets of quarters. The ones visitors saw stood near the Washington mansion. The Massachusetts school reformer and abolitionist Horace Mann described these quarters as "three or four most miserable looking dilapidated hutches." These were either a remnant of George Washington's slave quarters, built in 1792 with family compartments of roughly six hundred square feet each, or a new greenhouse slave quarter made of pisé (rammed earth), constructed adjacent to the old quarters in Bushrod Washington's era. Travelers had few qualms about peeping inside. So Benajah Ticknor, who visited ten days before Mann in 1848, deemed the dwellings "of course, so dirty as to be offensive to the sight." To a northerner's sight: slaves' meager habitations were a staple of abolitionists' critiques. Political views aside, dirt was endemic to agricultural life north and south. Walls were a barrier against the elements, not against the dust or mud that every pair of feet tracked in. The other slave quarters, which most visitors did not see, lay a mile north on the other side of the woods. Abutting Augustine Washington's "middle" fields halfway between the mansion area and Gum Springs, this compound contained five buildings: an overseer's house, a stable with an attached cornhouse, a "large Barrack" (perhaps for unmarried men), and two "negro quarters" that an insurance company listed as "out door kitchens," probably because they were one- or two-room family cabins each with a fireplace and a chimney. From the master's perspective, these quarters housed field laborers closer to their work. To their inhabitants, distance from the mansion afforded a modicum of privacy from the master's supervision and the visitors' curiosity.[32]

Sundays and evenings African Americans tended their garden plots, which probably adjoined the "far" slave quarters. Growing vegetables and raising chickens, the slaves pursued another economy in which they earned small financial rewards and some measure of self-determination. Augustine Washington occasionally gave his field hands a few hours' leave to work in their gardens, and his diaries mention "vegetables planted in the shop lot for negroes." Children like Sarah Parker helped their parents farm these little patches of land. Slaves could also make money working during holidays or after hours or performing additional tasks. Most commonly Augustine paid his enslaved people for cutting wood and for extra grubbing. The sums seem small—fifty cents for a cord of wood, for instance—but they revealed the implicit boundaries of daily, unpaid labors. Garden plots served the master's purposes by making slaves partially responsible for their own sufficiency, supplying vegetables and eggs to accompany the corn and pork that were the staples of their diet. Augustine sometimes bought chickens from his slaves, but the master's lands bounded the slaves' commercial autonomy. In December 1848 Augustine took neighbor Henry Triplett to court for "dealing with my negro Jim, unlawfully & without my consent, & having bought of him four bushels of corn, at 40 cts, four or five bushels of meal at 50 cts. the former having been stolen from me." Washington pursued the case relentlessly, winning a twenty-dollar judgment thirteen months later. The principle was inviolable: his slaves were not permitted to maintain an independent economic existence. As Jim's actions revealed, the slaves' practice did not always obey the master's principle.[33]

This episode of illicit commerce, recorded by Augustine because it ended up in litigation, is a rare window into these slaves' ties to the world beyond the plantation's borders. Augustine's slaves surely had friends and kin on the neighboring plantations, some of them owned by other Washington descendants. Work took some slaves off the farm; an adult man always served as wagon driver, taking grain to be milled near Dogue Creek or taking the Alexandria road into the city for supplies. Divided all week by their varied toil and by the two sets of slave quarters, Mount Vernon's African Americans may have used Sundays to congregate with one another and with their neighbors in recreation or worship. A strong black Baptist community existed in and around Fairfax County, including Alexandria's Colored Baptist Society but also decades-old traditions of worship among free and enslaved black people. Slaves traveled farthest at the Christmas holidays, when they might join relatives at Blakeley, and anytime the Washingtons journeyed to other family residences. At other times Blakeley was a refuge. Only a few months after Augustine Washington took command at Mount Vernon, Gabriel failed to return from a day's work. Suspecting that the slave had run away, Augustine went to the police in Alexandria to offer a reward. He imagined a wide radius of escape, for he also wrote to the police in Washington, Baltimore (fifty miles distant), and Hagerstown, Maryland (ninety miles away). Three weeks later he found Gabriel at Blakeley, with his parents and siblings.[34]

Slave hiring gave African Americans the most sustained exposure to other settings: different masters; different work; possibly the attractions and dangers of the city. It also separated families for extended periods, although not as irrevocably as sale. In November 1843 Augustine hired Eliza's daughter Amanda, then eight years old, to Miss Betsy Winter of Alexandria "for four years for her victuals & clothes," apparently as a maidservant to Winter's niece. When the niece got married, little Amanda got to return home. Particularly in the city, hired slaves might enjoy considerably more freedom than at home. This was probably truer for adult men, such as the industrial workers who lived in Richmond boardinghouses, than for women and girls, hired out as domestic servants and subject to more insistent supervision.[35]

In 1848 twelve-year-old Nelly Parker, Hannah's younger sister, was hired out to an Alexandria craftsman. Augustine renewed the arrangement the next year. Whether encouraged by the added freedom of the city or eager to escape her employer's attention, Nelly ran away in July 1849. She ended up in the Fairfax jail, costing Augustine the year's $10 hiring fee plus $17.75 in jail expenses. Nelly and her family paid a dearer price. The same week Augustine sold her for $350 to Bruin & Hill. Alexandria had another dubious distinction, as a northeastern terminus of the interstate slave trade. Nelly Parker may have been sent southwest, to the richer plantation lands and the harsher slave system of the Cotton Belt.[36]

For Jim Starks and Eliza Smith, the first slaves Augustine's parents had transplanted from Blakeley to Mount Vernon nearly two decades earlier, 1849 saw a more bittersweet farewell to their brother. Charles Starks had remained at Blakeley, married a free woman, and become the father of nine children, the oldest twenty-one and the youngest an infant. With Jane Charlotte Washington's encouragement, he had learned to read and write and developed his skills as a wheelwright. Jane Charlotte had emancipated him the week before Christmas the previous year so that he and his family could emigrate to Liberia. She also freed Lewis Wiggins, whom Bushrod Washington had specifically bequeathed her in his will. Wiggins and the Starkses went to Baltimore, boarded the *Liberia Packet* with forty-three other African Americans, and touched the western coast of Africa two months later. In Upper Virginia, outside Monrovia on the St. Paul River, Charles Starks planted coffee and kept in touch with the United States through *The African Repository*, the Washington-based organ of the American Colonization Society.[37]

Augustine Washington's notions of improvement owed more to agricultural reform and economic potential than to his mother's immersion in the benevolent reform enterprise. As 1849 drew to a close and a new year began, Augustine settled accounts with kin and neighbors. On the credit side, Edmund Parker, Sarah's son William, and Eliza's son John were doing day labor for a man named Wedge, each earning Augustine 62½ cents a day. Augustine's uncle Bushrod Corbin paid him $12 to continue housing and feeding Old Hannah, now a resident of Mount Vernon for nearly half a century. Debits ran from the trivial to the substantial. Augustine paid William Bell $1.50 for catching three escaped hogs and West Ford $206.72 for his previous year's work, extra blacksmithing, and hiring several hands. With other landowners in his neighborhood, he was seeking a charter for a turnpike from Alexandria, to replace the miserable roads that plagued visitors and planters alike. And on December 24 his mother asked him to retrieve a deed from her trunk of papers at Blakeley. After more than eight years of managing Mount Vernon, he would at last become its legal owner.[38] Augustine had arrived: justice of the peace; delegate to statewide Whig Party conventions; father of three daughters; master of nearly three dozen slaves. Fertility—his farms', his wife's, his slaves'—was the story of his early years as master of Mount Vernon. He was reversing the long decline that had begun with George Washington's death. But Augustine Washington's 1,225-acre Mount Vernon was not, nor could it ever become, the 7,600-acre estate of his most illustrious forebear's day. He was succeeding on a more modest scale, with increasing land under cultivation and a family consonant with the mid-century domestic ideal, southern style.

Augustine was not the only Mount Vernon resident to celebrate a festive Christmas in 1849. Dressed in their Sunday best, most of his slaves celebrated outdoors. They traversed the yard near the mansion, dancing and playing music on horn, fiddle, and tambourine. Augustine enjoyed the show and thought the slaves derived "infinite satisfaction" from the day's release. But old West Ford, who often oversaw Augustine's workforce, was appalled at the "unparalleled license" and mollified only when Augustine dispersed the gathering by distributing apple toddy. Perhaps Ford disliked the noise or was out of sorts that day. As a literate, free black man he may also have shared the abolitionist orator, writer, and ex-slave Frederick Douglass's belief, expressed in his recent autobiography, that masters encouraged such Christmas frolicking and drink only to take slaves' minds off their oppression. Meanwhile, in the slave quarters, Hannah Parker May neared the end of another pregnancy. On January 3, 1850, she delivered her fifth child and second daughter. For Augustine, a minuscule cost—the midwife's $1.50—helped add a new slave to his growing fortunes. For Hannah, who had been pregnant when Augustine sold her little sister Nelly the summer before, a new child might assuage some of the grief of that separation. She and Warner named their new baby Milly, after her mother back at Blakeley, reaffirming the kin ties that connected slaves across generations and distance.[39]

THREE

West Ford's Triple Life

One day in June 1850 old West Ford barred travelers from entering the Mount Vernon mansion. Before leaving for church in Alexandria, Augustine Washington had instructed him specifically to let nobody in without a letter from Augustine to West Ford himself. A party from the nation's capital arrived with a letter of introduction from Senator Daniel Webster but not the necessary authorization to Ford. Neither money nor the presence of a New York congressman would bend the old man's resolve, because previous travelers had chipped marble from the mantelpiece and mutilated other household objects in the incessant quest for mementos. However, West Ford gladly escorted a father and his young daughters, visitors from Norfolk, through the gardens and to the tomb and volunteered to tell them everything he knew about General Washington. As the little girls took some cedar sprigs already cut from a nearby tree, Ford told them how he cared for Washington's grave. Every so often he unlocked the iron railing, entered the alcove that contained the sacred remains, and brushed off the "leafy offerings" that reverent Americans and foreigners had thrown through the bars and onto George Washington's marble sarcophagus.[1]

Ever since Bushrod Washington's day, West Ford had occupied positions of trust and responsibility at Mount Vernon. He worked now for Augustine Washington, earning a hundred dollars a year as a carpenter, farm manager, and sometime labor foreman. When Augustine went away, West Ford often kept the plantation's accounts, disbursing money and settling up when his employer returned. Nearing seventy, the light-skinned man with a scarlike wrinkle on his left cheek still used the craft and the literacy that Hannah Bushrod Washington's will had prescribed for him.[2] Now too he assumed a role once played by Oliver and Phil Smith. His curly hair graying, Ford had become the superannuated servant ennobled by his memories and association with bygone days, even though he had been a free man for forty-four years.

Later that summer a United States census taker named Wilmer McLean neared Mount Vernon. At West Ford's own property on Little Hunting Creek, the sixty-five-year-old mulatto was not a hired carpenter but a farmer, his 214 acres valued at $2,100. His three horses, seven cows, ten sheep, and eight hogs were worth $268 in all. His farm had produced 500 pounds of butter and 250 bushels of Indian corn that year, plus smaller amounts of oats and rye. Paterfamilias to a three-generational household, Ford lived with his daughter Jane, her husband, Porter Smith, and their five children, ages eleven months to thirteen years. McLean proceeded from Ford's farm to Charles Washington's Wellington and then to Mount Vernon. Augustine Washington's real estate was worth ten times West Ford's, he owned far more livestock, and his acres yielded much larger crops, but he too was listed as a farmer.[3] For the purposes of the federal census, Washington and Ford were not employer and employee or planter and manager. They were fellow masters in a world where land conveyed a rough legal equivalency whatever the acreage.

Land could not erase other differences, however. By the laws of Virginia, as a free Negro West Ford could not carry a firearm, hold a religious meeting or preach at one, or sell or administer medicine of any kind. He could not acquire a slave, other than his wife or children. If his free children left the boundaries of Virginia to be educated, they could not legally return. And if he committed a felony, he would be tried and punished in the same manner as slaves. For West Ford, however, the greatest disparity between his situation and Augustine Washington's lay in another count that Wilmer McLean took that August, the roster of Augustine's thirty slaves, enumerated not by name but by age, sex, and color. Three were listed as 18-M-M, 12-M-M, 7-M-M: West Ford's kin, his sons or grandsons at Mount Vernon known as Joe Ford, West Ford, and Andrew Ford.[4] Old West Ford had not one legacy but two: the free children and grandchildren who would inherit his

Gum Springs property, and an enslaved family he was powerless to emancipate.

Witness to a hallowed past, employee and farmer, father and grandfather: West Ford's three identities mirrored Mount Vernon's own as shrine, farm, and home. At the same time, his fractured family tree, part slave and part free, became a microcosm of Mount Vernon's and the nation's divisions in a decade that was to split the Union. Just as travelers did not know the elements of Ford's life that Wilmer McLean totted up, most of them paid little, if any, attention to Mount Vernon as a working farm, where slaves performed the labor and where free black people lived nearby. America's gathering storm and Mount Vernon's own crisis made those connections more visible.

The escalating national conflict over slavery redoubled Augustine's public and private commitment to the institution. In the wake of the national Fugitive Slave Law enacted as part of the Compromise of 1850, Augustine and two fellow Fairfax County justices of the peace recommended tightening the Old Dominion's law governing "suits for freedom." At the very least, they argued, the state ought to pay the expense of keeping supposedly free Negroes while their cases were pending in county or circuit court. The presumption belonged on the owners' side, the justices wrote, because "Every Negro or mulatto is prima facie a Slave in Virginia." Closer to home, Augustine insisted that his children's governess be "sound (according to Southern views) on the subject of slavery." Alluding to Senator William Henry Seward's 1850 claim that scripture, "a higher law than the Constitution," mandated emancipation, Augustine refused to abide "the views of 'Higher Law Abolitionists' instilled into the minds of my children." When his overseer's house burned to the ground several years later, he may have wondered whether such views had infected the minds of his slaves.[5]

Augustine's commitment to slavery deepened too as he purchased more people. He bought a woman named Susan for $585 at a Jefferson County estate sale in 1852, then bargained with the sellers for a woman named Matilda. He purchased Matilda and her children Lucy (fourteen), Thomas (eight), Sam (six), and Thornton (two) for $1,575, $200 more than their appraised value. Each purchase sundered a family. Augustine did not buy Susan's husband and six-month-old baby boy or Matilda's husband and their other four children, who ranged in age from three to fifteen. Not surprisingly, the newcomers started their lives at Mount Vernon traumatically. Matilda unhappily helped Eliza cut fabric and preserve fruit, and Nelly Washington wrote her husband that Susan preferred to be sold rather than stay at Mount Vernon.[6]

Starting new families, the remedy Augustine encouraged, had mixed results. Susan became Edmund Parker's wife. Between 1853 and 1860 they had six children, including two sets of twins. Ned, one of the slaves raised at Blakeley, asked Augustine for permission to marry Matilda. The engagement cheered the bereft mother enough that Matilda rejected Augustine's offer two weeks afterward to sell her to his cousin in Jefferson County. Within a year, however, Ned's "tender solicitude" diminished, and Matilda's sadness returned. The newlyweds got to fighting, Ned attempted to run away, and Augustine sold him. The master offered to sell Matilda and her four children along with Ned, uprooting them together if she chose. When Matilda agreed, the slave dealers Bruin & Hill sent an employee to take her, Lucy, Thomas, Sam, and Thornton away. Lucy, who had made friends at Mount Vernon and flirted with Joe Ford, seemed particularly distressed. For his part, Augustine perceived his action as humane. He had honored Matilda's decision and, he thought, respected this family's integrity. But no evidence survives to reveal whether the slave dealer displayed the same respect. Nor do we know how the younger children reacted to their second displacement in as many years. We do know that the people left behind remembered them. The next year Betty Parker named her newborn daughter Matilda.[7]

On August 7, 1856, Augustine went to Annapolis and purchased a family. Nathan, his wife, Marietta, and four children, ranging from seven weeks to ten years old, cost twenty-seven hundred dollars, because the price of slaves had spiked. Nathan may have been a butler in his previous household, for that was the role Augustine Washington intended for him. Augustine spent seven dollars on "clothes for Nathan" the day after buying him and another ten dollars that December. In 1859 a writer described Nathan as the "chief house-servant, whose polite attentions are remembered by the thousands of strangers who visit Mount Vernon during the warm season." Marietta may have appealed to Augustine as a potential house servant; eight-year-old Joanna, as a young attendant for one of the Washington children. At the same time, buying Nathan's family told a story about Augustine Washington. He was purchasing the very picture of domesticity, four short years after *Uncle Tom's Cabin* had seared into Americans' consciousness a picture of the slave market ripping families apart.[8]

Sarah Parker, who turned twelve in 1856, had watched her own family grow as well. Her mother's marriage to Warner May brought a stepfather and five new half siblings, besides Isaac and Henry. Her uncle Edmund began his family with Susan. Her aunt Betty, like Hannah Parker May, first became pregnant as a teenage field hand and bore six children in all. And after Jane Charlotte Washington died in 1855, Augustine inherited still more Parkers from Blakeley. Grandmother Milly came to Mount Vernon, perhaps to take the place of her own mother ("Old Betty" had disappeared from Augustine's slave roster by 1856). Milly's adult children Jacob and Selina came too, the latter with a two-year-old, a one-year-old, and a baby on the way. Reuniting this extended family at Mount Vernon meant separating immediate families in Jefferson County. Milly had recently remarried, but her husband and Selina's stayed behind. Sarah knew this, even as family surrounded her: by the end of 1856 her grandmother, mother and stepfather, three half brothers, three half sisters, two aunts, two uncles, and nine first cousins.[9]

The Parkers at Mount Vernon had reason to rejoice, but Augustine Washington had inherited a problem, superfluous laborers. He sold Jacob Parker, and in December 1856 he did something new: he advertised NEGROES FOR HIRE in the *Alexandria Gazette*, breaking his long-standing custom of hiring out slaves to friends and neighbors. He did not list the NEGROES by name, but the descriptions of their skills help identify them. Milly, a "superior cook," and Sophy, a twenty-five-year-old "excellent sempstress and washerwoman," were hired to the Alexandria Theological Seminary for ninety and seventy-five dollars, respectively. Jenny, "a girl of 16 or 18, who is accustomed to cooking and general housework," went for sixty dollars to a farmer near Mount Vernon. A United States naval officer in Alexandria hired Selina Parker and her infant for sixty dollars. Augustine also advertised "one or two children" to be "put out for a term of years, free of hire." Accordingly, the final slave he hired out for 1857 was "little Milly," Sarah's seven-year-old half sister, "for five years for her victuals and clothes." Augustine could comfort himself that he had sold none of these people, divided no families permanently. For Selina and Hannah and the children from whom they were separated, it was cold comfort.[10]

Augustine repeated his advertisement in December 1857, this time with a different set of slaves. This was how Sarah Parker made her first appearance in print, as one of "three GIRLS" to be hired out for the year 1858. In addition to four women and a boy of ten or twelve, Augustine that year advertised girls of seventeen and thirteen, "accustomed to house work." Sarah was the only thirteen-year-old girl Augustine owned. His advertisement attested to the education she had received or at least the education that paid him dividends. He hired her to a Mr. Taylor of Alexandria.[11]

On or just before March 10, 1858, Sarah ran off from Mr. Taylor—but not away. Augustine, on business in Alexandria, wrote his wife that Sarah "had gone home this morning." The nine miles from Alexandria to Mount Vernon were not such a great distance. A thirteen-year-old girl could make her way between them on foot or stowed away in a wagon. Socially and culturally, though, a city of twelve thousand people was worlds apart from Mount Vernon's plantation quarters. Bustling by day, gaslit by night, Alexandria boasted dozens of craftsmen and merchants, including its slave traders. The Alexandria Canal (completed in 1843) and especially the Orange and Alexandria Railroad (1851) connected the city to northern Virginia's major wheat-growing counties and revived it as a hub of exports and imports.[12] In Alexandria Sarah surely lived and worked in continuous contact with her white employer's family. Housework could mean anything from carrying water to caring for children to answering the door to visitors, depending on how many other people the Taylors owned or hired. When she ran off, homesick, Sarah had been away from family for about nine weeks, probably for the first time in her life. Augustine instructed his wife to have her returned to Mr. Taylor, either in that day's coal wagon from the city or the following day.

" 'Shame, shame' on those who bear the name of Washington!"

Augustine reaped such scorn not for his slave management but for the neglect that visitors perceived at Mount Vernon. Even a traveler who compared Mount Vernon with the Grecian Patras, Jerusalem, and the Cities of the Plain, all likewise known for their historic associations with bygone glory, thought Washington's estate looked "deserted, forgotten, and despised." Ancient Rome and Greece were dead empires, powerless to preserve their historic sites. The United States was a young, vibrant nation, desecrating its great chief. The current Washingtons, like Bushrod before them, suffered accusations of "careless neglect." According to one visitor, Augustine had a reputation as a "good natured, indolent man, who takes the world easy, and does not trouble himself beyond his present wants & indulgencies." Another was closer to the truth: Augustine lacked the money to restore the place. It did not help that he was too young to have known the Father of His Country, or that he was an "accidental proprietor" rather than a direct descendant, or that he lacked the original furnishings and other treasured possessions that had once belonged to George Washington and Mount Vernon. No wonder visitors spilled so much ink describing the Bastille key and the marble mantelpiece. There was not much more to see inside the mansion.[13]

In September 1850, only three months after West Ford followed orders and kept visitors out of the mansion, Augustine Washington ended the three-decade ban on steamboats. He contracted with a boat company to land passengers at the Mount Vernon wharf twice a week on its route from Washington, D.C. The company built a plank walkway from the wharf to the tomb to the summerhouse, creating a mud-free, shaded path. The steamboat brought the Washingtons predictability as well as a quarter of the proceeds. Now they knew which days to expect the bulk of visitors, and they could decide whether or not to be at home. The experiment succeeded well enough that by 1853 the *Thomas Collyer* was making its run on Tuesdays, Thursdays, and Saturdays.[14]

Conditions and perceptions worsened. More visitors meant quicker dilapidation, decay, and ruin, more feet tramping over the grounds and through the entry hall of the mansion, more hands picking leaves and branches. Shortly before Augustine sold her and her family, the teenage slave Lucy pursued a thieving "lady visitor" all the way to the boat, trying in vain to retrieve a pair of newly cleaned nutcrackers that she had left to dry in the sun. Augustine closed the large dining room to visitors after one of them broke a cupid's arm off the mantelpiece. More visitors also meant more criticism of the appearance and upkeep.[15]

The onslaught of visitors owed much to larger developments especially in the North. The transportation revolution, witnessed in the completion of the Erie Canal (1825) and the massive expansion of railroads (nearly three thousand miles of track in 1840, triple that a decade later), made numerous American places accessible to those with leisure time and money enough. Most Americans could still not afford a sojourn in the nation's capital. But more could in 1850 than in 1820, especially city folk enjoying these years of commercial growth. Guidebooks to Washington first appeared in the mid-1820s and had proliferated by midcentury. Tourists listened to oratory in the galleries of Congress, examined relics in the museum at the Patent Office, and attended the president's weekly levees. They also went to Mount Vernon, described in the guidebooks. For decades, magazine and newspaper articles had told them exactly what to see and in what order: pass between the porter's lodges; admire George Washington's lemon tree; notice the Bastille key; worship at the tomb. Like Niagara Falls, Washington—and Mount Vernon—became a stop on the fashionable American Tour.[16]

The steamboat transformed the customary itinerary and the visitors' experience. Some still came by land at various times of the day and days of the week, but a ninety-minute excursion down the Potomac was far more pleasant than three or four hours on the muddy, stumpy paths from Alexandria. Once arrived, boat passengers toured a different geography from that which their land-going predecessors had. They climbed uphill from the wharf to Washington's tomb, now the beginning of the experience, not its culmination. They no longer saw, let alone entered through, the porter's lodges. Nor did they pass slave quarters before seeing anything "sacred." Before 1850 visitors had wangled letters of introduction to Augustine and Nelly Washington in order to get inside the mansion. Now entry to the first floor required no such formality. Most of all, the steamboat created a collective experience. Strangers arrived together, mingled everywhere, and left together. Some hailed the crowd's diversity as a welcome picture of the nation itself, where foreigner and Indian and native-born white

American all revered Washington. Others chuckled at the oddities of fellow travelers, like the white man who brought three barrels to fill with "sacred soil" and a pickax, a spade, and a black man to do the work.[17]

Not everyone appreciated the change. Writing in the *Southern Literary Messenger*, a traveler named Kennedy described the pilgrimage descending into tourism. "In these days of steamboats and rail roads every body visits Mount Vernon. They go thither in crowds, and they throng the old halls in troops, and long processions, and they—see everything." That last phrase was the tourist's language. The plankway to the tomb, the steamboat, the handbills and newspapers that advertised the journey: modern conveyances and conveniences had diminished the sense of solitary, thoughtful pilgrimage. In its place came curiosity seeking. A writer for *Harper's Weekly* depicted the mansion "filled with noisy young women in hoops and bright hats, who chattered and jabbered as they might have done at Barnum's. Some of them quarreled and fought to sit in the chair in which Washington spent many a thoughtful hour; others expressed their feelings in very natural 'Oh mys!' and 'You don't says!'—while their cavaliers gave vent to a higher form of enthusiasm in interjectional 'Jerusalems!' and 'Geminis!'" Writers such as these described an audience more than a citizenry, fashion more than reverence. P. T. Barnum's America had eclipsed George Washington's.[18]

Growing crowds encouraged more entrepreneurs. In 1854 Augustine signed a contract with a gas-lighting developer in Washington, not to illuminate Mount Vernon but to manufacture canes and other wooden souvenirs. Each commemorative disk produced by the Mount Vernon Cane Company bore a certificate of authenticity, testifying that the wood came from Mount Vernon trees. By early 1859, as the *Thomas Collyer* steamed down the Potomac, a photographer was distributing handbills: HAVE YOUR LIKENESS TAKEN AT THE TOMB OF THE FATHER OF HIS COUNTRY. When the boat docked, he raced up the hill, ahead of the crowd, to a small shanty by Washington's tomb. There he stood ready to take ambrotypes (cheaper to make than daguerreotypes) of people who wanted photographs of themselves with the tomb as background, for the same dollar as a picture without the tomb. He delivered these "Gems of Art" to buyers on the return boat trip.[19]

As critics assailed the specter of commerce, even black people, once imagined the truest relics of George Washington's Mount Vernon, came in for closer scrutiny. A poem that made the rounds of America's magazines ended with these lines: "the forests of Mount Vernon, / Guarding Washington's remains, / Are sold on speculation, / To be peddled out in canes." When elderly slaves such as Phil Smith and the century-old woman at the porter's lodges died, cane selling became the province of youth. But younger black people residing at Mount Vernon had even less claim than their ancestors to "historic associations." Confronted by "several black women and younger nig's" with canes for sale, one traveler refused the transaction altogether. "Are you sure these canes are *genuine?*" asked the visitor. "Oh, lor yes, massa! We would't lie for *nothing.*" "Certainly not for *nothing,*" replied the skeptical tourist, "but would you not for two and sixpence?" Unsatisfied with the slaves' "proofs," this visitor retreated to the woods "and cut a 'genuine' stick for ourselves." Another writer described the cane-selling women as "Vandals," implying that they desecrated what was historic or beautiful about Mount Vernon. He said nothing about the visitors who cut their own canes.[20]

Horrified at the dilapidation and apparent desecration, Americans called upon the government to act. Such requests dated all the way back to 1800, when Congress asked Martha Washington to relinquish her husband's remains for reburial under the Capitol Rotunda. Martha had acquiesced, citing her husband's lifetime of sacrifice at his country's request. Congress never made the necessary arrangements, even after renewing the appeal to Bushrod Washington in 1815, so George Washington's bones stayed at Mount Vernon. Similar appeals came roughly every sixteen years. John Augustine Washington rejected the 1831–32 incarnation, probably timed to coincide with the centennial of Washington's birth. After the Washingtons moved the patriarch (and their other dead) to the new tomb in the 1830s, they became less receptive to transferring his remains to the Capitol. By 1846 Jane Charlotte and Augustine were entertaining a different notion: to sell part of Mount Vernon itself, including the mansion and tomb, to the United States or to Virginia. However, at the time neither the national nor the state government would meet Jane Charlotte's asking price, a hundred thousand dollars for 150 acres. (Historic association accounted for most of the value.) Still, a decade of proposals and negotiations had begun, spurred after 1850 by well-publicized fears that Augustine Washington, now Mount Vernon's owner, would sell out to speculators who would make George Washington's home and tomb into a Barnum-esque theme park.[21]

The stage was set for innovative plans for Mount Vernon. Writers had long described Washington's tomb as an American Westminster Abbey, scene of reverent pilgrimage. In 1850, when President Zachary Taylor died after eating bad cherries at the Fourth of July dedication of the Washington Monument site, some embellished that vision. American leaders and heroes could be buried near George Washington, or a congressional cemetery could be located on the sacred grounds, which would thus become a national rural cemetery akin to Boston's Mount Auburn or Philadelphia's Laurel Hill. The British geologist Charles Lyell imagined a sort of time capsule: preserve Washington's mansion, outbuildings, and "negro houses" to showcase "the state of agriculture at the period when the Republic was founded, and how the old Virginian planters and their slaves lived in the eighteenth century."* Others looked to the future, not the past. Taylor's successor, Millard Fillmore, recommended the creation of an Agricultural Bureau within the Department of the Interior. Fillmore's interior secretary proposed concurrently to establish an American experimental farm—at Mount Vernon. Agricultural societies around the nation adopted the idea. One society inflated it into the Washington Agricultural Institute, which would do for the arts and sciences of farming what West Point did for military science. Where better to promote agricultural improvement than on land once tilled by Washington?[22]

The ultimately successful proposal imagined Mount Vernon not as a site of labor but as a shrine and a home. The basic story has been told

---

*Lyell's idea was 150 years before its time. In the 1990s Mount Vernon added "George Washington: Pioneer Farmer," a demonstration area with a replica of Washington's sixteen-sided barn. Interpreters in eighteenth-century dress tend livestock, cultivate a microcosm of his seven-field crop rotation, and invite visitors, especially schoolchildren, to perform the sorts of labor that enslaved people once did. The Pioneer Farm inhabits the ground those slaves knew as Hell Hole, long since drained and no longer malarial.

for 150 years, usually with a romantic sheen. In the fall of 1853 Louisa Bird Cunningham, mistress of South Carolina's Rosemont plantation and descendant of prominent revolutionary families in Pennsylvania and Virginia, took a steamboat down the Potomac on a moonlit evening. Passing Mount Vernon, she was shocked to witness its dilapidation. She wrote home to her daughter, and a movement began. An unlikely leader for America's first nationwide historic preservation movement, thirty-seven-year-old Ann Pamela Cunningham was a semi-invalid in lifelong, recurrent pain, the result of a riding accident years earlier. At first she launched the Mount Vernon crusade from the privacy of Rosemont. Under the pseudonym "A Southern Matron," Cunningham published an appeal to "Ladies of the South" in the *Charleston Mercury*. She exhorted southern women to raise Augustine Washington's asking price, now two hundred thousand dollars, to give Mount Vernon to the state of Virginia. She also wrote to Nelly Washington, in an unsuccessful attempt to bring Augustine around.[23]

For five years Cunningham and the movement navigated around political shoals. The Southern Matron's appeal initially galvanized fund-raising in Virginia, Alabama, and Georgia. By fall 1854 northern women were expressing interest, but they were reluctant to purchase Mount Vernon for Virginia rather than the United States. To allay this concern, Cunningham and her male advisers sought a legislative charter, incorporating the Mount Vernon Association with a Central Committee of women from across the nation. When passed in early 1856, the charter named the Mount Vernon Ladies' Association of the Union (MVLA), stressing feminine character and nationwide appeal. But Augustine Washington rejected the legal particulars: Mount Vernon was to be conveyed to the state of Virginia by the MVLA, ostensibly leaving him out of the transaction. Cunningham went to Mount Vernon to salvage the association's efforts. Washington was initially unmoved, but fortuitously Cunningham missed the return boat and had to stay overnight. As she recounted a decade later, she realized that evening that the problem lay in Augustine's wounded pride. Commiserating with his outrage, she unlocked the floodgates of sentiment. "What a change in his face! Unawares, I had . . . touched the 'sore spot,' the obstacle no money could have removed." Back in Richmond, the revised charter fell victim to a split within Virginia's Democratic Party. Recog-

nizing at last that the legislature would never consent to take possession of Mount Vernon, Augustine Washington agreed to sell two hundred acres to the MVLA, which would hold the title. The legislature
approved the charter on these terms, and Washington and Cunningham signed a contract on April 6, 1858. It required the MVLA to pay
two hundred thousand dollars (plus interest) in five installments: an
eighteen-thousand-dollar down payment, fifty-seven thousand dollars
by January 1, 1859, and the remainder in equal parts by the subsequent three Washington's Birthdays, concluding in 1862. If the MVLA
failed to maintain Mount Vernon adequately, its title would be forfeit
to the state of Virginia.[24]

Ann Pamela Cunningham knew her diverse audiences. The early
appeal to southern women painted northern commercial, industrial
culture as the threat: heaven forbid that Washington's home be "surrounded by blackening smoke and deafening machinery!" Once northern women joined the crusade, Cunningham changed her script. Now
women north and south were taking up a cause men had abandoned.
As male politicians steered the nation toward the abyss, in the form of
the Kansas-Nebraska controversy and South Carolina congressman
Preston Brooks's 1856 caning of Massachusetts senator Charles Sum-
ner, women united would regenerate American nationalism. Domestic
affection lay at the heart of the MVLA's appeal. Women's patriotism
fueled the movement, and the object of their endeavors was a home,
not a battlefield. As Augustine Washington's experience and the controversy provoked by *Uncle Tom's Cabin* demonstrated, however,
southerners' domestic ideal differed from northerners'. Mount Vernon
was a Virginia plantation, in Washington's time and their own. Some
northern MVLA supporters wanted a commitment that the association would employ only free white workers, but fearful of southerners'
reaction, Cunningham demurred. Because the immediate objective
required transcending, or appearing to transcend, politics, the Ladies
resolutely skirted the issue surest to inflame sectional tension.[25]

The MVLA created an unprecedented fund-raising pyramid. Once
the legislature endorsed Cunningham's deal with Augustine Washington, the Southern Matron became the regent of the Mount Vernon
Ladies' Association of the Union. In each state a vice regent, appointed
by Cunningham, was to enlist a network of lady managers to oversee

the effort within their own cities, towns, or counties. The vice regent for New York, Mary Morris Hamilton, Alexander Hamilton's granddaughter, raised about forty thousand dollars. Her Ladies' Standing Committee included the wives of former president Fillmore, Senator William Henry Seward, the historian George Bancroft, and the architect Andrew Jackson Downing, as well as the novelist Caroline Kirkland. Across the nation, less heralded women at the local level solicited donations of fifty cents or a dollar or two, aiming to involve as many Americans as possible in the movement. Balls and concerts raised significant sums in the South and especially in cities. Edward Everett, the nation's premier orator, toured the United States speaking on the character of Washington, the proceeds of nearly seventy thousand dollars filling the MVLA's coffers. While the unionist Everett lauded Washington as a nationalist, the states' rights champion (and soon-to-be fire-eating secessionist) William Lowndes Yancey raised money in the South with his own lecture on Washington as a revolutionary against governmental tyranny. Despite the nationwide economic depression of 1857, the MVLA raised the $200,000 (nearly $4.5 million in today's dollars) within two years and made each scheduled payment early.[26]

Although the overwhelming sentiment supported the MVLA, its summons was not irresistible. The vice regent for Maine reported that some northerners refused to contribute to a project they associated with the South, even if failing to contribute meant "yielding Washington as [southerners'] exclusive property." In August 1858 Mary Morris Hamilton invited Elizabeth Cady Stanton to become a lady manager in upstate New York. At home in Seneca Falls, site of the pioneering women's rights convention a decade earlier, Stanton replied that the MVLA had its priorities wrong. All her energy, Stanton wrote, was "pledged to a higher and holier work than building monuments, or gathering up the sacred memories of the venerated dead." As long as America's laws contradicted the essential truth in the Declaration of Independence that all people—"black and white, male and female"—were created equal, righting that wrong remained the purest tribute to Washington's memory. The abolitionist press as far west as Wisconsin hailed Stanton's refusal. Elizabeth B. Chase declined a similar invitation from Rhode Island's vice regent that November. "The cries of four millions of slaves, crushed beneath the iron heel of this wicked nation," reminded her that the United States had violated its principles ever since its founding. Mount Vernon's "moral value" derived from its association with America's fight for liberty. How could America's women claim to commemorate that struggle "when, with their consent, and approval and aid, every sixth woman in the land is liable to be sold on the auction-block, and is often so sold, for the vilest purposes?"[27]

Within eight weeks the connection between slavery and the Mount Vernon Ladies' Association hit closer to home. A correspondent to the *New York Tribune* happened upon the December 25, 1858, *Alexandria Gazette*, containing Augustine Washington's third annual advertisement: NEGROES FOR HIRE — FIVE WOMEN AND GIRLS AND TWO BOYS. The *Tribune's* editor, Horace Greeley, elaborated on the theme:

> Here we have Mount Vernon transmogrified into a regular slave shamble, where human beings are sold out to the highest bidder—the proprietor living on their wages—until they are returned on his hands. Five women and girls are so dealt in by the illustrious descendant of the Father of his Country! Women that cook, and bake, and brew, and do the work of the housewife, and are entitled before God and man to the earnings of their heads and hands, these Mr. Washington sells out, and pockets the proceeds. So, too, "boys" (men) who have an equal right to the product of their brawn and their brains. To such a cadence has Mount Vernon reached. Oh, save it, Americans, from further profanation! Stop rattling these bones in public, figuratively speaking, lest they turn over in their coffin through immortal indignation.[28]

The *Tribune's* article appeared under the title "Playing on the Bones," wordplay on the bones player who was a staple of every minstrel show. This time, though, the player was Augustine Washington, extorting every possible cent from the bones of his revered forefather while renting out the bones and bodies and minds of his own slaves. Greeley supported the MVLA's efforts, in the name of taking Mount Vernon from Augustine's clutches.

Other abolitionists argued that the rescue was not worth a slave-holder's ransom. A Republican newspaper in New Bedford, Massachusetts, scoffed that Washington could be poor enough to need the hiring fees from his slaves on top of the money the MVLA was collecting. If Augustine had agreed to free the slaves "who have supported him in idleness all his life" and provide for their futures out of the two hundred thousand dollars, the price might be defensible. Even so, a Protestant United States had no business salaaming at Washington's grave, the sort of obeisance associated with Islamic or Catholic pilgrimages. The MVLA, founded to save Mount Vernon from commerce and fashion, found itself tarred with the same brush, accused of assisting Augustine Washington's moneymaking schemes and peddling "Mount Vernonism" as the latest Barnum-esque humbug.[29]

Having signed the contract with Ann Pamela Cunningham and accepted the down payment, Augustine Washington looked for a new home for his family. He found it two counties and sixty miles west. For thirty-five thousand dollars he purchased Waveland, an 866-acre plantation three miles south of Marshall, in Fauquier County. For another ten thousand he renovated and enlarged the mansion, adding an Italianate wraparound porch, a large wing in the back, and an indoor plumbing system modeled on the one recently installed in the White House—none of which he could have done at Mount Vernon, where obligation to historic integrity and lack of money had forestalled architectural and mechanical innovation. Between the Blue Ridge Mountains to the west and the Rappahannock Range on the east, Waveland lay in the grain-producing piedmont of north-central Virginia. Its agricultural promise outstripped Mount Vernon's, and it was distant from the incessant annoyance of tourists.[30]

Abolitionists would have seethed to learn what else Augustine Washington bought with the MVLA's money: more slaves. He needed them because he sold the MVLA only a sixth of his Mount Vernon acreage, the part with George Washington's mansion and tomb. Augustine retained the most productive farmland, a thousand acres that included the compound of slave quarters, barn, and overseer's house a mile from the mansion. Now Augustine required two forces of field laborers, at Mount Vernon and at Waveland. As he received the MVLA's payments in 1858 and 1859, he spent $8,575 in all for seven adult men and a thirteen-year-old boy. Most came from Fauquier County planters who would soon be his neighbors. Strenuously as the MVLA avoided the topic of slavery, the money it raised throughout the Union financed the expansion of Augustine Washington's slaveholding and plantation operations, an irony that went unseen by steamboat travelers.[31]

Instead most Americans continued to imagine Mount Vernon to be America's unifying shrine, especially when events seventy-five miles north shook the nation. On September 18, 1859, Nelly Washington and the children were at Blakeley, their refuge from Mount Vernon's annual malarial miasma. Augustine was preparing to join them. He wrote to his cousin Lewis, who lived at nearby Beallair, about some papers he hoped to retrieve before his family relocated to Waveland. Four weeks later the militant abolitionist John Brown and his small army of like-minded white and black men began their long-planned raid on Harpers Ferry, site of a federal arsenal just twelve miles from Blakeley. After capturing the arsenal, they seized Beallair, armed its slaves, and ordered them to hold Lewis Washington captive. The role reversal ended within two days, when Brown and his surviving followers were captured by United States troops under the command of Robert E. Lee, George Washington Parke Custis's son-in-law and now master of Arlington House. By then Augustine's brother had also become part of the story. Richard Blackburn Washington, a crack squirrel hunter, joined the Jefferson County sheriff's posse. From an upstairs window, as legend has it, he took aim and killed Dangerfield Newby, a free black member of Brown's army.[32]

For the residents of Mount Vernon, black and white, John Brown's raid was local history. The uppermost topic of conversation in north-eastern Virginia and across the nation, it touched the master's family directly. White people discussed it, perhaps in hushed tones in the rooms where slave attendants came and went. Out of Augustine and Nelly Washington's earshot, their slaves must have talked about it too, in their own quarters when the day's work was done. But it was not their only news. Two of Betty Parker's daughters, seven-year-old Jenny and two-year-old Caroline, died that year, and Betty had a new baby girl. Her brother Edmund and sister-in-law Susan welcomed their seventh child, a boy. And the butler Nathan's wife was suffering a difficult pregnancy in the months before Brown's men invaded Harpers Ferry.

The next record of Marietta appeared in an invoice: $5.00 for a coffin for "Nathans wife"; $1.50 for another for "Nathan's child."[33]

For Americans not personally involved, the events at Harpers Ferry portended national disintegration, and Mount Vernon was its perfect symbolic foil. On December 4 a New York traveler sat in a hotel room in Charles Town, the seat of Jefferson County, where John Brown had been executed two days before. At Mount Vernon earlier in his journey, this New Yorker had received a rare privilege. Someone, perhaps West Ford, had opened the iron gates and allowed him to enter George Washington's tomb. Inside, he knelt by the sarcophagus and swore an oath to live by the words of the Farewell Address and safeguard Washington's legacy to the nation. If conservative, Christian men could only meet and exchange views at Mount Vernon, he wrote, "the present unfortunate violence of party spirit" could be defused and the Union saved. The same year a southern novelist painted the opposite picture. In his imagined America, abolitionists and secessionists in Congress agree to disband the United States, and "Border War" quickly ensues. The president, a unionist southerner, refuses to vacate his office and determines to preserve the nation. Forced from Washington as northern armies invade the South, he establishes headquarters at Mount Vernon. As northern forces and their British allies continue their pursuit, the evacuating unionists witness a true American's nightmare. A "dark column of vapor" reduces George Washington's home to the kind of ruin that no MVLA could save.[34] North and South, Mount Vernon symbolized the American nation. Northerners and southerners argued over the presence of slavery there—and the MVLA studiously avoided the issue—precisely because George Washington's home and grave possessed such powerful meaning for all.

Unlike the cane sellers, or the slaves hired out for their owners' profits, or the black soldiers in John Brown's army, West Ford seemed a fitting representative of the nation's shrine. Now the African American repository of Mount Vernon's lore, Ford did not recount the story of George Washington's death, the way Oliver Smith had once done. Instead he told of another demise, one he had actually witnessed, that of Billy Lee, the Revolutionary War manservant Washington had freed in his will. Back in the 1820s West Ford had bled Billy to relieve the parox-ysms of delirium tremens, but one morning the blood did not flow. The old man was dead. The popular historian Benson John Lossing heard this story in 1858, when he visited Mount Vernon to prepare an article for *Harper's New Monthly Magazine*. Lossing encountered Ford making a plow outside the burned-out ruins of the old greenhouse. He also learned a bit of Ford's own history: his service to Bushrod Washington, his plantation on Little Hunting Creek. An artist as well as an author, Lossing asked to sketch Ford's portrait the next morning. Ford donned a black satin vest and silk cravat and arranged his "curly gray hair . . . in the best manner." The old carpenter, who had probably been sweat-ing the day before, knowingly explained his careful self-presentation: "The artists make colored people look bad enough anyhow." As Augus-tine and Nelly Washington prepared to move to Waveland, West Ford built them new wooden plows as well as packing crates. His eldest son, William, free since birth, now worked at Mount Vernon as well, tend-ing the gardens once tilled by Phil Smith.[35]

West Ford created a different legacy on his own land. Not waiting for the uncertainty that might follow his death, he divided the 214 acres into four sections and gave one to each of his free children. His younger children, son Daniel and daughter July, soon sold their por-tions. Porter and Jane Smith and their children, who had lived with old West for decades, stayed. William Ford and his wife, Henrietta, who had resided in Alexandria for much of the 1850s, returned with their children to take possession of their fifty-two acres. Their land became and remains the African American community of Gum Springs, where a state historical marker identifies West Ford as the founder.[36]

By a fluke of the 1860 census, West Ford was listed twice. On July 1 he was at Waveland with Augustine Washington's family, listed as a seventy-six-year-old mulatto carpenter. Augustine may have brought Ford there to work; there was plenty to do with the renovations to the mansion and the new farm. Perhaps too, Ford wanted to spend time with his enslaved kin, whom Augustine had transported west to a new set of slave quarters. Ford may have remained there on October 9, when Nelly Washington died unexpectedly. Friends and relatives del-uged Augustine with sympathy, but one cousin struck a harsher note. The tragedy was a sign that Augustine needed to forsake his preoccupation with material things and get right with God, for the salvation of his own soul and the benefit of his seven "motherless children." His wife's death, his cousin's admonition, or both stirred Augustine, who began assembling the family in regular prayer. By November 29 West Ford was back at Mount Vernon, but not with his children at Gum Springs. As at Waveland, Ford lived on Augustine Washington's acres, in the household of the white man Augustine had hired to oversee the landed and human property he still owned there.[37]

When the Washingtons went to Waveland, one visitor hoped that Mount Vernon would no longer "be disfigured by decrepid [sic] or youthful negroes, miserably clad, who are made to sell canes, shrubs, and other souvenirs, for the profit of others." Eschewing slave labor and the controversy it might provoke, the MVLA hired a different group of Negroes to work on the hallowed ground: West Ford's free grandchildren Dandridge and Priscilla Smith and his free son William, the gardener. Ann Pamela Cunningham also hired a distant cousin of the Washingtons', Upton Herbert, to begin restoring the collapsing piazza and several outbuildings when it became clear that the MVLA's financial campaign would succeed. Herbert welcomed the streams of visitors through 1860, notably the prince of Wales in October. Cunningham conducted the association's business from Philadelphia and made plans to move to Mount Vernon. Her new secretary, a New Yorker named Sarah C. Tracy, shopped for mattresses and other necessities lacking in the mansion, which Augustine Washington had left almost bare. Soon after Cunningham and Tracy arrived on December 1, a contingent of Connecticut notables called the Putnam Phalanx made a ceremonial pilgrimage from Hartford. They peeped inside buildings and took canes, leaves, and twigs. Like most visitors, they encountered black people: a "venerable negro" selling nuts, acorns, and locust beans; "a smart looking colored cook of the true old Virginia stamp" presiding in the old kitchen. These were the people recently hired, in the absence of Augustine Washington's slaves.[38]

Just through the woods, half a mile from the ground now rendered exclusively historic, Augustine's agricultural operation persisted, fueled by his slaves' sweat. The population on that land reflected its absentee ownership: ten adult men and a fourteen-year-old boy, just three adult women, eight children. They appear to have included Jim

Michum, Jim Starks, Edmund Parker, Edmund's sister Selina and her children, and Gabriel and Mary and their daughter, among others.[39]

For West Ford and for the black people who belonged to Augustine Washington, the purchase of Waveland, occasioned by the very success of the Mount Vernon Ladies' Association, divided families and community built over the past three decades. Sixty miles were not an unbridgeable distance for people who had long visited family at Blakeley. West Ford traveled back and forth between Mount Vernon and Waveland, and Augustine almost certainly dispatched slaves from one plantation to the other. Nevertheless, as the election of a new president stirred talk of American disunion, many of them must have wondered whether a whole new era of separations had commenced.

FOUR

Andrew Ford's America

Born sixteen months apart, Andrew Ford and Sarah Parker both assumed adult responsibilities in the turbulent spring and summer of 1861. Even before Virginia formally seceded from the United States that May, Augustine Washington joined Robert E. Lee's staff as an aide-de-camp. He took Andrew, seventeen and unmarried, to wait on him and care for his horse. Lee's troops encamped in the Alleghenies that rainy August, as Federals and Confederates contended in the mountains and valleys for control of northwestern Virginia. Lee, Washington, and Captain Walter Taylor shared a tent, which doubled as office and sleeping quarters. No evidence reveals where Andrew or Lee's body servant Perry slept. Andrew Ford went off to war, a black man serving a master who fought for an independent slaveholding nation. He left behind—forever, as it turned out—the slave quarters at Waveland. While Andrew was striking tents and carrying his master's provisions on horseback, sixteen-year-old Sarah was nursing her new baby. It was a particularly fertile year at Waveland, for Andrew Ford's two sisters-in-law, Sarah's nineteen-year-old aunt Jenny, and fifteen-year-old Charlotte all gave birth that spring as well. Sarah's son Smith was born on June 1, 1861; the facts of his paternity are as elusive as those of Sarah's own.[1]

Andrew and Sarah entered adulthood miles away from where they had been raised. Back at Mount Vernon, different tableaux of daily life played out against the national cataclysm. Mount Vernon itself became an American borderland, and not simply because it lay between Union troops headquartered at Alexandria and Confederates at Manassas. The MVLA sought to insulate America's transcendent shrine as best it could from hostilities and politics. The association has told this story for a century and a half, about Virginian Upton Herbert and New Yorker Sarah Tracy living at Mount Vernon during the war, their partnership a symbol of the neutrality that preserved Washington's home in the nation's darkest hour. It is a true story with an enduring purpose. It places Mount Vernon safely outside and above politics, a rejoinder to whatever divides America, from immigration at the turn of the twentieth century to partisan rancor at the turn of the twenty-first.[2]

The rest of the Mount Vernon that Andrew Ford and Sarah Parker knew, the thousand acres that Augustine Washington still owned, became an entirely different sort of borderland, military and political and economic. No-man's-land rather than demilitarized zone, this was the ground where African Americans crossed boundaries of property relations, social status, and economic possibility. On this land, men and women tested the meanings and the limits of newfound freedom. In pursuit of that freedom, several of them told their stories after the war ended. So did Andrew and Sarah. Largely unknown and unremembered, their individual narratives bespoke America's war for emancipation, not the MVLA's quest for union.

In the presidential election of 1860, Abraham Lincoln was not on the ballot in most southern states and many Virginia counties. The southern Democrat John C. Breckinridge won most of the slave states, including Maryland and Delaware. In a tight contest, however, Virginia gave a 156-vote plurality to the Constitutional Union ticket, headed by John Bell, whose running mate was the Massachusetts orator and MVLA champion Edward Everett. Lincoln got just 1,887 votes in the Old Dominion, 1.1 percent of the state's total. Most came from the northwestern counties that formed West Virginia three years later, but a scattering came from Mount Vernon's neighbors the Quakers of Fairfax County. Virginia continued divided as the lower South rang with calls for secession. Some Old Dominion Democrats promoted secession immediately after Lincoln's election. They were opposed by a coalition of unconditional unionists, particularly in the northwest, and others who would stay in the United States if Lincoln pledged not to coerce the seceding states. On February 4, 1861, Virginians elected delegates to a state convention on secession. Although seven lower South states had seceded by then, the convention chose the path of moderation. Unionists outnumbered secessionists and kept the upper hand as late as April 4, when a secession ordinance failed by a 90–45 vote. Pressure against conditional unionism mounted as Lincoln was reported to be planning to resupply Fort Sumter. After South Carolinians fired on the fort on April 13 and Lincoln called for seventy-five thousand troops to quash the southern insurrection, the course changed. An ordinance of secession passed the convention on April 17 and went to Virginia's voters a month later.[3]

Tension mounted at Accotink Precinct, four miles from Mount Vernon, where local residents were to cast their ballots on May 23. About forty unionist voters congregated outside the polling place, hesitating to enter. The election judge sat inside, a loaded revolver on the table. He swore to shoot the first man who tried to vote for union. Jonathan Roberts, a Quaker farmer and surveyor, exhorted his neighbors to stare down the threat. Roberts entered first and announced his vote before the scowling Judge Windsor. The others followed suit, and unionists outpolled secessionists at Accotink, 76–19. But Fairfax County as a whole supported secession by a vote of 942–289, echoing the decision of voters across the Old Dominion.[4]

War had already touched the neighborhood. An anxious George Mason, Augustine Washington's old Fairfax County neighbor, wrote General Lee on May 5 about the perilous situation. The Potomac and its tributaries, surrounding the vicinity on three sides, offered limitless opportunity to slaves bent on escape and "Kansas ruffians and murderers" who filled the nearby Union armies. Augustine, now a lieutenant colonel on Lee's staff, replied on the general's behalf that the army had insufficient resources to protect every locality and that Mason and his neighbors should form home guards and devise signals to collect their forces if marauders attacked. Residents became refugees, secessionists fleeing southward, unionists (including many recent northern emigrants) northward. A few hundred rebel cavalry, carrying breech-loading carbines and short swords, patrolled the fifteen miles between Washington and Mount Vernon to support local secessionists. Along the Mount Vernon Road from Alexandria, mounted men patrolled every half hour, but not on the hallowed grounds now owned by the MVLA.[5]

On May 24, the day after the secession vote, Union armies occupied Alexandria with little resistance. The remaining Confederates in eastern Fairfax County spent the next eight months under the hard hand of war, even though only one pitched battle took place in the county, at Manassas in July. Flouting their governments' policies and their commanders' orders, Union and Confederate soldiers terrorized civilians who sympathized with the other side, and they confiscated and destroyed residents' property. Noncombatants also joined the conflict. His Quaker faith precluded Jonathan Roberts, who had defied the judge to vote his unionist conscience, from taking up arms. He volunteered his services as a scout and spy and mobilized a network of African American informants, free and enslaved. Anne Frobel, who lived five miles north of Mount Vernon, marveled at how her slaves informed her and her sister what the armies would do next: "They seem to have a perfect telegraphic system of communication all over the country." With their decades-long connections off the main roads, African Americans often proved the best intelligence gatherers of all.[6]

Secession and war turned the Ladies' Mount Vernon upside down. The regent, Ann Pamela Cunningham, had left for South Carolina in late December 1860, to put her affairs in order before the crisis that was expected to follow Lincoln's inauguration in March. She did not return for six years. By the time she got home, South Carolina had seceded from the Union. Her widowed mother, an ardent secessionist, beseeched her to stay at Rosemont and manage the plantation, where 138 slaves formed the bulk of an estate worth $194,000. Forty-five years old, pained by chronic rheumatism and weak eyes, Cunningham complied. The regent felt herself increasingly isolated from her life's work during the war. The cotton had to be harvested, and mail traveled sporadically at best between Mount Vernon and remote northwestern South Carolina. Sarah Tracy remained at Mount Vernon, joined by a friend from Philadelphia, Mary McMakin (to deter any hint of impropriety between Tracy and Herbert). The booming of cannons from

Manassas, thirty miles away, roused the little community at six in the morning on Sunday, July 21. Mount Vernon lay within sixty miles of other scenes of battle: Ball's Bluff (October 21, 1861), Chancellorsville (April 30–May 6, 1863), and the Wilderness (May 5–7, 1864).[7]

Strife outside fortified Tracy and Herbert's resolve to keep Mount Vernon neutral inside, especially as northern newspapers rumored that Herbert and Cunningham harbored secessionist sympathies. The regent never abandoned her love for Mount Vernon or her intention to return, but distance and daily cares left her with an enormous void. The notion of a Ladies' Confederate Navy Association helped fill it. As she had done nine years earlier, Cunningham began with a pseudonymous appeal. Friends assured her that citizens across the Confederacy would rally to this new movement once they knew that the MVLA's tested leader carried its banner. Cunningham imagined a structure much like the MVLA's, with a presiding officer in each state and lady managers for districts and counties. She started at the top, imploring South Carolina's first lady, Lucy Pickens, to lend "your time, your talents, & your influence as an offering to be laid upon [your country's] Altar." The catch: Cunningham could not publicly announce her own involvement. Northern newspapers had already condemned her "treasonous proclivities" (their words, not hers) and wondered whether she had "turned Mount Vernon into a secession rendezvous." What would they say if they knew that the MVLA's founder was creating a kindred Confederate organization?[8]

More important, what might Union troops or the United States government do? The government confiscated Robert E. Lee's house when his wife failed to appear in person to pay taxes on it during the war. To symbolize what happened to traitors' property and what the Union was fighting for, the United States soon planted two new communities on the land around Arlington House. One was a city of the dead, the graveyard for fallen United States soldiers now known as Arlington National Cemetery. The other was a farming community of very much alive black families that had escaped as "contrabands" to Union lines. Freedmen's Village persisted for more than thirty years. Had the MVLA not purchased its two hundred acres before the Civil War, the United States might have seized Mount Vernon from the absent Augustine Washington. The ground around George Washington's mansion could have become, like Arlington, a national cemetery or a showplace for emancipation. As Cunningham wrote to Pickens, Washington's home and tomb were "now <u>within</u> the lines of the enemy, and <u>at their mercy</u>!" Only the MVLA's unflinching neutrality protected America's shrine.[9]

By fall 1861 the bulk of visitors were military men stationed nearby or passing through, almost entirely Federals now that the Union controlled Alexandria. To visiting Union soldiers, Mount Vernon embodied their cause. They had been taught from childhood to revere George Washington, America's founder in an earlier war. Echoing the MVLA's own rhetoric, they believed Mount Vernon a national shrine, all the more reason to defeat the rebellion and prevent Washington's home and tomb from falling into the Confederate States of America. At the same time, soldiers simply enjoyed the chance to play tourist. Hailing from as far away as Maine and Michigan, many had never before left their small towns and family farms. They might never again pass near the nation's capital. Like their antebellum civilian counterparts, they wandered the grounds, drew sketches of the buildings and the Potomac view, and wrote home to relatives about what they had seen. Some carved their names on the tree trunks or in the bricks of Washington's mausoleum, sometimes identifying their regiment. Cunningham had dictated that soldiers stack their weapons outside the grounds. Further, they could not enter the property in uniform, a real hardship for those with no other clothing. They covered their uniforms with shawls or blankets, making for unusually raggedy clusters of visitors. Given the MVLA's small staff, Sarah Tracy beseeched commanding officers to let soldiers visit only in small groups, a request that the troops usually honored.[10]

Money was tight throughout the war. Union commanders allowed the steamboat to run intermittently through midsummer 1862, then stopped it entirely after the second battle of Bull Run late that August, shuttering the primary source of income. By then most visitors were soldiers coming by land. Many could not afford the 25-cent admission fee, which merely matched what the MVLA received for each steamboat passenger. Receipts plummeted. For all of 1862 and 1863, entrance fees and garden sales totaled $1,264.43. Revenues for 1864 were even worse: $348.03, including only $230.65 from visitors. Expenses from May 1861 to early 1864 ran much higher: "miscellaneous house expenses, servants, &c."; groundskeepers, carpenters, and other day workers; repairs and farm and garden costs. Including the deferred salaries owed to Herbert, Tracy, and McMakin, total expenses came to more than $8,000.[11]

As best they could, Herbert and Tracy tried to create a self-sufficient community. Their skeleton workforce grew wheat, corn, potatoes, and fruit, some of which they sold to visitors. Tracy and McMakin caught Potomac shad and herring for breakfast, and the secretary and superintendent themselves policed the grounds against larcenous or vandalizing visitors. Each of them concocted fund-raising ventures. Tracy had coffee beans from a Mount Vernon tree strung into necklaces for sale. Herbert sold some of the bricks removed in the restoration as souvenirs. Most controversial was a fee, imposed sometime before April 1862, for admittance to the room where George Washington had died. One visitor that spring encountered a black man at the door to Washington's bedchamber. "Sah, you must give me twenty-five cents," said the attendant. "Why so?" asked the visitor. "General Washington died in that room and you can't go in without a quarter of a dollar." The visitor took offense. Could not the Ladies' Association make its money in some other way than charging pilgrims for their worship? This traveler calculated that the MVLA had made more than fifty dollars in boat fees that day. He did not realize that such days were rare.[12]

Declining income took a toll on Tracy and Herbert's workforce, composed almost entirely of free black people. The gardener was William Ford, old West Ford's son. Three of West Ford's grandchildren were also on the payroll in 1861, Dandridge Smith as "a jack of all trades" and his sisters Priscilla and Caroline as housemaids. A washerwoman came in once a week. In the early weeks of war George Washington Riggs, the MVLA's banker in Washington, advised Herbert to lay off all but two workmen. "Dissatisfied" with Dandridge Smith and Emily, a housemaid, Herbert dismissed them. The employee rolls remained unsettled that spring. As finances tightened, Sarah Tracy volunteered to pay Priscilla Smith herself; Herbert decided to "hire a boy" at lower wages than an adult man's. This young employee, Eugene, did various chores for Herbert and cleaned the walkways, "which have been entirely neglected on account of the expense." That fall or the fol-

lowing year Mary McMakin described the reconstituted little community as just a "parlor circle" of herself, Herbert, and Tracy; and a
"kitchen cabinet" of "Emily (cook), Priscilla (chambermaid) Frances
(charity maid of all work) George (coachman & general assistant),"
plus a gardener and one or two additional hands.[13]

Provisioning this community meant traversing a war zone. Once
Union troops occupied Alexandria, transportation into the city required a pass, authorized by the Union commander. Superintendent
Herbert, suspected of Confederate sympathies, could not obtain a
pass without forswearing allegiance to Virginia. (From a sense of duty
to Mount Vernon, Herbert resisted several appeals to join the Confederate army, as his brothers and other relatives did.) Travel thus became
the province of Sarah Tracy and a succession of African American
drivers. Six city passes survive in the Mount Vernon archives. One,
signed by General Winfield Scott on October 2, 1861, allowed Tracy to
move between Mount Vernon and Alexandria. The other five were for
black employees, specifying the routes, locations, and purposes of
travel permitted for each man.[14]

Once-routine trips into Alexandria became adventures, in which
African Americans' knowledge of the landscape proved invaluable.
Tracy and her attendants regularly encountered Union pickets watchful for Confederate sympathizers. At five-fifteen one October 1861 afternoon, she and her driver left the city. A barricade three miles en
route forced them to retrace the journey and take another road, leading to an unexpected, large body of troops. An officer, not the typical
sentinel, informed Tracy that she could go no farther that night. Wield-
ing her pass, Tracy persuaded a series of officers to let her proceed,
barricade after barricade, her horse growing palpably skittish. At the
Mount Vernon Road, still several miles from home, a high fence
seemed impassable until the soldiers helped Tracy's driver locate a little gate. They led the horse through and lifted the buggy over. "If once
around the barricade," she thought, "I could reach the blacksmith's
whose children worked at Mount Vernon," Porter Smith, son-in-law of
old West Ford. Smith could keep her horse and buggy overnight and
lead her on foot, through the woods, back to Mount Vernon. Unfortunately, the soldiers told her there was no way out that night. It was
getting dark. She "begged a night's lodging" at a house near the soldiers'

encampment and made it to Mount Vernon with a military escort the next day.[15]

Like many other white people in Fairfax County in 1861, Sarah Tracy and Upton Herbert felt boundaries tightening: between Mount Vernon and Alexandria, even between the land the MVLA had bought and the thousand neighboring acres that still belonged to Augustine Washington. Tracy of course had never known "Mount Vernon" as Augustine's entire twelve-hundred-acre plantation. To her, the phrase meant the MVLA's property, the sacred ground. Herbert understood how locals used the phrase "Mount Vernon" to refer to the entire tract or even to the much larger property once owned by Bushrod Washington, but his loyalty to Virginia and implicitly to the Confederacy virtually confined him within the MVLA's grounds. At the same time, communication grew more difficult. Mail service was interrupted when the post office at Accotink was closed after the Union occupation of Alexandria. Thenceforth Mount Vernon's residents could get mail out only through Alexandria or through the Occoquan post office eight miles south. Before Mary McMakin's arrival Sarah Tracy lamented the isolation of having "not a white woman within three miles of me."[16]

In contrast, African Americans, especially those who had lived at greater Mount Vernon for decades, found all sorts of borders increasingly fluid. Black people moved far more freely than whites in this Union-controlled terrain where they knew the byways and back roads. In mid-June 1861 Tracy wrote to Cunningham about recent difficulties. With a Scotsman named Fraser who had recently done some carpentry for the MVLA, Dandridge Smith (apparently reemployed at Mount Vernon) had taken to drink and, worse, gotten into the habit of selling whiskey to other employees. After Herbert had dismissed both men, Fraser spread word that Herbert was a secessionist who had fired Fraser for his politics, a charge that helped cement the superintendent's isolation at Mount Vernon. Meanwhile, following troubles on Augustine Washington's land, Edmund Parker ran off to Alexandria. "Now he with Dandridge and Fraser"—an enslaved man, a free black man, and a white Scotsman—"are trying what mischief they can make," Tracy complained. Smith, Parker, and Fraser were trying to scare the MVLA's employees into leaving, she thought. Mount Vernon

employees received messages summoning them to Alexandria to answer charges. The gardener William Ford became a particular target,
perhaps because his nephew Dandridge had some family score to
settle. Black people's mobility did not always advance the MVLA's
agenda. It furthered their long-standing hope to create a life story of
their own, beyond Mount Vernon's boundaries.[17]

On the morning of July 14, 1861, a picket from the Sixteenth New
York Infantry reconnoitered along the Mount Vernon Road. At Augustine Washington's property, the soldiers saw what they estimated to be
seventy-five barrels of fish and eight thousand pounds of bacon. They
also met the slaves Washington had left behind. Colonel Thomas A.
Davies, who commanded the picket's brigade, told his commanding
officer that "some person" associated with the Confederate army
planned to send for the provisions that night. Davies acted fast, taking
possession of three horses. The slaves helped, harnessing four mules to
one army wagon and two to another. Ten of the slaves drove the wagons to Davies's camp "of their own accord," as he described it. He later
returned for the fish and bacon but found far less bacon than his men
had estimated; had somebody made off with the rest in the meantime?
Then he had second thoughts. Whatever his own views about confis-
cating rebel property, the case was not clear-cut even though Augustine Washington was a high-ranking Confederate officer. So Davies left
a guard to watch the provisions, mules, and wagons until he received
further instructions. The black people were another matter. Without
"law or orders" either to leave them on Washington's property or "to
prevent them from volunteering to do team duty in my brigade," Davies
kept them in his camp.[18]

Not for long. His commander's rebuke appeared in the next day's
official records: "Colonel Davies has been instructed to immediately
withdraw his pickets to within a proper distance in front of his brigade,
to respect private property, and to send back to the farm the negroes his troops brought away." That last clause—"his troops brought
away"—admitted no trace of black self-determination. It was a far cry
from Davies's description of black people as volunteers in their own
confiscation and willing workers for the Union cause. In this first sum-

mer of war, when Lincoln still worried about secessionist sentiment in the remaining border states, Union policy limited the confiscation of rebel property. The month after Davies accepted the Mount Vernon slaves into his camp, the president rescinded General John C. Frémont's order declaring the slaves of rebel combatants in Missouri to be "contrabands of war," subject to seizure. For now those slaves would remain in place, as private property. So would those at Augustine Washington's Mount Vernon, for all their efforts to capitalize on an opportunity.[19]

Augustine recognized how tenuously he controlled his Mount Vernon property, human and otherwise. From the soggy mountains of northwestern Virginia, he sought to maintain his mastery at least of Waveland. When he went off to war, the widower left his children in the care of his aunt, his farm in the immediate charge of an overseer, and the entire operation under the supervision of Edward Carter Turner, a fellow Fauquier County planter. Augustine cautioned his daughter Lily to be careful with money, for "all my property except that at Waveland has either been taken by the enemy or has been rendered useless to me" behind enemy lines. Instead of an income of ten or twelve thousand dollars, the Washingtons earned nothing except the proceeds of Waveland's farm. "In one word, instead of being well off we are poor." The doctor had to be paid for every visit, so his daughters should "learn to doctor yourselves." If house servants were "laying up sick," he had a familiar solution: hire them out. Assigning them to farmwork would do no good; "they will then lay up altogether. They will be better off at good homes with something to do."[20]

Augustine Washington was dead two weeks later. On the night of September 13, on an ill-advised reconnaissance at Cheat Mountain, he and Robert E. Lee's son came within twenty yards of a concealed Union picket. A quick volley surprised them, and three bullets tore into Augustine's body. Within four days the news from northwestern Virginia reached the papers of Warrenton, seat of Fauquier County. Friends and neighbors lamented the death of Waveland's master and worried for his orphaned children and for their own loved ones. At the funeral on Saturday, September 21, neighbors from miles around viewed Augustine in his wood coffin in the library, so recently remodeled according to his design. The Reverend Joseph Packard lamented the sting of death, familiar in a season of war, and celebrated the victory in death over earthly woes, equally familiar in midcentury evangelical culture.[21]

For southerners and northerners alike, the death of George Washington's great-grandnephew assumed symbolic meaning. How fitting, Packard preached, that "one who bore his name" should have been appointed to high station within Virginia's army for independence. In one of his last letters home, Augustine had told his family that he would gladly die in the "just and sacred cause" if God willed it. Thus he became a "blessed martyr" in that cause, even more so because he had embraced religion in the last year of his life, since Nelly's death. The life and death of Augustine Washington united evangelical Christianity, the Father of His Country, and the Confederate struggle, precisely the combination that ministers and political leaders employed to arouse Confederate nationalism that first year of the war. A correspondent to a Vermont newspaper drew the opposite message: "This mean descendant of the Great Washington, after steeping his crabbed soul in avarice all his life, as a final act of meanness, chose to take the traitor's path, and has met with a traitor's fate." Martyr or traitor, Augustine Washington provoked divided reactions in death as he had in life.[22]

Father and master, Augustine Washington disrupted a household and a community yet again when he fell at Cheat Mountain. For his children, his death meant a second uprooting in as many years. Richard Blackburn Washington, now the executor of his brother's estate, decided that the seven children should move to Blakeley, which he had inherited from Jane Charlotte Washington. There they would be among family: "Uncle Dick," his wife, and their six children. Augustine's teenage daughters took tearful leave of their Fauquier County friends at the end of September. They would also miss their new home, with its gleaming woodwork and indoor plumbing. The following week Dick Washington took his nieces and nephews to Jefferson County in the family carriage. Their clothing and other personal possessions followed in wagons. A few weeks later Fauquier County neighbors took inventory of what the Washingtons left behind at Waveland. Furniture, the family silver, a well-stocked cabinet of liquors and wines; livestock, farm equipment, and the year's harvest: all constituted about 45 percent of Augustine Washington's estate. The larger part lay in the human

property, forty people in all, valued at $18,425. Each slave was as-
signed a value, recorded with the rest of the inventory. The most valuable men, as well as a few women bundled with their infant children,
were appraised at $1,000. Teenage boys capable of field work were
valued at $700 to $900; children of three or four, $125 or $150. By
the appraiser's eye, Sarah Parker and four-month-old Smith were
worth $800.[23]

Andrew Ford was not listed because he had run away from the Confederate army once his master was killed. The well-ordered Waveland
inventory concealed the extent to which Augustine Washington, and
now his estate, had lost control of the enslaved population. It listed
seven adult men, nine adult women, nine boys ages three to sixteen,
nine girls ages three to thirteen, and six younger children appraised
with their mothers. However, the 1860 slave censuses for Fairfax and
Fauquier counties had enumerated more than sixty slaves in Augustine's name. In other words, the inventory left out more than twenty
people, those still at Mount Vernon, now behind Union lines and beyond the executors' reach. These were the people Colonel Davies's
picket encountered in July 1861. In addition, Andrew's brothers Joe
and West Ford had fled Waveland shortly after the battle of Manassas
that month, leaving their wives and children and escaping to Union
lines. They worked for the Union army in the campaign on Virginia's
peninsula that fall and into 1862. Andrew escaped to Alexandria.[24]

Sarah remained at Waveland. Her stepfather, Warner May, and two
other men ran away in late October or early November. Less fortunate
than Edmund Parker and the Ford brothers, they were captured and
thrown into jail at Warrenton. By this time Augustine Washington's executors were arranging for the disposal of his possessions. Edward
Carter Turner started selling off Waveland's provisions on November 7. A three-day estate sale the following January raised more than
twelve thousand dollars, as Augustine's neighbors bought everything
from pots and pans to fifty-year-old bottles of sherry and finely bred
horses. The most difficult decisions involved slaves. Dick Washington
apparently intended to maintain some farming at Waveland. He had
sixty head of cattle taken there in December 1862, and he sold Wave-

land corn, wheat, and pork as late as January 1865. But he shrank the
scale of operations. The estate accounts include no expenses for slaves
(food, clothing, doctor's bills), occasional mention of a manager, very
modest harvests. It appears that Dick did not leave his late brother's
slaves there but instead hired a white resident manager to run the farm
with his family's labor. From Dick Washington's perspective, Blakeley
was no better an answer, though a nanny and a few other slaves were
ultimately sent there. He already had a household and farm full of servants; most of Augustine's slaves would be surplus laborers.[25]

In Dick's mind, there was only one option. Restive, difficult to control, expensive to maintain, owned by a dead man whose household
was being broken up: in slaves, these characteristics all pointed toward
hiring out or sale. On November 12, 1861, Turner spent $17.36 to take
"servants to Rich'd," specifically the widowed butler Nathan and his
fifteen-year-old son, Stephen. In Virginia's capital he bought new
clothes for both and shoes for Stephen, the better to present them as
household servants. On the seventeenth Turner returned to Fauquier
County alone, having sold or hired out father and son. Three days later
three more Waveland slaves—Sarah's young aunt Jenny Parker, her
husband, Stephen, and their young child—joined Warner, Frank, and
Armistead in the Warrenton jail. In early December they were taken to
Richmond, and all except Warner May were sold.[26]

Sarah and Smith were sold as well. They fetched nine hundred
dollars, a hundred more than their appraised value. At this point Sarah's
whereabouts become difficult to trace. On February 6, 1862, the slave
auctioneer's ledger books include the "Sale of woman Sarah & child" to
N. M. Lee & Co., another Richmond slave dealer, for a thousand
dollars. If this was the same Sarah, all we know is that the auctioneer unloaded her on a colleague for a one-hundred-dollar profit. It is
likely that she spent the war years in Richmond, for that was where
the Mount Vernon Ladies' Association found her when the conflict
ended.[27]

In wartime Richmond, Sarah would have experienced an urban
maelstrom utterly different from what she had found in Alexandria a
few years earlier. Richmond's 1860 population of thirty-eight thousand
more than doubled in the first weeks of war. Soldiers from across the
Confederacy poured into the capital. Soon they were joined by refugees

from the countryside seeking relief or employment, as well as slaves hired for factory work or impressed (forced into service) for war work, building fortifications or serving the Confederate army. Before the war black people in Richmond—especially male slaves hired out there, away from owners in the countryside—enjoyed considerable freedom of movement. Long-standing laws requiring slaves to carry passes went largely unenforced, as did restrictions governing blacks' hiring themselves out. Wartime restrictions circumscribed black mobility. Guards, watchmen, and judges enforced the pass and self-hiring laws with renewed vigor. The hardships of war, notably the food shortages that led white women to riot in Richmond's streets in April 1863, fell heavily on slaves. Most enslaved women remained domestic workers in private homes or businesses, unlike enslaved men, who were encouraged or impressed into government service. Whether sold or hired out, Sarah probably worked harder than ever before. As the price of buying and hiring slaves skyrocketed, employers burdened fewer workers with more chores. A woman who once worked as a cook might now also be a washerwoman, chambermaid, and nurse. At seventeen, with little Smith in tow, Sarah may have performed all of these roles during the war, as she certainly did afterward.[28]

Back on home ground, a reunion was occurring. On June 20, 1862, the local miscellany in the *Alexandria Gazette* included this item: "Most of the negroes on the Mount Vernon estate have returned, but they are generally idle, and consider themselves free." Two-thirds of this statement was accurate. That summer black people returned to the land Augustine Washington had left behind. In addition to those who had remained all along, several men who had decamped to the Union army joined them: Joe and West Ford, Jim Starks, Edmund Parker. Somehow, Joe's wife, Fanny, and West's wife, Ellen, and their eight children, who had been counted at Waveland for the inventory, made their way back too. So did Andrew Ford, who may have learned in Alexandria that his brothers, sisters-in-law, nieces, and nephews were reuniting. By July some sixty African Americans, including as many as forty children, were living on the Mount Vernon property. Most of them formerly Augustine Washington's property, they reconstituted their community without the master. Parents cared for their children; when Andrew contracted smallpox, Gabriel Johnson nursed him back to health. A Quaker named Thomas Wright, who lived four miles southwest, nominally managed the property.[29]

The black people on Augustine's land indeed considered themselves free, but not idle. The previous summer the commanding general had ordered Gabriel Johnson to harvest the corn crop as his own, while the Union army took the wheat, oats, horses, and livestock. By the time Gabriel's compatriots returned in 1862, the Union had consolidated its control of Alexandria and eastern Fairfax County. Poor people and African Americans streamed back in search of war-related employment. The Mount Vernon estate afforded a wooden opportunity, its old-growth forests a prime source of timber for fuel and construction. Jacob Freese, judge of the Union's provost court at Alexandria, gave Edmund Parker permission "to take care of his family and three orphaned children that belonged on the estate," perhaps his sister Selina's fatherless children. Thomas Wright told the brothers Ford "to go to work and take care of the women and children," cutting oak, hickory, and cedar.[30]

These African American men imagined their new life on Augustine Washington's ostensibly abandoned property as exactly the "free labor" that northern Republicans championed, the economic system that distinguished freedom from slavery, North from South. It meant the chance to make one's own living, to support self and family by the sweat of one's own brow. Not everybody saw it this way. To the *Alexandria Gazette*, it looked like idling, perhaps because the women and children were not toiling the way slaves were supposed to. To an outsider's eye, black men chopping down trees may have appeared more destructive than productive.

At the start of 1863 unionist residents elected Jonathan Roberts, the Quaker who had opposed secession at Accotink Precinct and organized a largely black spy ring, to replace the Fairfax sheriff, who had left to join the Confederate army. Somebody told the county court about "depredations . . . being committed upon the Mt. Vernon estate," and the court appointed Roberts to take charge of the Fairfax County land that now belonged to Augustine's heirs. Visiting the property, Roberts found cords of cut wood at the ferry landing and scattered around the woods. The overseer's house had been stripped of its windows and doors. The barn was also heavily damaged. Roberts found black people on the estate, some of them Augustine's former slaves and some from parts unknown, all cutting timber and carrying it away.[31]

Whose timber, and whose land, was this? To the African Americans, free labor principles applied; their work and its fruits belonged to them. Despite his sympathy for slaves and free black people, Roberts applied a different principle. The land and its resources belonged to Augustine Washington's heirs, not to the people squatting there. On the last day of January, Roberts rented the land for seven hundred dollars to a man named George Johnson. To put this new tenant in "quiet possession," he ran the African Americans off the land and confiscated the timber they had cut. All the profits from selling the wood were turned over to the court, presumably to be held for Augustine Washington's children. We do not know where the African Americans went once Roberts rented the property to George Johnson. Some apparently remained as tenant farmers, suspended between slavery and freedom.

Their dispersal and the unsettled state of affairs on Augustine Washington's Mount Vernon may help explain why Sarah Tracy and Upton Herbert provided old West Ford with a place of refuge that June at the MVLA's Mount Vernon. In the summer of 1863 Tracy and Herbert visited Ford and "found him very feeble." Fearing the "excitement" would hurt the old man and feeling a duty to provide for him, they brought him back to the mansion to which he had come with Bushrod Washington sixty-one years before. On July 31, 1863, the *Alexandria Gazette* reported that West Ford, seventy-eight and "well known to most of our older citizens," had died the previous day "at his home" on "the Mount Vernon estate." It did not report that he had been free more than half a century or that he had possessed his own farm for nearly thirty years.[32]

Two summers later, after the war had ended, most of the others came back—and told their own stories in the form of claims with the Bureau of Refugees, Freedmen, and Abandoned Lands. Better known as the Freedmen's Bureau, this agency in the War Department supervised educational and relief efforts for emancipated African Americans, negotiated and enforced labor contracts between freedpeople and employers, and adjudicated claims of violence against freedpeople. On August 1, 1865, Captain George A. Armes took command of the Freedmen's Bureau office for the counties of Fairfax and Alexandria. His supervisor instructed Armes about the bureau's philosophy and policy toward the freedmen: to "encourage them to industry and economy, by assurance of all necessary aid in securing a fair remuneration for faithful labor, and all necessary protection in the enjoyment of the fruits of that labor." In settling claims between freedmen and others, a simple consideration ruled: What would the claimants get if both parties were white? If freedmen were being "held and worked as slaves," a violation of United States law, the miscreants were to be punished harshly enough to deter others. In "aggravated cases," Armes could even confiscate land (though not houses or gardens, defined as domestic rather than economic space) and let the freedmen work it "for their own benefit." Because the Emancipation Proclamation had applied to slaves in this district, they were "entitled to full compensation for their services" since January 1, 1863. Finally, the bureau did not permit employers to force family separations or to cheat freedmen in contracts. By early October the Freedmen's Bureau office for northeastern Virginia had begun organizing schools for black children in Fairfax County and had established an employment office in Alexandria. Simply put, the bureau sought to extend northern free labor ideology to the conquered states of the former Confederacy: contract, not force, ruled economic relations; such relations required an educated workforce.[33]

On August 18, Sarah's uncle Edmund Parker went to the bureau office in Alexandria to file his complaint against Jonathan Roberts for "expulsion from his house and charge and appropriation of his property." According to Parker, back in snowy February 1863, George Johnson had driven him and other black people off the estate too quickly to find another home. Parker and his comrades had had to abandon the wood they had cut. A Freedmen's Bureau officer sought information from Roberts and other officials. The inquiries apparently worried George Johnson, who visited the bureau office on August 29 to tell his side of the story: that he had rented the estate from Roberts and paid his rent regularly. On Saturday, September 2, the brothers Joe and young West Ford filed their own claim, recalling that their families had also been driven off, forfeiting $250 worth of wood they had cut. They remembered that thirteen men had each had "his own work," not gang labor reminiscent of slavery, but individual initiative and implied contract. The following Saturday Gabriel Johnson and James (formerly Jim) Starks filed a third complaint against Sheriff Roberts. According to Johnson, the commanding general had given him "a paper" that should have prevented anyone's interference with his woodcutting. But Roberts had taken twenty-five cords that Johnson had cut, as well as eighty-five dollars in cash. Roberts had even intimidated two "old servants on the place" into surrendering twenty dollars that Johnson had given them.[34]

Edmund Parker, the Ford brothers, Gabriel Johnson, and Jim Starks displayed a remarkable comprehension of contract relations and legal process. They wanted to know what authority had placed George Johnson there, whether he had possessed the right to turn them off the land, and whether they were entitled to compensation for their labor, the wood, or both. They wanted reparations "for the damage done them." As a witness to their veracity, Parker and Johnson and Starks all named Dr. Lewis Linton, who owned the nearby property across Little Hunting Creek from Mount Vernon. Edmund Parker now lived on Linton's property, perhaps a refuge for people forced off the Mount Vernon land. On September 21 the Freedmen's Bureau notified George Johnson that it was claiming the Mount Vernon estate, the part Augustine Washington's heirs owned, as abandoned land and required him to report its condition. The case records end here, and the following month the Freedmen's Bureau began restoring confiscated Fairfax County land to its antebellum owners. But four months after the Civil War ended, it was the freedmen who asserted legal rights to the fruits of their labor at Mount Vernon.[35]

Men were not the only ex-slaves who sought assistance from the Freedmen's Bureau. Sarah's aunt Selina Parker reported a case of assault and battery, begun that summer over a pair of pants. Selina and her family still lived on the land George Johnson rented, as tenant laborers in a shanty some three hundred feet from Johnson's house. Her eleven-year-old son, John, had done some work for another tenant farmer there, a white man named Chapman Renoe, who promised "a pair of pantaloons" in return. Renoe bought some linen and gave it to his daughter, who gave it to Selina, who got another woman to sew the pants. But then Renoe shooed Selina's children off and began to harangue her. The cloth was meant for his own pants, he claimed, and he wanted $1.80 for it. Selina responded that he owed her son more than that. Her self-assertion surprised and angered Renoe, who was accustomed to dealing with black women as slaves, if at all. "By God," he swore, "I will let you know that you have not Pomp [his son] to fool with now," and he threw a rock at her. It missed. Selina ran for Johnson's house. On the way she picked up an ax, to defend herself if necessary. Renoe kept hurling rocks at her and eventually hit her in the back of the head, knocking her briefly senseless. The next morning he returned to her house and "beat her with a pole." She started to run; he kicked her in the side. She came into Alexandria "to get protection and security in her person and rights." The Freedmen's Bureau sent an agent to investigate Selina's complaint, but after that the record is silent.[36]

No less than her brother Edmund's claim, and though seemingly unresolved, Selina Parker's revealed an understanding of legal rights, in this case the right to be free from violence and the implied contract between her son and Chapman Renoe. Edmund's and Selina's appeals to the Freedmen's Bureau shared something fundamental: both sought to protect their families. During the war Edmund subsumed Selina's brood under his own paternal care. By the summer of 1865 his sister employed the mechanisms provided by the United States government to stand up for her son and for herself.

Andrew Ford had left Mount Vernon long before his brothers Joe and West filed their Freedmen's Bureau claims. Around March 1863 Andrew encountered Ennis Smith, regimental surgeon to the Ninth Michigan Infantry. Dr. Smith's tour of duty was ending, and he was returning home to Calhoun County, about a hundred miles west of Detroit. Offered a job on Smith's farm at seven dollars a month, Andrew followed. He spent the summer and early fall planting and harvesting there, familiar work with the still-novel pleasure of earning his own wages. When the harvest was done, he moved into the nearby town of Marshall, made acquaintance with other black men, and took a job at Brown's Hotel. Fifteen days later an army recruiter came to Marshall, seeking volunteers for the First Michigan Colored Infantry. Andrew enlisted on December 28.[37]

Private Ford found himself in a company of strangers trudging to Detroit. For three months they stayed in spartan, uncomfortable barracks—board walls, straw bedding, wood stoves for heat. As he remembered years later, his rheumatism began there. He felt its first effects, in his right big toe, in the Toledo train station in March 1864. His whole foot had swollen by the time the First Michigan boarded the train for Baltimore. "If you can't keep your place in ranks," his commanding officer ordered, "get out of the way and let these men go on." Ford fell out and hobbled alongside his unit, with his gun for a cane. By the next morning the inflammation had spread up both legs to his hips. At Baltimore he was placed in an ambulance. Slipping in and out of consciousness, he was taken to a military hospital in Annapolis. While his regiment proceeded to Beaufort Island, South Carolina, where it was organized as the 102nd Regiment, United States Colored Infantry, Private Ford spent most of summer 1864 in Maryland hospitals. He finally joined his comrades at Beaufort Island in August or September. His feet, ankles, and knees swelled when he marched, and sunstroke felled him for a few days, but he kept pace as the company marched around South Carolina and to Savannah in the aftermath of General Sherman's march to the sea. In late summer 1865, when the war was over and while his brothers claimed restitution for the Mount Vernon wood they had cut, Andrew Ford marched through a series of South Carolina towns with unfamiliar names: Boykin's Mills, Bradford Springs, Branchville. On provost duty at Orangeburg and Winnsboro that summer, his regiment kept the peace among white and black South Carolinians who reacted very differently to the sight of black soldiers in blue.

One such South Carolinian was Ann Pamela Cunningham, whose family plantation lay within seventy miles of the 102nd's encampment at Winnsboro. Toward war's end Cunningham had devised a private microcosm of the MVLA's structure right at Rosemont, a hierarchy of black men instead of white women. Hiring a reliable white overseer had proved impossible, with most of the eligible white men off at war. Resolving not to hire an unskilled white man, Cunningham instead appointed an experienced slave as manager and others as "sub-managers" reporting to him. The system worked for months after Lee's surrender, and Cunningham told her now-former slaves that she would try to keep them together and fed if they stayed. She imagined Rosemont to be the "model plantation," with its freedpeople continuing to work and "every thing going on as formerly."[38] Outside, rumors of race reversal unsettled the neighborhood and frenzied Cunningham. In the mild version, freedmen were preparing to demand that whites rent them land. In the dangerous version, insurrection loomed. Ex-slaves were plotting to kill all the white men, preserve the white women—"you may guess why!"—and seize land and property for themselves. Cunningham came to believe that white people were now "at the mercy" of blacks, who could burn down whites' houses even if armed insurrection came to naught. Her black manager announced that he and the rest were free and planned to depart. Like many a plantation mistress, she was shocked, angry, and resentful. She believed that her family had always treated its slaves well, so their departure seemed the vilest ingratitude. Cunningham blamed "Yankee malice" most of all for turning freedpeople into ingrates. Northern Radicals, she fumed, were spreading abolitionist propaganda throughout the South Carolina countryside and distorting ordinary black people's perspective. The trouble was a Union army full of "black soldiers, or the scum of Europe or their own wicked cities."[39]

The 102nd Regiment mustered out at Beaufort Island on September 30, 1865, twenty-one months after Andrew Ford had joined up. The twenty-two-year-old veteran lived another sixty-three years. He returned to Marshall and worked odd jobs, mostly at day wages. On the sixth anniversary of his enlistment, he married Almira Coleman, who had been born free in Michigan. The newlyweds moved to Chicago, where Andrew worked in a paper mill. After Almira died of scarlet fever less than a year later, Andrew went back to Michigan, "jobbing around" from Saginaw back to Marshall. He married a black woman from Canada in 1873, and in 1876 moved to Cedar Rapids, Iowa, where he earned twenty-five dollars a month as a school janitor. In the early 1880s he was ordained a deacon and then an elder of the African Methodist Episcopal Church in Iowa. The Reverend Andrew Ford moved from town to town in Iowa and Wisconsin as a traveling elder, taking farmwork to make ends meet. He belonged to a local post of the Grand Army of the Republic, the Union veterans' organization, as well as the Colored Masons and other lodges. He never returned to live at

Mount Vernon, but one of his nephews, perhaps inspired by his uncle's example, moved to Cedar Rapids around 1920. Andrew Ford's rheumatism never left him. Neither did his memories of the people among whom he had grown up or of the way he had taken his freedom and his manhood.[40]

"My son, sir." Sarah spoke these words at Mount Vernon on September 4, 1865, while Andrew Ford was encamped in Winnsboro, South Carolina. She was introducing her son Smith, now four years old, to John Townsend Trowbridge, a Massachusetts writer who had taken the steamboat that day. Whether the "pretty looking colored girl" or the well-dressed tourist ever learned each other's name is a mystery. Trowbridge saw an "intelligent and cheerful" woman "industriously scrubbing over a tub." Sarah saw a man scribbling into a little notebook, different from most visitors because he spent time talking with her. She told him that she had been born on the place. Sarah Parker's Civil War ended back at Mount Vernon—not the land Augustine Washington's heirs still owned but the Ladies' Association's national shrine.[41]

The visitors and the steamboat had returned as well. Anticipating crowds, Sarah Tracy placed an advertisement in the *Alexandria Gazette*, reminding the public "that the MANSION and GROUNDS at MOUNT VERNON are closed to ALL VISITORS on Sundays." Union soldiers mustered out at Washington in May and June, thousands participating in the Grand Review on May 23 and 24. Many of them trooped to Mount Vernon: tourists enjoying their final days before returning to far-flung homes. Civilians also flocked to Washington, no longer the epicenter of war and once more a travelers' destination. As of June 1, they could follow the Potomac to Mount Vernon. The steamboat *Wawaset* (replacing the old *Thomas Collyer*) resumed round trips from Washington and Alexandria, bringing 150 or more passengers twice a week. Once more thousands of people visited Mount Vernon, as they had before the war. After a straitened four years, Upton Herbert and Sarah Tracy welcomed the ability to make ends meet. Admission receipts from May to December totaled $2,784.49, nearly double the previous three years' admissions combined. By late August all the deferred expenses except the superintendent's outstanding salary had been covered. Herbert's employees had harvested enough wheat for the year's consumption, and he expected to grow sufficient corn and vegetables as well. Soldiers eagerly bought bouquets of flowers, which Sarah Tracy and Mary McMakin arranged. Business was so brisk that Tracy sought permission to hire another gardener for the rest of the summer.[42]

Prosperity brought its own perils, however, as old complaints resurfaced on all sides. Because the crowds were so large, and because this was Tracy and Herbert's first experience of such an onslaught, it all seemed overwhelming, even destructive. The MVLA arranged in mid-June for a guard from the Seventy-ninth New York Infantry to protect the property and preserve order, but some visitors still behaved badly. They broke pieces off the marble mantel and sliced wood from George Washington's bedstead with their penknives. They spit tobacco juice into the fireplace in the large dining room. They broke branches off the shrubbery. Herbert posted signs to police their behavior, prompting one frustrated newspaper columnist to carp that "every pilgrim is esteemed a poacher." But poachers abounded, the pickings easier in crowded rooms. Tracy wrote to Cunningham and various vice regents about the vandalism that "pilgrims" and "relic-hunters" perpetrated. Similar stories found their way into newspapers because Herbert complained publicly about the depredations. Despite the continued destruction, most visitors seemed to show the same combination of reverence and curiosity that had motivated their predecessors in Augustine Washington's day.[43]

Other tensions simmered aboard Potomac steamboats. By July many African Americans were traveling on the boats as part of daily life because the river was a thoroughfare for local citizens going to market or to work. The *Wawaset*, for example, ran several trips a day between Washington and Alexandria; only one morning and one afternoon trip, twice a week, went as far as Mount Vernon. On an afternoon trip from Washington on July 5, a black man on the *Wawaset* "spat upon, and soiled a lady's dress." Reproved for his "impoliteness," the black man allegedly responded in "grossly insulting language," egged on by other African Americans, whereupon white passengers attacked and whipped them. Fearful of what the white crowd might do next, three black people jumped overboard and swam to shore. In a culture where white tourists spit tobacco into George Washington's fireplace and spittoons could be found in the halls of Congress, "ladies" (a term reserved for white women) in mixed crowds were hardly immune to having their dresses soiled. In the aftermath of emancipation, however, black people mixed with whites without the accustomed deference of slavery days, aboard ship and in myriad other settings. Like a disputed pair of pants, a wad of tobacco expectorated in the wrong direction could ignite latent resentment, even violence.[44]

John Townsend Trowbridge, the Massachusetts reporter who visited Mount Vernon on the exceedingly sultry September 4, 1865, recounted the African American perspective on recent history. One of the founders of the *Atlantic Monthly* in 1857, Trowbridge had made a minor literary sensation with his antislavery novel *Cudjo's Cave* (1864), which romanticized abolitionists and fugitive slaves. When the Civil War ended, a Hartford publisher asked him to tour the defeated South and write a book about its condition. Trowbridge began at Gettysburg, then proceeded to Harpers Ferry and Charles Town, where fire and war had obliterated traces of John Brown's trial and execution. He talked with African Americans nearly everywhere he went, revealing their responses to freedom and to the collapse of the Confederate regime, along with much of its physical architecture. In this way he was unlike most of the other people who wrote about Mount Vernon in 1865, who took their stories and their cues from Upton Herbert as he guided them around the grounds and into the mansion.[45]

At the center of Trowbridge's detailed description of Mount Vernon and its "little village" of outbuildings was Sarah, her words an autobiography in miniature.

On her early life: Augustine Washington "kept me hired out; for I s'pose he could make more money by me that way—tho, sir, I don't think twas altogether right . . . After the war was over, the Ladies' Association sent for me from Richmond, and I work for them now." Trowbridge summarized more of her story: "She told me that she was twenty years old, that her husband worked on the place, and that a bright little fellow four years old, running around the door, handsome as polished bronze, was her son." He used Sarah's story to editorialize: "I looked at her, so intelligent and cheerful, a woman and a mother, though so young; and wondered at the man who could pretend to own such a creature, hire her out to other masters, and live upon her wages!" Sarah did not tell—or Trowbridge never asked—anything about the black family and community in which she had grown to adolescence.[46]

Sarah's husband was Nathan Johnson, the butler Augustine Washington had purchased in 1856. Nathan's first wife, Marietta, had died shortly before the war, and he too had been sold or hired to Richmond in late 1861, after Augustine's death. How Sarah and Nathan came to marry is another historical mystery, but perhaps their common experience of Mount Vernon and Waveland encouraged them to maintain contact in frenzied wartime Richmond. In all likelihood, the Ladies' Association sent for Nathan after the war, and Sarah returned with him. Tracy and Herbert would barely have known Sarah—a teenage girl, always hired out—but they would have known Nathan as Mount Vernon's butler. Alternatively, the neighboring presence of Sarah's uncle Edmund Parker, aunt Selina Parker, and various cousins and longtime friends could also have drawn Sarah home. In any event, Sarah and Nathan Johnson were working for the association when Trowbridge came to visit. They were not the only former slaves of Augustine Washington to find employment at the MVLA's Mount Vernon.

On her wages: "I gits seven dollars a month, and that's a heap better 'n no wages at all!" Sarah laughed with pleasure as she answered Trowbridge's question about her compensation. The previous year several vice regents had convened in Washington, the first MVLA assembly since war broke out. They paid long-overdue salaries and devised a scale of monthly wages and salaries. Sarah Tracy received $150 a month to cover her own pay, household expenses, and "servants' wages." She quickly realized that this was $25 less than expenses required. Upton Herbert got a budget of $60 a month for "laborers." In the summer of 1865 Sarah and Nathan Johnson's monthly wages probably came out of Tracy's allocation, because they served the household as well as the tourists. When Trowbridge found Sarah Johnson scrubbing over a tub, she was probably doing Herbert's, Tracy's, and Mary McMakin's laundry as well as her own family's. Sarah contrasted freedom with slavery in exactly the terms Trowbridge appreciated. She cast herself—and he was happy to cast her—as the epitome of northern free labor, industriously and happily earning wages for her toil.[47]

And on her work ethic: "The sweat I drap into this yer tub is my own; but befo'e, it belonged to John A. Washington." Trowbridge failed to catch her meaning at first, so she tried again.

You know, the Bible says every one must live by the sweat of his own eyebrow. But John A. Washington, he lived by the sweat of my eyebrow. I alluz had a will'n mind to work, and I have now; but I don't work as I used to; for then it was work to-day and work to-morrow, and no stop.

Sarah was describing a choice that freedpeople made across the postwar South. Rather than work without stop, as masters and overseers had compelled them to do, they insisted upon making time for other things: family life, community life, leisure. As early as the fall of 1865 some white observers attributed that determination to laziness. Sarah knew better, for she had always been willing to work.[48]

When he put Sarah's story at the center of his story of visiting Mount Vernon, John Townsend Trowbridge understood something important. Certainly he had his own blinders. He wanted to see black people as individuals earning their own wages in a free market society. Although he praised Sarah as a mother, he had no inkling of her extended communal life. He did not see or could not know, for example, that malaria ravaged the Mount Vernon workforce that summer or that Sarah Johnson had an aunt and an uncle on neighboring ground that locals still called the Mount Vernon estate. Nonetheless, he knew that Mount Vernon was both George Washington's and Sarah Johnson's—a place where the sacred past and an emancipatory present, no less glorious, met.

Andrew Ford's Civil War, as he told it himself in a pension application in the 1880s, offers the dramatic version of African Americans' wartime experience. A field slave goes into war with his master but runs away to Union lines, where he rises from menial labor to the blue uniform of the United States Army. It was not all drama. He saw far more time in hospitals than in battle. Nor was it entirely unfamiliar. Mount Vernon's slaves had always enjoyed a modicum of mobility, and an army uniform was as scratchy and ill-fitting as a slave's annual ration of clothing. Freedom was not without its own trials, a lifetime of aching joints and odd jobs. Yet the war transformed Andrew Ford's life completely. In slavery, his passage into manhood might have meant an abroad marriage, children bound to a white master, and labor increasingly skilled but no less unpaid. Instead he crossed the boundary from enslaved to free labor with an odyssey across the United States.

Sarah Johnson could not join the Union army, nor did she travel as far away as Andrew Ford did. Unlike him, she returned to Mount Vernon. But Sarah too knew that the war had changed her life. She expressed the same sense of justice and of family that her aunt Selina, uncle Edmund, and the others did in their Freedmen's Bureau claims. She took pride in working for the Ladies' Association, in raising her handsome little son, in owning her own sweat, and in earning her seven dollars a month. Simply, eloquently, she got the economics of freedom just right.

FIVE

The Johnsons' Neighborhood

Sarah, Nathan, and Smith Johnson lived in a little white house that had probably never been slave quarters in George Washington's day. Situated less than a hundred feet west of the mansion, with only the old family kitchen between, the Johnsons' probable abode had served multiple functions in the eighteenth century. Its front room, which opened onto the central bowling green and had small glass-paned windows on both sides, had stored tools and supplies for the mansion house farm. The rear chamber, with a small hearth and a ladder stair to the attic, had housed a succession of white men, Washington's clerks. The door to that apartment opened onto the south lane of work buildings—smokehouse, washhouse, coach house, barn. Until 1860 a solid wall had separated the "circle storehouse" from the "clerk's quarters." In one of the MVLA's early restoration efforts, Upton Herbert added a well-framed doorway between the two chambers, replaced and re-framed the windows, and installed a larger, curving staircase.[1]

What had been a storeroom and a single white man's compartment was now a commodious dwelling for a black family recently freed from slavery. The two first-floor rooms provided about five hundred square feet of living space, with pine floors throughout. The attic was partitioned into two more spaces, eleven feet high where the faces of the roof met, well suited for sleeping quarters. The house was not perfect. The fireplace was barely large enough to heat the whole first floor. The cellar, accessible through a bulkhead door in back of the house, was chronically damp. Visitors could peep through the windows and imagine, mistakenly, that they were seeing old-time slave housing. Nevertheless, it had considerable advantages. Nathan and Sarah were always close to their work, a mixed blessing for them but a boon to their employers. Their young son could play on the spacious lawns and in the surrounding woods. On historic grounds, the Johnsons began to build the domestic life that freedpeople across the South craved in the heady aftermath of emancipation.*

One afternoon in mid-October 1867 Nathan Johnson went out with his gun. Returning around dusk, he went into the washhouse, perhaps to visit Sarah as she laundered clothes for their family or for Miss Tracy and Mr. Herbert in the mansion. He left the gun outside, propped against the wall. When he came out, he took the muzzle in his left hand. The gunlock hit the washhouse step, and the entire load discharged into his left arm, tearing the flesh from wrist to elbow and wounding his upper arm as well. Tracy and Herbert bandaged his arm, applied cold cloths to stop the profuse bleeding, gave him laudanum, and waited four hours for the doctor to arrive from Alexandria. They watched Nathan closely for six days, then obeyed the physician's command to send him into the city for closer medical attention. Sarah went with him. Amazingly, though "every nerve, tendon & muscle" had been laid bare, and even though his wound came within an eighth of an inch of an artery, none had been cut. He would regain the use of his arm and elbow.[2]

Nathan Johnson became familiar to Mount Vernon's visitors over the next years as the "majordomo" of the mansion, the well-dressed, courteous butler who took their admission tickets and sold photographs. One of those visitors was Ella Bassett Washington, whose direct ancestors included George Washington's sister, Martha Washington's sister, and Robert "King" Carter, the wealthiest man in the early eighteenth-century Old Dominion. Ella Washington received attention befitting

---

*New architectural evidence opens another possibility. In the summer of 2007 Mount Vernon was restoring the house inhabited by George Washington's hired white gardeners, directly across the bowling green from the "circle storehouse" and of identical size and dimensions, though without a cellar. In removing the 1860s-era door frames, the restoration manager discovered handwriting on the backs of two boards: "Nathan house" and "Nathan house door facing." The Johnsons may have lived in the "gardener's house" before they relocated to the one described above, where documentary sources suggest they resided by 1878. Given the different sorts of evidence, both fragmentary, definitive conclusions remain elusive.

her pedigree and her status as the MVLA's vice regent for West Virginia. When her carriage stopped in front of the mansion, Nathan helped her alight and took her overnight bag.[3] She probably had no idea of his injury, long since healed. Indeed, she might not have welcomed the knowledge that this "fine-looking middle-aged man" owned a gun at all. Eleven years earlier black members of John Brown's band had stormed her family's home and taken her husband, Colonel Lewis Washington, hostage at gunpoint.

In the eighteenth-century world that the MVLA sought to recreate, black men did not carry firearms. Neither did they vote. After the Civil War, however, the black men who helped present Mount Vernon to the public and worked its farm and gardens when visitors were not there did both. On October 22, 1867, when Nathan Johnson was still in the doctor's care in Alexandria, his fellow employees and neighbors walked the four miles to Accotink village to line up before a ballot box and a brace of white registrars. Six years earlier the site had witnessed a very different election, as white men determined whether Virginia would secede from the Union. Then Gabriel Johnson had been Augustine Washington's property. Now he was a free man, voting just ahead of old West Ford's son-in-law Porter Smith, who had been free decades before the war. Behind them were other Mount Vernon exslaves, returned to the vicinity during the war: the Ford brothers Joe and West; Jim Starks, born at Blakeley sixty-two years earlier; Sarah Johnson's stepfather, Warner May. The 227 black voters at Accotink Precinct included men whose ancestors George Washington had emancipated and men named James Madison, Thomas Jefferson, and George Washington. All the men voted to call a state constitutional convention and voted for Radical Republican delegates to represent them in it. White men, many of them Quakers who had moved into the vicinity since the 1840s, voted the same way as their black neighbors but dropped their ballots into a separate box.[4]

In this new Old Dominion, black women and men shared public space in unprecedented ways. They negotiated for wages, stood up to discrimination, and gathered to celebrate their emancipation. The standard story of American historic preservation ignores them. Its main characters are white women such as Ann Pamela Cunningham, Ella Bassett Washington, and the other vice regents, women of enormous energy and distinguished lineage. Soon after Robert E. Lee's surrender, groups of such women mobilized across the defeated South. They were responding to a world turned upside down. By glorifying fallen Confederates and preserving cemeteries and historic sites, white southerners found ways to assert the present-day value of a past properly understood.[5]

Mount Vernon's story was not as different as it seems. Certainly the MVLA was re-creating George Washington's day, not an antebellum plantation fantasy. Its membership and its story alike were national, not sectional. Because its efforts have continued for a century and a half, its reconstruction of an authentic eighteenth-century past appears little connected to America's far briefer Reconstruction. Yet at Mount Vernon in the 1860s and 1870s the roots of historic preservation found their ground in the political and social history of black and white Americans. We can see the connections in the experience of Ann Pamela Cunningham, who returned to live there, her own politics unreconstructed. We can see them too in the lives of African Americans employed where many of them had recently been enslaved. Like black people all over the South, freedmen and freedwomen at Mount Vernon reconstructed their lives, reshaping family and community and exercising newly won economic and political rights with everyday actions, not just ballots and guns.

Her racial and sectional attitudes hardened by her own postwar experience, Ann Pamela Cunningham returned to Mount Vernon the month after Nathan's accident and Virginia's election. As she moved into the mansion, her vision was unchanged from the 1850s: to restore Mount Vernon to its "original" state, meaning its appearance in George Washington's lifetime. Achieving her goal required ascertaining that appearance and raising more money. The mansion and outbuildings needed immediate structural repairs, the house had to be furnished, and the entire estate required long-term maintenance. First, however, Cunningham needed to reassert her own control after seven years away. Within weeks she had a falling-out with Sarah Tracy, who she thought had grown too fond of running Mount Vernon. Worse, Tracy— "a ---- Yankee!"—would introduce "sectionality" into the MVLA's deliberations, setting northern against southern vice regents. Tracy, who had spent four grueling years keeping sectionality off the premises, soon departed, insisting to another vice regent that she had no desire to usurp Cunningham's rightful place. A year later, when a northern paper criticized Cunningham's management and Mount Vernon's up-keep, the regent wrote that the attack must have come from Radical Republicans.[6] Ever politically savvy, Cunningham knew better than to express such views outside private correspondence with the most trusted vice regents.

Instead she met the public with a face that befitted the Mount Vernon Ladies' Association of the Union. Mount Vernon remained plagued by relic hunters, a familiar scourge noticed by visiting officers from nearby Fort Washington. When the fort's commanding general offered in May 1868 to send soldiers free of charge to protect the place, Cunningham "jumped at the idea," as she put it, "not only for the preservation of the House, but for political effect." (She volunteered to pay five soldiers each twenty-five cents a day.) Radical Republicans had all the money in postwar America, she wrote, and many of them still thought the MVLA was "too southern! So the appearance of soldiers here on guard—gives the place such a Northern aspect that it will tell favorably!" As a fringe benefit, the soldiers' band played at Mount Vernon twice a week, attracting still more visitors. That November Cunningham invited the general and his wife to dine at Mount Vernon, even though—or because—he was a Radical Republican. "I thought it politic to take this trouble in order to aid in doing away the feeling about secessionist here!"[7]

Such exertions mattered more than ever because in 1868 and 1869 the MVLA was seeking an appropriation from the United States government. The old greenhouse remained a burned-out shell. Other out-buildings were in disrepair. The roof of the mansion leaked, and plaster peeled from the walls inside. Revenues were anemic, despite increased visitation after the war. The proprietors of Washington's Willard Hotel ran the steamboat and collected most of the profits. Sales of flowers and canes netted paltry sums. Backed by well-connected vice regents, Cunningham lobbied Congress for seven thousand dollars, approximately the revenue lost when the United States confiscated the steamboat during the war. She emphasized Mount Vernon's wartime neutrality. Except for the Masons, only the MVLA had preserved a nationwide organization once the war broke out. Cunningham herself met with congressmen and with President Johnson, the way she had lobbied Virginia legislators for the MVLA charter a dozen years before. The campaign succeeded in 1869, and General Nathaniel Michler of the U.S. Corps of Topographical Engineers came from Washington to supervise the structural repairs.[8]

Far more needed to be done. Ever since the immediate postwar rush, visitors had tramped through the mansion, even the second and third floors. With the Washingtons gone, visitors expected to see more than before. Instead they found some rooms empty and others closed off because Sarah Tracy, Upton Herbert, and then Ann Pamela Cunningham lived in them. "Quite like Barnum," huffed one newspaper reporter. A "negro boy" took tourists' money but couldn't make change. The parlor, which doubled as the current residents' dining room, contained only Nelly Custis's harpsichord and new placards prohibiting smoking and spitting. The room where Washington died housed "only a bare and cheap old bedstead, a *fac-simile* of the original." That report and similar stories riled the MVLA through the late 1860s. Upton Herbert's departure at the end of 1868 made things worse. Welcoming visitors to the grounds and mansion, this relative of Fairfaxes and Washingtons had seemed a link to Virginia gentlemen of the past. On a practical note, most of the furniture in the mansion belonged to him; he had brought it when the Washingtons moved out in 1860. Once it was gone, the mansion seemed emptier. One tourist complained in 1869, "Well this don't look like I want to see the <u>home</u> of Washington look. I want it to look <u>comfortable</u>." Another groused, "they have not done anything to the house—there aint a room furnished."[9]

Nancy Marsh Halsted, the new vice regent for New Jersey, devised a plan to solve the problem. Cunningham's chief lieutenant in 1868 and 1869, Halsted was the descendant of seventeenth-century Scottish immigrants to the colonies and the wife of a New York dry goods merchant who had commanded two Trenton camps during the Civil War. From their thirty-three-acre Hudson County estate, Nancy Halsted raised money for her local Presbyterian church as well as for the MVLA. Halsted envisioned a fund-raising campaign across her state and collected contributions large and small. In September 1868 she spent twenty-seven dollars to have three thousand appeals for donations printed in Newark. Three months later she persuaded the printer to donate some of his services and supplies too and got another three thousand for just fifteen dollars. At Halsted's request, a Newark nursery gave Mount Vernon thirty-nine kinds of vegetable seed (from asparagus to turnips and including five varieties of cabbage), plus little packages with herbs and flower seeds. Cunningham also asked Halsted to buy new furnishings in New York, a cheaper market than Washington. So on January 16, 1869, a steamer left Newark for Virginia with table linens, blankets, towels, and tableware; along with these were garden tools, a shovel and pitchfork, and two hoes all donated to Halsted for Mount Vernon's farm and gardens.[10]

To address the larger challenge of the empty rooms, Halsted proposed that vice regents from the original thirteen states each furnish one chamber in the mansion. Her colleagues adopted this resolution, a reprise of the strategy that had worked in the 1850s, when each vice regent coordinated fund-raising within her own state. Now the quarry included furniture and objects as well as money. If it succeeded, Halsted's plan would solve several problems. First, George Washington's possessions had been scattered among heirs and collectors. Vice regents could more easily procure colonial-era, or even newly manufactured colonial-style, furniture. Second, the furnished mansion would provide lodgings for the vice regents when they came for the annual council meetings. Each would occupy the room she had furnished, a practice that continued into the early twentieth century. Cunningham offered New Jersey a plum assignment, the second-story bedroom where Lafayette had stayed and where until recently Upton Herbert had lived. On December 14, 1868, the sixty-ninth anniversary of George Washington's death, she stationed Sarah Johnson in the Lafayette bedchamber. Sarah's assignment was to explain to the public what would soon occur in the empty room. Thus a black employee, not Cunningham herself, was the first person to tell visitors about the incipient process of historic restoration. Over the next two years Nancy Halsted tirelessly collected furniture and objects for the Lafayette bedchamber, now known also as the New Jersey Room. It was done by April 1871, "nearly every article having some Revolutionary interest."[11]

Meanwhile Cunningham began her own quest for the authentic Mount Vernon, starting with the walls. She stood in the stairwell, her back surely aching, scraping layers of wallpaper down to the original. As for paint, she wondered, was "the testimony of a scraped wall . . . good guidance"? If not, maybe the testimony of old black employees was. Jim Mitchell, who claimed to have come as Bushrod Washington's slave in 1802, remembered that the largest room had "always been yellow." Cunningham hated yellow—eighteenth-century fashion confounded modern taste—and preferred a lovely rose color. While George Washington and his contemporaries had chosen deep, vivid colors, Victorian Americans preferred "delicate tints." But the MVLA should try to maintain Mount Vernon's "Ancient look." For better or worse, "We ought not to try to modernize Washington Home. We must try to keep it to the spirit of his age—only to make the best of it in that line."[12]

"Furniture of antique style," "the spirit of his age": such phrases invited diverse approaches to restoring the mansion. Over time Mount Vernon became a Victorian cabinet of curiosities, a display of the quaint and unusual not unlike many other contemporary museums. To house the relics that Americans might donate, Cunningham got glass cases from the Smithsonian Institution. At first she imagined designating one room of the mansion as a museum, but soon there were cases in many rooms. Washington's old house now doubled as a new museum of early American relics.[13]

The result was a hybrid historic house, suspended between alternative visions of nationhood and between conflicting notions of authenticity. Within Mount Vernon's public rooms, an older union of separate states would reign, each vice regent furnishing her room with little coordination of the whole. An indivisible United States became America's official ideology during Reconstruction. The Fourteenth Amendment, ratified in 1868, created for the first time a constitutional definition of national citizenship, extended to African Americans. But sectionalism lived and burned within Cunningham's private correspondence, as it did in the hearts and conversations of countless other white southerners. Nancy Halsted's idea, to furnish Mount Vernon room by room, addressed the practical problem of an empty house.[14] In full flower, however, it stood at odds with an approach derived from scraping walls down to the original paint and paper. The spirit of Washington's age was soon embodied by the colonial revival of the late nineteenth century, when "period" objects were so venerated that furniture makers around the United States competed to manufacture "antique-style" selections with names such as the Martha Washington Chair. Pale Victorian colors remained on Mount Vernon's walls deep into the twentieth century.

To some visitors, the most vivid authenticity appeared not in paint colors or period furniture but in the person of old Jim Mitchell. In June 1868, Charles Douglass, a son of America's foremost black orator and abolitionist, visited Mount Vernon with Frederick Douglass's German friend Ottilie Assing. Assing wrote to her sister how a black gardener claimed to have been a teenager when George Washington died. Assing figured that this was impossible but also that it was Jim Mitchell's act, devised to make money from travelers less enlightened or more gullible than she. As Mitchell, Assing, and Douglass conversed, a white American woman excitedly interrupted. "I must shake hands with you!" she gushed to Mitchell, who "put on a mask of neutrality" as the interloper continued: "I think there is no position more venerable and honorable in the country than to have been the slave of General Washington." Assing chimed in with an implicit rebuke: "And I will shake hands with you because we are so lucky to meet here on free soil." One tourist celebrated an imagined past, the other an abolitionist present. The black employee was shrewd enough to accommodate both.[15]

Mitchell told another visitor, a Methodist abolitionist from Boston, more: he had been purchased by Bushrod Washington, whose heirs sold Mitchell's children to keep Mount Vernon running. "Human flesh was cash in those days," the Methodist editorialized. All the evidence, however, suggests that Mitchell had not been at Mount Vernon since "a year and a half after Washington's death," but that he had been among the Blakeley slaves who came in the 1830s and early 1840s. The story of children sold away harked back to Oliver Smith's experience almost a half century earlier. Like Oliver Smith, Phil Smith, and old West Ford before him, Mitchell recognized and played on visitors' predispositions, recycling stories from a previous generation of black workers. He adjusted his own life story to provide what each visitor wanted to hear. The Methodist also inspected Mitchell's dwelling place, the decrepit old greenhouse slave quarters still unrepaired from the fire of the 1830s. He made a novel suggestion: if the MVLA in-

tended "to preserve the place yet more carefully," it should leave "the
negro quarters . . . these huddled huts" standing. No other site could
testify so starkly to Washington's measly treatment of his slaves or
show how far America had come. This idea would have horrified the
MVLA in 1869. To the Ladies, authenticity meant restoring the mansion in the mode of eighteenth-century gentility, which might include
a well-dressed, well-spoken black butler like Nathan Johnson. It did
not include revisiting the horrors of slavery.[16]

Sarah Johnson was sick in early March 1869, the week Ulysses S.
Grant's inauguration brought thousands of visitors to Washington and
hundreds to Mount Vernon. Ann Pamela Cunningham had little sympathy for her ailing employee. Already annoyed by Grant's victory, the
regent wrote to Nancy Halsted, "I have had mostly to wait on myself,
meet all the duties arising from the great crowd & this—with former
fatigue & a fearful cold . . . makes me—quite sick." Two months later,
as Cunningham penned another letter to her New Jersey comrade,
Sarah interrupted her. Was the regent writing to Mrs. Halsted? asked
Sarah. When Cunningham said yes, Sarah asked her to send "a <u>thou-
sand thanks</u>" from herself and Nathan. Amid the printer's fees and the
vegetable seeds, Nancy Halsted's receipts contain this item: "Newark
April 6, 1869—Nathan's bill—$19.66," addressed to "Nathan at Mt.
Vernon." Nathan Johnson's purchases consisted entirely of fabrics:

12 yds	Mouslin de Laine	@20.	2.40
8½ "	Fine Muslin	@16.	1.36
20 "	" "	@17.	3.40
2¾ "	Cassimere	@2.	5.50
1¾ "	do [ditto]	@4.	7.00
			————
			19.66

The cloth arrived at Mount Vernon a few weeks later, along with
farm implements for the gardener and more household items for the
regent.[17]

    By tracing each step of this transaction, we can weave the larger
tapestry of Sarah Johnson's work and world in 1869, the year she

turned twenty-five. Why did a well-heeled woman from New Jersey go shopping for a black family at Mount Vernon? What would become of the cloth after it had reached the Johnsons? Who would see Sarah, Nathan, and Smith in their new clothes? And what did those clothes mean to the people who wore them?

The Johnsons did not work merely for the MVLA; they also worked for the women who constituted it. The previous November six of those women—Cunningham and the vice regents for Michigan, Georgia, Delaware, Rhode Island, and Louisiana—had convened at Mount Vernon for the council meeting. Some surely brought their own maids, but Sarah served them all. She prepared their bedrooms in the mansion, cooked their meals, waited on their table, and ensured that their needs were met. Both Nathan and Sarah waited on MVLA women and their personal guests throughout the year. Their small courtesies created deeper bonds with vice regents who visited frequently, including Nancy Halsted. During one of those sojourns Sarah or Nathan probably seized an opportunity to mention that they desired some new clothes. Women like Halsted provided the Johnsons access to the marketplace of New Jersey and New York, with wider selection and better bargains than could be had at Alexandria.

They got fabric, not ready-made garments. Living at the margins of gentility, the Johnsons could afford to spend nearly a month of Nathan's salary, which Cunningham had recently, grudgingly, raised from $17 to $20, on material for nice clothes: muslin at 16 to 20 cents a yard, cassimere a splurge at $2 and $4 a yard. But the manufacture had to occur at home. Halsted addressed the package to Nathan because he represented his family in financial dealings. Like other freedmen, he took pride in this responsibility. The opportunity to act as the head of his own household marked the distinction between slavery and freedom, between having a master dictate his wife's and child's lives and being a patriarch himself. Also like other freedmen, Nathan Johnson belonged to a family economy in which the income derived from his wife's labors as well as his own. Seen another way, $19.66 was about 70 percent of Nathan's and Sarah's monthly wages combined. Muslin and cassimere in hand, Sarah had more work to do, not as the MVLA's servant but as Nathan's wife and Smith's mother. On Sundays, or by firelight in the evening after a day's paid labor, she made her family's shirts, trousers, and dresses. Or she might have hired another woman, a more skilled seamstress somewhere in the neighborhood or even in Alexandria, to sew the new clothes. If so, the finished products provided further testimony to the Johnsons' purchasing power and their participation in an economy beyond Mount Vernon's boundaries.

Either way, manual work made up a considerable portion of their days. Nathan kept the mansion clean as well as tended to visitors. He scrubbed the walls and floors and woodwork, washed the windows, and cleaned up after the men who hung wallpaper and replastered ceilings and walls during the government-funded 1869 repairs. Sarah washed and ironed not only for her own family but also for the white people who inhabited the mansion: Sarah Tracy and Upton Herbert until 1868; then Ann Pamela Cunningham and a series of her secretaries. Sarah also preserved fruit and made jelly. At Augustine Washington's Mount Vernon, with its much larger white and black population, these duties had been divided between a dairymaid and a seamstress, and washdays had involved teenage girls as well as adult women. Now these chores fell to Sarah with little or no assistance. In the late spring and summer of 1869, as her illness persisted, she struggled to manage them all. She "suffered a good deal" in early June, then improved, then worsened by July 3. She could perform her regular duties, selling milk to visitors every morning except Sunday and twice a day on Tuesdays and Thursdays, when the steamboat made an extra early-evening trip to Mount Vernon. But the heavy, hot work of ironing was too much for her, and Cunningham's secretary hired someone else to do it several times that July.[18]

The fine muslin and cassimere from New Jersey would not have been worn during such sweaty labors. Rather, they would enhance the third dimension of the Johnsons' work, where appearance counted most: dealing with tourists. Nathan ushered them into the mansion and sold photographs. Sarah sold cups of milk in the old kitchen, the building to the right of the mansion. On special occasions she worked in the mansion. After Upton Herbert left, Nathan assumed some of the former superintendent's role, conversing with those who walked through the mansion and guarding against thieves and vandals. When a woman tore a strip from a picture in the parlor, Nathan pursued her until he learned her name. When another woman asked who kept the mansion so clean, Nathan replied that he did. She told him, "[W]ell, I

don't want to know any more—I wish you would go and live with me."
As representatives of the MVLA and as public stewards of George
Washington's memory, the Johnsons needed to look neat and present-
able, respectable more than fashionable.[19]

The package from Nancy Halsted also provides clues about Sarah's
world beyond her work as servant, housewife, and attendant to the
public. Consider what the vice regent did not send from New Jersey:
thread, an essential for transforming muslin and cassimere into pants
and dresses. Nathan and Sarah had access to a general store in the little village at Accotink, four miles west of Mount Vernon, where several
grocers and other storekeepers lived and worked. Or they could take a
wagon or the steamboat north, all the way to Alexandria, to purchase
staples and enjoy an occasional day in town. Sarah's uncle Edmund
Parker lived there with his wife and children. So did her stepfather,
Warner May, and perhaps one of her half sisters. Either Sarah's
mother, Hannah, had died by then, or the war and the dispersal of Augustine Washington's estate irrevocably separated her from her husband and children.[20]

Imagine too where Sarah and Nathan and Smith Johnson wore
their new clothes besides Mount Vernon. These garments bespoke respectability not only—maybe not even primarily—to strangers who
took the steamboat from Washington. They were also for special days
with friends and neighbors. Perhaps Nathan wore a new suit on July 6,
1869, when he went into Accotink to cast his first vote. Fellow MVLA
employees Warner May, Thomas Mitchell, and young West Ford went
too, as did Jim Starks and Joe Ford from slavery days at Mount Vernon.
They were among 122 white and 177 "colored" men who voted there
that day to ratify the new Virginia constitution and elect a slate of officials, from governor to congressman to members of the state legislature. This time, though, the Radicals were no longer in the saddle. The
constitution passed overwhelmingly. However, two of its provisions—
disenfranchising former Confederates and requiring candidates to
swear that they had never borne arms against the United States or supported the Confederacy—had been separated into a different ballot
and could thus be defeated, allowing conservative whites to return to
political power. The new General Assembly ratified the Fourteenth
and Fifteenth Amendments that October, and on January 26, 1870,

President Grant signed Virginia's readmission to the Union. The Old Dominion's Reconstruction was over, but Nathan Johnson and his comrades had enjoyed the opportunity to vote for an African American, the unsuccessful Republican candidate for lieutenant governor. They may have envisioned similar chances in future elections.[21]

New clothes were also for church, probably at Bethlehem Baptist, the new house of worship that freedpeople built near Gum Springs in 1863. Many of its founders descended from slaves freed by George Washington. Samuel K. Taylor, who had escaped slavery in Caroline County, Virginia, and fled to Gum Springs during the war, conducted the services. Because Taylor had not been ordained, the Reverend Samuel Madden of Alexandria's First African Baptist Church also ministered to the Bethlehem congregation, performing communions and baptisms. Here Sarah, Nathan, and Smith Johnson would have mingled with an African American community of more than a hundred souls: landowners such as William Ford and Porter Smith and their families, who owned half of old West Ford's Gum Springs land; tenant farmers and farmhands who worked the ground that had once belonged to Bushrod Washington and now belonged to Quakers; women who stayed at home to raise their children and others who found employment as domestic servants or washerwomen.[22]

Black families lived on the land abutting the MVLA's property. The trustees of Augustine Washington's estate put his 1,025 acres there up for public auction in June 1869, dividing the land into ten lots ranging from 33½ to 155¾ acres. Edward C. Gibbs, a New Jersey Quaker, bought lots three and four, the 216 acres just north of the Ladies' Association. That was where Augustine's "far" slave quarters had stood, the land to which dozens of his slaves had escaped during the war. The following year, Gibbs lived there with his wife and four children—and with thirty-three African Americans, most of them in five other dwellings on the property. Several of them had once belonged to Augustine Washington: Jim Starks and his sister Eliza; Joe Ford, his wife, Fanny, and five of their children, the eldest of whom was now a twenty-year-old farmhand. Most of the men were farmhands; most of the women were "keeping house," not laboring as someone else's domestic servants. These families had sixteen children below thirteen years of age, some of whom may have been playmates of nine-year-old Smith Johnson.[23]

Though none of those children attended school in 1869–70, Smith Johnson did. He likely wore his new clothes not only to church but also to Gum Springs School. Like former slaves across the South, Virginia's African Americans embraced schooling as soon as the war ended. Because the Old Dominion had no public school system, and because the postwar state government made no provision for financing public schools, freedpeople took matters into their own hands. By September 1867, according to the superintendent of freedmen's affairs in Virginia, 198 schools across the state educated twenty thousand students. "In many cases," he reported, "freedmen have erected houses without the aid of the [Freedmen's] bureau, and without an immediate prospect of procuring teachers." Black people in eastern Fairfax County erected one-room schoolhouses at Gum Springs and near Woodlawn. With financial support from the local Quakers and the Friends' Association of Philadelphia for the Aid and Elevation of the Freedmen, education commenced at the Woodlawn school in October 1866 and at Gum Springs three or four months later. By February 1869 fifty-four students were attending the latter. Enrollment dropped during spring farming, and attendance was spotty—about half the enrolled students attended each month—but students and parents alike exulted in the opportunity for education.[24]

The 1869–70 Gum Springs term, when Smith Johnson attended school, ran only from October to February. The teacher, Josephine Baker, was a twenty-two-year-old white woman, the daughter of a Poughkeepsie, New York, Quaker who had bought land on the Wellington estate (once the home of Augustine Washington's cousin Charles) and moved his family to Virginia after the war. When school started in October with two-and-a-half-hour sessions in the morning and afternoon, eleven boys and eighteen girls were registered, although the average day's attendance was only sixteen. Most of the students were ten to sixteen years old, and their levels of education varied greatly. Many already knew how to spell; a handful had progressed as far as the third or fourth McGuffey's reader. They studied arithmetic and geography, but owing to the lack of resources, four-fifths of them had to write on slates, not in books. Progress was slower than Baker hoped, because books were scarce and pupils disorderly. Even though more students registered during the year, on average only twenty attended each day. Distance from school surely impeded regular attendance. For example,

Smith Johnson had to walk three miles, a long way for an eight-year-old even if accompanied by fourteen-year-old Barney Ford (young West's son), who also lived at Mount Vernon and attended school that year. By December, though, Baker could announce some success after an official visited the school and commended her students' progress.[25]

Smith Johnson was among the youngest scholars in a one-room school. Most students' fathers were farmers or farmhands. By the summer of 1870 many of the students themselves were working as farmhands and domestic servants. Perhaps some would return to class the following fall, when the "colored schools" became part of the public school system mandated by the new state constitution. Thanks to the alliance between Conservatives and white Republicans, that system was segregated, as Virginia's public schools remained for almost ninety years. Even so, parents like Nathan and Sarah Johnson knew that education was their son's best chance for improvement and economic mobility.[26] As she handled the fabric that Nancy Halsted had sent from New Jersey, Sarah may have imagined a time when Smith would be able to afford the store-bought garments she saw every day on the visitors who purchased milk from her in the Mount Vernon kitchen.

Her hopes must have been rekindled every time well-dressed black excursionists toured Mount Vernon. On Thursday, August 19, 1869, Frederick Douglass stepped off the steamboat *Arrow* with a party of men, women, and children, members of Washington's black elite. They had a large number of fellow passengers that ninety-degree day. Ninety-one people in all, some from as far away as Cincinnati and Mexico City, signed the visitors' register. Douglass's companions included Carter M. Stewart, a Washington barber with five thousand dollars in real estate, as well as Stewart's wife and infant daughter. Also aboard the *Arrow* but not in Douglass's party were a Mr. and Mrs. Montague, a black man and a white woman married in Washington's city hall two days before. Douglass, his friends, and the other passengers debarked, climbed the stairs to Washington's tomb, and made their way up to the mansion and its surrounding gardens and outbuildings. Douglass was not publishing a newspaper in 1869—his *New National Era* debuted the following year—and many of his papers were destroyed in an 1872 fire. His thoughts on his fellow excursionists or on the largely unfurnished mansion and the greenhouse slave quarters just then being repaired are memories erased from history. Two weeks earlier Douglass had addressed an emancipation celebration in western New York on the topic of discrimination against black people in trades and professions. There he had expressed suspicion about the results of Virginia's recent election. But without any written record, his encounters with Mount Vernon's black employees have been forgotten.[27]

Likewise, we do not know how those employees reacted at the sight of the venerated leader and his party of genteel black people. Perhaps they shed any "mask of neutrality" and displayed their enthusiasm palpably, gathering around to shake Douglass's hand. In school Smith Johnson would have learned about Douglass, whose life story offered stirring testimony to the power of reading and writing. Teachers used such examples to inspire their young African American charges, farmhands and domestic servants, to lives of richer potential. Sarah and Nathan Johnson could take particular pride in their family's appearance as they met Frederick Douglass that day. After all, their income, and perhaps Sarah's handiwork, enabled them to greet their distinguished visitor as respectable representatives of their race, not only of the Mount Vernon Ladies' Association.

Possibly, however, Sarah Johnson did not meet Frederick Douglass at all. One week later the MVLA's secretary reported that she had taken Sarah, still badly ailing, to Washington for medical treatment. What caused Sarah's prolonged suffering that year, beginning in March well before Mount Vernon's annual malarial season? The only clue appeared more than forty years later, in a census question to women in 1910 asking how many children they had ever had. Two, answered Sarah, the only evidence in any surviving source that she ever had a second child. The long illness of spring and summer 1869 may have been a pregnancy: morning sickness in March, something gone direly amiss over the summer, and no baby at Mount Vernon when the census taker came the following year. Or perhaps Sarah's second child had already been born and died, and her 1869 suffering left her unable to bear more children. Despite relatively high child mortality rates among African Americans (and poor people generally), it is striking that Smith Johnson remained an only child in this era before the availability of reliable means of birth control.

Frederick Douglass's visit discomfited Ann Pamela Cunningham. He and the other men "behaved well," she reported to Nancy Halsted, but the "boys & pretended Ladies" in his party were noisy and trying. To the regent of the Mount Vernon Ladies' Association and many fellow white southerners, only white women could be true ladies. Yet Cunningham refrained from chastising the women and children for fear of criticism from Washington's Republican newspapers. Even if Reconstruction was drawing to a close in Virginia, Radicals remained in command of the national government five months after President Grant's inauguration. The MVLA had already endured bad press that year. An article entitled "Washington's Home Going to Ruin" in the *New-York Observer and Chronicle* had deplored the apparent carelessness on the MVLA's grounds. A Boston paper, criticizing her arrogance and disorganization, had called for abolishing Cunningham's regency. James Craig, the Scottish gardener Cunningham had recently hired, was less discreet that August day. He asked Douglass to control the "negro boys" in the party and fully expected to find his admonition reported in the papers. Once Douglass's group left, Cunningham lectured the MVLA's black employees. Such conduct would never again be tolerated from visitors. She had borne it this time, she said, only to show them that she objected to "the conduct & not the color." As a result of her own postwar experience in South Carolina, Cunningham had difficulty separating the two.[28]

Given Cunningham's druthers, Mount Vernon's farmworkers would have been "white entirely." She described the black employees as "eye servants," a biblical term that slaveholders had long used to describe bondspeople who labored only when the overseer was watching. She complained that black people all around the nation's capital expected to be paid without working and that laborers around Mount Vernon ate enough to fill two stomachs. She wondered how white farmhands were boarded in the North.[29] Many northern women, however, would have disputed Cunningham's belief that white workers would be any better. Commiserating with her plight, a Massachusetts woman speculated that African Americans' supposed ingratitude stemmed from a nationwide problem, often labeled the servant question. Good help was hard to find and harder to keep, went the familiar refrain; northern women treated their Irish servants with the same kindness southern whites showed to blacks, only to see them leave at the slightest opportunity to better themselves. On seeing Mount Vernon's stuffy third-floor bedchamber where Martha Washington had supposedly spent her final years, a society journalist made a similar point: "No modern 'Bridget' would be content to occupy for a week such a room as this." Whether they attributed it to black restlessness or "the nature of service," Cunningham and the MVLA had a labor problem.[30]

From African Americans' perspective, it was not a problem at all, but the power of opportunity and choice. Demand for workers exceeded supply in and around Washington. Laborers could afford to be selective about their wages and accommodations. Nathan Johnson made seventeen dollars a month in early 1868, but the MVLA voted that November to increase his regular monthly salary to twenty dollars "or even more . . . if his services cannot be obtained at the above price." The majordomo of the mansion learned of the council's decision probably because he or Sarah had been within earshot as the Ladies deliberated. Seven weeks later Cunningham complained that "Nathan compels me to give him 20 p. month after February," notwithstanding her efforts to prevent the raise. Until immigrants from other parts of the United States or from Europe flooded the nation's capital in search of work, she wrote, there would be no remedy. The calendar proved unfriendly too. Because labor contracts in the vicinity generally began with the new year, the MVLA had to hire employees for the full year even though visitors were scarce until April. When Mount Vernon needed extra workers to meet the summer rush, it competed with employers hiring farmworkers for harvest season.[31]

The MVLA struggled to support a year-round workforce on an eight-month tourist season. Visitation had sagged, and money had grown tight again. Some years the admission fees and sales of flowers and photographs helped finance needed repairs; more often these revenues paid only for essential maintenance and expenses. With only twenty-five acres in cultivation, the MVLA made little money from farm products. Even feeding the resident workforce could be difficult. The farm, orchard, and gardens provided a very limited supply of fruit and vegetables, plus Indian corn and oats to fodder the livestock. Meat had to be purchased entirely, because the livestock included only a single horse, two mules, four milk cows, four other cattle, and a single hog.[32]

Not only did a labor shortage give unprecedented leverage to people who had been until recently enslaved, but black families now also made their own decisions about whether and how long wives and children would work. Workers such as Sarah Johnson had more freedom to take breaks than they had ever been allowed in slavery. No master would put her son to work at a tender age, educating him for a lifetime of bound labor. To many white Americans, the sight of black people at leisure, at Mount Vernon or anywhere else, looked like "shiftlessness." One New York reporter even suggested that Mount Vernon dismiss some of its workers to save money better used for repairs, even though he had no idea what they did when he wasn't there. Like the regent, he equated the choice of leisure, or even a brief respite from work, with a proclivity to laziness.[33]

Mount Vernon's isolation and miasmic conditions made white employees hard to find, much less keep. Cunningham hired an Irishman to work the farm and garden but feared that loneliness and homesickness would soon drive him away. Moreover, having never worked with blacks, "he feels the idleness of the other laborers here." With her usual vigor, she decried the challenge of hiring a new secretary: "This is anything but a comfortable house, in the winter especially. We are 9 miles from a church, a clergyman, physician, P[ost] office & market—& a stranger (like myself) coming to live here—must make up their mind to the sameness of life imposed by never having a friend to visit—or a friends house to procure a little variety from." All true, for an Episcopalian or a Presbyterian or a Catholic new to the area. Nine miles from Alexandria, Mount Vernon was surrounded by Quaker farmsteads cultivated by their transplanted northern owners and by black farmhands. There were churches nearby: Bethlehem Baptist and the Friends' meetinghouse near Woodlawn. Margaret Comegys, the vice regent for Delaware, offered a more measured analysis than Cunningham's: it was difficult to entice any new laborers to come to lonely, sickly Mount Vernon. Malaria still afflicted the workforce every August and September. Even Sarah Johnson, who thought that she was "chill proof" from having grown up there, came down with the miasma in 1870.[34]

Cunningham spared her solicitude for the more valuable, harder-to-replace white employees. When the Scottish James Craig's six-month-old baby boy took sick with chills in September 1870, she feared Mount Vernon would lose its gardener. Two-day waits for ten-dollar doctor visits exacerbated the problem. She considered paying Craig's doctor bills, even though she recognized that the black employees, less able than he to afford such expenses, would resent not receiving the same benefit. For his family's health, Craig took a job in northwestern Virginia a year later. His replacement lost his wife to the Mount Vernon malaria the year after that.[35]

Frequent turnover characterized not only the white secretaries and gardeners but the black labor force too. Twenty-two people lived in six dwellings on the MVLA's property in 1870. Many of them had not been at Mount Vernon a year before. The secretary Sarah Tiffey lived in the mansion with Ann Pamela Cunningham. Gardener Craig, his English wife, and their baby inhabited one of the neighboring out-buildings. The third dwelling housed Nathan, Sarah, and Smith Johnson, Warner May (listed as a farmhand), and a white gardener named Frank Sherwood. With its two ground-floor rooms and capacious attic, this building had space enough for the Johnsons and Sherwood to have separate apartments. Three black farmhands and a seventeen-year-old white gardener had the fourth house. Young West Ford lived with his wife, Ellen, and their five children, ages five months to fifteen years, possibly in part of the old greenhouse quarters. Old Jim and Agnes Mitchell had the sixth dwelling, another compartment of those quarters. Of the eleven people listed as employees (farmhands, gardeners, secretary) in 1870, just four were still at Mount Vernon two years later, along with a half dozen newcomers.[36]

The potentially long-term employees were the most familiar faces: African American men, and Sarah Johnson, who had been at Mount Vernon in slavery. Sarah had a long connection to them all. Warner May was her stepfather. Jim Mitchell had watched her and young West Ford, six years her senior, grow up in the 1840s and 1850s. Thomas Mitchell, hired as a day laborer in 1870 and soon added to the regular payroll, had been a free black apprenticed to Augustine Washington until he turned twenty-one in 1856. Now he was married to Sarah's half sister Milly, Warner and Hannah May's daughter. To white newcomers such as Ann Pamela Cunningham, Sarah Tiffey, and James Craig, Mount Vernon was isolated, friendless, even like "solitary confinement" in Tiffey's words. To the Johnsons and Mitchells and Mays and Fords, it was home. More than this, it was a home Augustine Washington no longer owned. Unlike ex-slaves who became tenant farmers or sharecroppers where they had once been enslaved or who returned to work for their former masters, Sarah and Nathan and their compatriots found new employers on familiar ground.

One problem remained: the MVLA could not be certain that these people would stay. Warner May's primary residence in 1870 was not Mount Vernon but Alexandria, where his own family lived. At Mount Vernon he boarded with the Johnsons when he stayed overnight. One of the unattached farmhands at Mount Vernon also had dual residences, one at Mount Vernon and one in Alexandria, just three households away from May's family. Both men probably took the steamboat from Alexandria to Mount Vernon for work on Monday mornings and returned to their families on Saturday afternoons—not a recipe for long-term employment in a labor market with other choices. The MVLA recognized as much. At its 1870 council meeting a three-woman committee on "wages, farm, and garden" reviewed what it called "the labor question in general." To ensure more permanent labor, the committee recommended providing houses for Warner May and West Ford, giving the Fords something better than a hutchlike greenhouse compartment. It authorized James Craig to prepare the houses as quickly as possible. It also recommended that the MVLA make yearlong contracts with May and Ford, to solidify their employment.[37]

The problem of Ann Pamela Cunningham was more delicate. Many vice regents were beginning to consider their leader a liability. Newspapers consistently criticized her management, particularly the secrecy with which she administered the finances. The American people had purchased Washington's home, many argued, and deserved to know how the MVLA managed the money. Decades of using laudanum and other medicines, not to mention long-standing grudges against Republicans, blacks, and other adversaries real or perceived, had taken a toll on Cunningham's stability. Long afterward Margaret Sweat, the vice regent for Maine, expressed the problem best. A visionary and brilliant organizer, Cunningham had been the right person to achieve the

MVLA's initial goals: forging the association, winning the legislative charter, raising the purchase money. All had required precisely the single-minded passion that she brought to the cause. As an administrator she was less skillful. "She could not coldly calculate the more prosaic claims of the outside world . . . [H]er feelings would not allow of any deep respect for the unfeeling multiplication table." The restive vice regents recognized a pivotal moment, the point at which a sacred cause required a long-lasting institutional structure, "more business-like methods," and "an administration open to public scrutiny." Cunningham could not or would not heed their suggestions.[38]

At a tense council meeting in June 1872 the vice regents began the yearlong process of ousting their regent. They voted to search for a superintendent, a man who would run the farm, supervise the employees, and relieve Cunningham of day-to-day control. In fact they had already found him, a Mexican War veteran named J. McHenry Hollingsworth, who began work at Mount Vernon later that year. Still, Cunningham remained, bunkered in the mansion, her personal secretary and the secretary's family ensconced in the building next door that was supposed to be Hollingsworth's home. The regent and the secretary's family made incessant demands on the employees, especially Nathan and Sarah Johnson, treating them as personal servants. Cunningham grew more unbalanced. The Johnsons had to "work to keep her in her room." Sometimes she went to the window "in a state of undress," and Sarah had to pull her back. Cunningham claimed all the chickens on the property as her own, even though the MVLA's grain fed them. She tried to compete with Hollingsworth to sell ice cream on the premises—more precisely, to have Sarah sell ice cream for her—and demanded the profits.[39]

During that difficult council meeting the vice regent for Michigan interrupted the proceedings with an announcement from one of the gardeners: the employees were striking for higher wages. The strike did not last long. The vice regents turned to their colleague Betsey Mason of Virginia, as the member most familiar with labor conditions in the vicinity. Mason replied that there was no reason to meet the workers' demand. The vice regents interpreted the strike as a protest against Cunningham's management and thus as confirmation of their own instincts. They informed the gardener that the demands would not be entertained and that any employees who left would be replaced. And that was that. "[T]he sudden storm abated," and nobody quit.[40]

The following month ten Mount Vernon workers earned a total of $204.25. The gardener, also responsible for the greenhouse and farm, made $50. Nathan Johnson, who (in the words of the MVLA minutes) "has charge of the mansion, receives entrance fees & sells photographs," earned $25.25, while Sarah, "who has charge of the cooking & general housework with an occasional housemaid," made $13. Eleven-year-old Smith got $8, likely for minor services around the estate. Together, then, the Johnson family made $46.25—nearly as much as the white gardener. Equally significant, it was more than most farm families, black or white, made in 1872. In the quarter of Fairfax County that included Mount Vernon, a farmhand's average monthly wages were $11 if the worker boarded, $21 if not; the average unboarded domestic servant made $2.50 a week. Warner May (who made $22 a month), West Ford ($20), and Tom Mitchell ($20) earned about the going rate for farmhands. On the basis of their wages, they all probably paid for their own food, except for the fruit, vegetables, and chickens they raised themselves. Jim Mitchell, described in the minutes as "an old negro brought here many years ago by Judge Washington," remained on the estate with his wife and received $6 "for such small services as he is able to render." All was not rosy; extra seasonal labor still required extra hands, often at high prices. However, by accepting the necessity for African American workers and by meeting their price—market-conscious salaries and housing—the MVLA seemed to have surmounted its labor problem.[41]

Mason and her colleagues may have read the strike accurately. Ann Pamela Cunningham was a difficult employer with little sympathy for black workers. With their access to Cunningham and the vice regents, Sarah and Nathan Johnson knew the MVLA's internal politics. They or their fellow employees may have seized the opportunity to assist the vice regents in deposing the regent.

Then again, they may have imagined another kind of opportunity in the MVLA's turmoil. If the vice regents were concerned for Mount Vernon's stability, they might be willing to pay more to keep the workforce so recently secured. The council's rebuff did not negate the significance of the moment. Black workers across the South knew their own power in local and regional labor markets. Soon after the war they had exercised that power by refusing to accede to unacceptable demands, that they return to gang labor systems and that employers determine women's and children's hours. Sharecropping began as a compromise between freedpeople who wanted a measure of economic autonomy and landowners who wanted a steady workforce. By 1872, as federal troops departed and Reconstruction ended in most of the South, many of those workers were becoming trapped. Sharecropping contracts tied families through indebtedness to land they had once tilled as slaves. Violence and intimidation began the decades-long process that stripped black men of the vote. Nevertheless, freedpeople seized local opportunities to assert the value of their labor, reflecting in the 1870s more a nationwide impulse than a national movement.[42]

Mount Vernon's black employees recognized their centrality to the working of both a national shrine and a Fairfax County farm. Their strike did not have to succeed for change to happen. Ann Pamela Cunningham departed the following year, bowing to the vice regents' threats to depose her and to her own failing health. She tapped Lily Berghmans, the vice regent for Pennsylvania, as her successor and returned to Rosemont, leaving Mount Vernon forever. Cunningham's retirement opened a new era of divided government, between Superintendent Hollingsworth in residence and the regent and vice regents in their annual council meetings, their correspondence, and their intermittent visits. The upcoming centennial of American independence promised record numbers of visitors. Both these developments afforded Sarah and Nathan Johnson new chances for self-determination.

SIX

Nathan Johnson's Enterprise

June 22, 1878, began like a typical Saturday at Mount Vernon. Nathan and Sarah arose at daybreak and began the morning's chores. As the majordomo of George Washington's mansion, Nathan made sure visitors saw nothing amiss. He swept and dusted the first-floor rooms that received the most traffic, and he opened the windows to admit light and fresh air. After an hour or two he closed the windows and placed screens in front of the doors, to guard the rooms against relic hunters. Sarah, who managed the poultry and dairy, collected the day's eggs from the henhouse and retrieved the day's milk from the young man responsible for tending the cows. Shortly after eleven o'clock Nathan and Sarah took their posts in the old kitchen, just southwest of the mansion, and domestic servants transformed into businesspeople. The steamboat from Washington arrived around eleven-thirty with the day's excursionists, who could now buy a modest lunch at Mount Vernon for fifty cents. Nathan served as "steward and caterer," collecting patrons' money, selling photographs of the mansion and grounds, and supervising the uniformed young black waiters whom he had hired from the neighborhood. Sarah prepared plates of sandwiches, fruit, and ice cream, made coffee, and served milk. Their son, Smith, now seventeen, was one of the waiters. Nathan and Sarah would happily have paid the Mount Vernon Ladies' Association a monthly fee to conduct the lunchroom themselves and pocket the profits, but those proceeds helped balance the MVLA's books. So when the last steamboat whistle blew at two-fifteen to summon straggling visitors for the return trip, the Johnsons totaled the day's receipts to turn over to Superintendent Hollingsworth. While Sarah and the waiters cleaned and put away the dishes and teacups, Nathan returned 'to the mansion, removed the door screens, and closed the doors to keep out the flies and the dust.[1]

Most Saturdays the steamboat's departure would have marked the beginning of the black residents' Sabbath. Hollingsworth would have taken the boat back to Washington, where his wife and several nieces lived in a large house in Georgetown, leaving Nathan in charge of the quiet premises until Monday morning. This June day, however, the steamboat's passengers had included two of the vice regents, New Jersey's Nancy Halsted and Connecticut's Susan Hudson, bearing overnight bags. When the afternoon boat steamed away up the Potomac, Halsted, Hudson, Hollingsworth, and his two young clerks remained behind on the now quiet grounds, anxiously awaiting distinguished guests. At about five o'clock a government barge docked at the Mount Vernon wharf, and the president and first lady alighted. Rutherford and Lucy Hayes were spending two nights in George Washington's mansion, leaving the "position and dignity of office" back at the White House and allowing "holy reverence" to fill their hearts. They slept in the Lafayette bedchamber, which Halsted had furnished with contributions from the Garden State. On Sunday morning they worshiped with their hosts at Pohick Church, as Washington had done, and visited several landowning Quaker farmers on the return trip to Mount Vernon.[2]

Weekend guests meant Sabbath work for Nathan and Sarah. Nathan, who had surely voted for the Republican Hayes twenty months earlier, tended to the first couple's needs in the mansion. Sarah killed, plucked, and fried or roasted one or two of the chickens, baked bread and cake, and cooked vegetables and potatoes from Mount Vernon's gardens. Then she changed her clothes, perhaps into one of the nice garments she had ordered through a vice regent. As she served dinner to the Hayeses and her employers, Sarah may have spoken only a few words of thanks for their compliments. Her "good and simple meal," Halsted wrote, was "better than a feast of fat things." Just as likely, however, the vice regents invited her to describe for the president and first lady her own thirty-year connection with Mount Vernon. Sarah, her unadorned culinary arts, and her hospitality seemed like survivals from a sacred past, supplanted in the White House and in

Gilded Age mansions by lavish entertainments. Served quietly in the small dining room in George Washington's house, the meal must have seemed equally removed from the crowded lunchroom that the Johnsons had managed in the afternoon.

Nathan Johnson's commercial pursuits had begun soon after the Civil War, when Ann Pamela Cunningham relaxed her opposition to photography at Mount Vernon. The MVLA contracted with Alexander Gardner, the famed battlefield photographer who had a studio in Washington, to take several dozen views of Mount Vernon. Gardner kept the negatives and supplied prints exclusively to the MVLA, which sold them on the grounds for a profit. At first Sarah Tracy hired one of old West Ford's grandsons to sell the pictures, but she soon entrusted them to Nathan. He was "very anxious to sell," Cunningham's secretary wrote in 1869, and he kept this responsibility for more than fifteen years.[3]

One of Gardner's photographs depicted haystacks in front of the mansion, revealing Mount Vernon as a landscape of work. Farm labor was the domain of Tom Mitchell and Warner May, along with other employees who came and went over the 1870s. In the half dozen years after the war Mount Vernon's farm produced just hay for the horses and cows, small amounts of other grains, fruit in the orchard, a few vegetables and herbs, and dairy products. The younger West Ford, now in his early thirties, worked in the garden—the only Ford brother in the MVLA's employ—under the supervision of a series of white gardeners. Every day Mitchell and May and Ford performed their farmwork before eleven and after two-thirty. While visitors roamed the grounds, they and other employees wore uniforms and badges and guarded the premises against vandals and relic hunters. Each longtime employee also had special duties. Mitchell drove the "ambulance," a small carriage that transported visitors uphill from the wharf to the mansion for ten cents. Ford sold bouquets of flowers. May earned a few dollars a month for cleaning the outhouses, a disgusting task that no employee would perform without extra compensation.

The vice regents hired Hollingsworth to take charge of these day-to-day operations. The great-grandson of Samuel Chase, a signer of the Declaration of Independence and justice of the Supreme Court,

Hollingsworth had grown up on a Maryland farm. Decades before, he had sought adventure and fortune across the continent. He volunteered for the Mexican War in 1846, at the age of twenty-three, and sailed around South America and to California with a New York regiment whose special mission was to "assist in colonizing the country." Mustered out at Los Angeles in September 1848, Hollingsworth stayed in California's mining country. He earned no riches, but he did serve as a member of the territory's constitutional convention in 1849. He returned east soon after, gained an appointment as collector for the Chesapeake and Ohio Canal, and bought a house in Georgetown. When the Civil War broke out, he mustered in for a three-month stint as major of the District of Columbia's Potomac Light Infantry. He left the service when his enlistment expired in July 1861, returned to his home and profession, and married four years later. By the time the MVLA hired him, Hollingsworth was accustomed to relating to women because he had a house full of them: his wife, her mother and her two sisters, and two nieces. In an earlier era he might have become the master of a farm or plantation, not the employee of a women's organization.[4]

In Hollingsworth the vice regents found several desirable qualities. His revolutionary lineage and broad experience suited him to meet Mount Vernon's daily excursionists. Self-possessed and commanding, he answered tourists' questions fluently and patiently without "the vulgarity of a showman." His early farming life and later commercial pursuits fitted him to manage the agricultural and business operations, and he quickly expanded the acreage under cultivation. Hollingsworth wisely elected to live not in the mansion, as Cunningham had done, but in the building immediately to the north known as the law office, allowing the entire mansion to be opened to visitors.[5]

In his first months on the job Hollingsworth asked Betsey Mason of Virginia if Sarah Johnson reported to him. Working for an organization of women, Hollingsworth logically wondered whether they, not he, directed the endeavors of a female domestic servant, much as his wife supervised the two young black domestics in their Georgetown home. Mason replied that everyone at Mount Vernon, including Sarah, was "subject to your control." In addition to managing the milk and the chickens and assisting Nathan in the mansion, Sarah soon became

Hollingsworth's personal servant. She cooked and cleaned for him, as she had for Cunningham. She even sewed carpets for his lodgings, using needles provided by Susan Hudson, Hollingsworth's closest friend among the vice regents.[6]

"We can't run a restaurant," Hudson wrote Hollingsworth in September 1872, but over the next four years a business developed in the old kitchen. Hudson was protesting Cunningham's idea to have her secretary's mother open a lunchroom but not the entire notion of selling food to visitors. The MVLA had neither staff nor resources to sell visitors a seated midday dinner, Hudson explained, but perhaps there was another way: call it a lunch, serve it picnic style, and "charge very high." The MVLA, which still ran at the edge of financial solvency, found in the lunch table a source of income to augment the entrance fees and photograph and garden sales. Visitors appreciated the service because an excursion to Mount Vernon consumed much of a day. The steamboat left Washington around ten o'clock and returned to the capital around four. No restaurant operated in the vicinity of Mount Vernon's relatively isolated grounds. Some visitors brought their own repasts, but many were tourists in Washington without kitchen facilities to prepare lunch baskets. Visitors were happy to be "served a lunch by colored people" in the old Mount Vernon kitchen. The nation's centennial in 1876 brought more visitors than ever before, often hundreds a day, many of them making a circuit to Washington after visiting Philadelphia's Centennial Exhibition. Early that summer Hollingsworth authorized construction of a tent-shaped pavilion behind the old kitchen, to accommodate fifty more "hungry people" at a time. The new lunchroom required more cooks and waiters, while the unprecedented crowds required additional watchmen to guard against "desecration."[7]

The lunch table brought the MVLA into sustained contact with its neighbors, white and black. The sandwiches were usually filled with ham, beef, or lamb, washed down with coffee, tea, and milk. Potomac oysters, ice cream, and cake were occasional treats. Many of the staples, especially dairy products and fruit, came from Edward Gibbs's neighboring farm because Mount Vernon's own cows and orchard could not supply enough. Paul Hillman Troth, another New Jersey Quaker who had bought Augustine Washington's Potomac tract just west of the MVLA's land, sometimes sold Hollingsworth corn and meal, for the lunchroom or for fodder. Other local farmers in the "Mount Vernon District" often supplied the meat. Hollingsworth also bought supplies nearer to his own home, from a grocer and butcher in Georgetown and a baker in Washington. Equally important, Nathan Johnson drew upon his own local connections to hire waiters. Some were relatives, including his son, Smith, and Esau Parker, Sarah's first cousin, who tended Mount Vernon's cows as well as waited tables. Other young men, probably people Nathan and Sarah had known for years, came from Gum Springs. The MVLA paid its waiters roughly ten dollars a month, plus board from the lunchroom and housing.[8]

Commercial interests tied Mount Vernon to the surrounding farm-steads but also produced recurrent strains. With an eye to the riparian trade that took local farmers and their produce to Alexandria and Washington every day, Paul Hillman Troth launched a steamboat busi-ness in 1874. He appealed to the MVLA's council that June for per-mission to land his *Mary Washington* at the Mount Vernon wharf. However, the MVLA's contract with the proprietors of Willard's Hotel in Washington, which ran the *Arrow* to Mount Vernon every day except Sunday, mandated exclusive access. Thus rebuffed, Troth established a wharf on his own land, primarily for the more lucrative commercial traffic. Soon he was competing with the MVLA. He offered a cheaper excursion rate from Washington and a carriage to take passengers from his landing to Mount Vernon's land entrance at the old porter's lodges. When the MVLA lowered its admission fee to stave off the unwanted competitor, a battle of words followed. Prodded by Troth or other neighbors, newspapers criticized the MVLA "monopoly." For her part, Nancy Halsted decried the "steamboat belligerents" and complained that everyone living within forty miles harbored hostility toward Mount Vernon. One of the neighbors, a transplanted northerner, even ob-jected to "Nathan's holding such a position of trust."[9]

A new threat materialized at five o'clock in the morning on Sunday, August 6, 1876. As the sun rose, Edwin Howland, a dentist from New York who lived in Washington and owned the property just north of Troth's, sneaked onto the Mount Vernon grounds with photographic equipment and six other men. The MVLA's black employees awoke to find Howland's party taking unlicensed pictures of the mansion, Wash-ington's tomb, and other parts of the property. When the residents

protested, Howland and his compatriots threatened them with bod-
ily injury. The employees confiscated the photographic apparatus and
shooed Howland's band off the premises. The next morning the would-
be photographers returned at the same early hour with new equipment. This time the black residents drove them away, cameras intact.
Hollingsworth took the matter to Fairfax County chancery court and
won an injunction against Howland and his conspirators.[10]

At bottom, the steamboat contretemps and the photography lawsuit were conflicts over property. The MVLA's critics had always argued that Mount Vernon belonged to the people of the United States,
whose subscriptions had purchased it. Now they also claimed that the
MVLA had become an unchecked monopoly. In response, the MVLA
claimed legal title *and* superior stewardship. Without its so-called mo-
nopolies, the MVLA could not make ends meet. By driving down the
admission fees or by flooding the Washington market with unlicensed
pictures, competitors cut into the revenue from which the association
paid its employees and maintained the estate. If local landholders
somehow got possession of Mount Vernon, they would convert sacred
ground into a "Beer Garden" or amusement park. The MVLA's legal brief argued that when the photographers invaded the hallowed
grounds on a Sunday morning, they violated "the duty and respect they
owed to the name, memory, and resting place of General George
Washington."

Nathan Johnson and his fellow employees neither held legal title nor
testified in chancery court, but they too possessed a sense of property
in Mount Vernon. It was this sense of ownership that propelled them to
stop Howland that Sunday morning. Howland likely assumed he would
meet no resistance, because Hollingsworth was home in Georgetown.
He failed to anticipate that African Americans would defend the
land—not just because it belonged to the MVLA, George Washington,
or even the American people but because it was their home.[11]

The photography fracas marred what was otherwise a smashing
centennial season, peaking with 13,040 visitors in October 1876 alone.
Mount Vernon's receipts that fiscal year totaled more than ten times
the previous year's. Also that year, the MVLA authorized publication of
its first guidebook, sold on board the *Arrow*. Except for entrance fees,
the lunch table was the largest single source of revenue, helpful particularly during the steamboat fare war.[12]

The centennial also advanced the refurnishing of George Washington's mansion. Halsted's summons notwithstanding, vice regents had been slow to claim and furnish most of the rooms, although familiar relics such as the Bastille key remained and a venerable-looking bed gave material interest to the room where Washington died. "Centennial furor" sped the process. Harking back to the MVLA's initial fundraising campaign of the 1850s, vice regents sponsored entertainments across the United States. The most popular, Martha Washington Tea Parties, became a staple of women's benevolent and patriotic associations in 1876 and for decades afterward. Attended by well-heeled guests in "colonial" attire, these balls proved moneymakers for such organizations as the MVLA. Several of Mount Vernon's first-floor rooms were not furnished until 1878, and most chambers on the upper stories were even slower to completion, but the momentum was now unstoppable.[13]

Because most of the vice regents lived far from northeastern Virginia, they relied not only on Hollingsworth but also on Sarah as they planned the furnishing. For example, Delaware's Margaret Comegys asked the superintendent for the dimensions of her tiny second-floor bedchamber, which could barely accommodate a bed. She also peppered him with questions about wallpaper, paint, and furniture. One query, however, fell beyond his ken: Of what fabric were the curtains in the room, chintz or cambric? "Gentlemen are not au fait at these things," Comegys told him, so "if you will get <u>Sarah</u> to describe it—it will be less trouble to you & <u>plain</u> to me." Sarah contributed farm labor as well as fashion sense. For the Connecticut room she provided the chicken feathers to make pillows for a lounge.[14]

Newly appointed, painted, and curtained, the mansion became Mount Vernon's premier attraction in the late 1870s. Visitors could now see the house from bottom to top. In the main hall they signed the guest book, writing their hometowns or states beside their names. Guided by Hollingsworth or one of his clerks, they walked through the East Parlor, adopted by Ohio's vice regent, Elizabeth Broadwell, into the State Dining Room, which New Yorker Justine Van Rensselaer Townsend had just begun furnishing. There visitors admired George Washington's marble mantelpiece, as had generations of their predecessors, but now a life-size Charles Willson Peale portrait of Washington was the pièce de résistance. After inspecting the first-floor rooms, they ascended the central staircase to find five bedchambers, four of them furnished (including the Lafayette Room). After walking through the one empty bedroom and into the back hallway, visitors came to the most sacred spot in the house, the room where George Washington died. Some pronounced the bed too small for the general's six-foot-two frame, and so many visitors carved pieces from the pine windowsill that Hollingsworth had to replace it several times a year. Nevertheless, some pilgrims experienced here the sort of somber reflection about nationality and mortality that Washington's tomb had long stirred. Up a small stairwell in the back hall, visitors approached the third story's single furnished room, where Martha Washington supposedly spent her final years in solitude, looking out the window at her husband's grave. Another set of stairs, beginning on the central landing of the second story, led to the third-floor landing and four empty bedchambers. From there an enclosed spiral staircase brought visitors into the cupola. Gazing far across the Potomac, they could imagine George Washington surveying the same landscape nearly a century before. Hundreds of them also left traces of their own presence. They scrawled their names on the cupola walls, a second and unauthorized guest book at the top of the mansion. Visitors wanted to see every inch of the house, and the MVLA encouraged their curiosity.[15]

By restoring the mansion, the MVLA also restored George Washington's image for a nation transformed. The end of the Civil War altered the way many Americans remembered the revered leader. Veteran and civilian now knew a far bloodier war than the Revolution, firsthand. Washington's tomb, long America's most popular pilgrim shrine, now had competition everywhere in the hallowed graves of newly fallen patriots North and South and especially at Gettysburg, where local entrepreneurs were packaging the battlefield and cemetery for tourism. Northerners had a new heroic martyr in Abraham Lincoln, a man of humor and pathos, approachable and human. As a congressman visiting Mount Vernon for the first time in 1866, Rutherford Hayes wrote that the setting and views were beautiful, but the "sentiment" from "the tomb, and the like, did not strike me." If it were not sacrilegious, Hayes wrote, "I should say that Lincoln is overshadowing Washington." Both men were necessary "to complete our history," but Washington seemed "formal, statue-like, a figure for exhibition."[16] Lin-

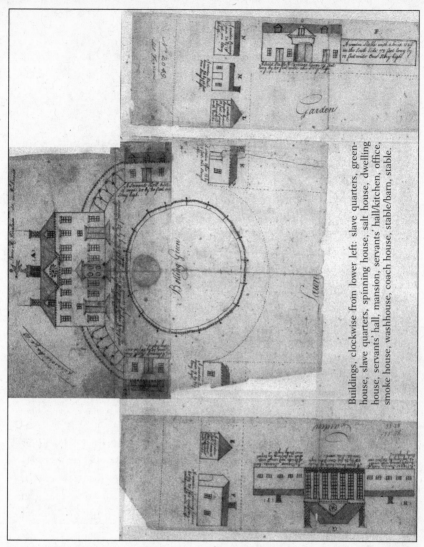

An 1803 insurance policy shows the main buildings of Mount Vernon in Bushrod Washington's day. After the Civil War, the building called "office" would become Sarah Johnson's home. (The Library of Virginia)

Buildings, clockwise from lower left: slave quarters, green-house, slave quarters, spinning house, salt house, dwelling house, servants' hall, mansion, servants' hall/kitchen, office, smoke house, washhouse, coach house, stable/barn, stable.

Garden

Bolling Green

Lawn

Bushrod Washington (1762–1829), Mount Vernon's owner from 1802 until his death. (Virginia Historical Society, Richmond, Virginia)

West Ford (c. 1784–1863) gained his freedom in 1806, continued to work as a carpenter and farm manager for three generations of Washingtons at Mount Vernon, and owned the 214-acre tract that became the Gum Springs neighborhood. (Courtesy, Mount Vernon Ladies' Association)

John Augustine Washington (1820–1861), known as Augustine, the last Washington family owner of Mount Vernon. (Courtesy, Mount Vernon Ladies' Association)

NEGROES FOR HIRE.—I have for hire for 1858, several WOMEN, among whom are a good Cook, a good House Servant, a Laundress, and Dairy Maid. Three GIRLS, one of 17, and one of 13 years of age, accustomed to house work, and one to put out for a term of five years. A BOY of 10 or 12 years old. Persons who may wish to hire any of the above NEGROES, may do so, by making personal application to the undersigned, at Mount Vernon, on any day after Christmas day, when they can see and examine the Negroes for themselves.
JOHN A. WASHINGTON.
Mount Vernon, dec 18—eo2w

In the late 1850s, Augustine Washington hired out surplus slaves; in this 1857 advertisement, the thirteen-year-old girl is Sarah. (Courtesy, American Antiquarian Society)

This engraving from an 1850 sheet-music cover shows African Americans' practice of selling wood canes at George Washington's tomb. (Virginia Historical Society, Richmond, Virginia)

After visiting Mount Vernon in the 1850s, the painter Eastman Johnson depicted a mother and children in the old kitchen. (Courtesy, Mount Vernon Ladies' Association)

Mount Vernon had become dilapidated by the time of this 1858 photograph, which also depicts at least eight African Americans, probably Augustine Washington's slaves. The bottom image shows a detail. (Courtesy, Mount Vernon Ladies' Association)

An 1858 bird's-eye view of Mount Vernon shows the new family tomb (at left), the old tomb (built into the hillside, center), and the summerhouse constructed in Bushrod Washington's day (right). (Courtesy, Mount Vernon Ladies' Association)

Joachim Ferdinand Richardt's 1858 drawing includes several house slaves in the covered walkway between the kitchen and the mansion. (Courtesy, Mount Vernon Ladies' Association)

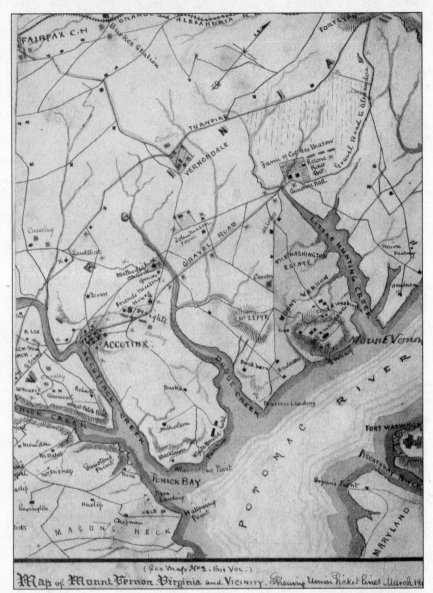

Robert Knox Sneden's 1861 map shows Union pickets in the Mount Vernon neighborhood, as well as Augustine Washington's property and the Quaker town at Accotink. (Copyright 1996, Virginia Historical Society, Richmond, Virginia)

During the Civil War, Union soldiers made up the bulk of Mount Vernon's visitors, as the sketch artist Alfred R. Waud depicted for *The New-York Illustrated Journal* in December 1861. (Courtesy, Mount Vernon Ladies' Association)

Well-dressed visitors at Washington's tomb in the 1860s. (Courtesy, Mount Vernon Ladies' Association)

Ann Pamela Cunningham (1816–1875), founder and first regent of the Mount Vernon Ladies' Association. (Courtesy, Mount Vernon Ladies' Association)

Sarah C. Tracy, the MVLA's resident secretary in the 1860s, who worked to maintain Mount Vernon's neutrality during the Civil War. (Courtesy, Mount Vernon Ladies' Association)

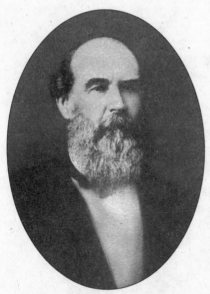

J. McHenry Hollingsworth, Mount Vernon's superintendent from 1872 to 1885. (Courtesy, Mount Vernon Ladies' Association)

Harrison Howell Dodge, Mount Vernon's superintendent from 1885 to 1937. (Courtesy, Mount Vernon Ladies' Association)

A cane seller transacts business with a white visitor at Washington's tomb. (Courtesy, Mount Vernon Ladies' Association)

Haystacks near the mansion suggest Mount Vernon's agricultural operations in 1869. (The Library of Virginia)

In 1873, Ann Pamela Cunningham and eleven MVLA vice regents sat for this photograph with Jean-Antoine Houdon's bust of Washington. Standing (left to right): Elizabeth Willard Barry (Illinois), Letitia Harper Walker (North Carolina), Ella Bassett Washington (West Virginia), Nancy Marsh Halsted (New Jersey), Matilda Emory (District of Columbia), Abby Wheaton Chace (Rhode Island). Seated (left to right): Martha Reed Mitchell (Wisconsin), Mrs. James Brooks (New York), Margaret Jane Mussey Sweat (Maine), Ann Pamela Cunningham (regent), Margaret Ann Douglas Comegys (Delaware), Philoclea Edgeworth Eve (Georgia). (Courtesy, Mount Vernon Ladies' Association)

Between 1850 and 1892, most visitors to Mount Vernon arrived by Potomac steamboat. (Courtesy, Mount Vernon Ladies' Association)

An early MVLA guard at Washington's tomb, 1860s–1870s. (Courtesy, Mount Vernon Ladies' Association)

An MVLA employee on the south lane of outbuildings, 1860s–1870s. (Courtesy, Mount Vernon Ladies' Association)

A uniformed MVLA employee at the entrance to Mount Vernon's gardens, probably between 1876 and 1885. (Courtesy, Mount Vernon Ladies' Association)

Marriage of the long-time housekeeper at Mount Vernon.

The pleasure of your company is requested at the marriage of

Sarah Johnson

to

William Robinson,

Thursday, October 25th, 1888,

at 6 o'clock P. M.

Mt. Vernon, Fairfax County,

Virginia.

Reception from 7 to 9.

Sarah Johnson and William Robinson's 1888 wedding invitation, preserved in a scrapbook with handwritten notation by Margaret Sweat, vice regent for Maine. (Courtesy, Mount Vernon Ladies' Association)

The one known picture of Sarah, sketched in 1891 for *The Washington Star*. (© *Washington Post*, reprinted by permission of the D.C. Public Library; photograph by Franz Jantzen, Apollo Archival)

In September 1892, the Grand Army of the Republic encampment in Washington brought Mount Vernon more visitors than ever before. Behind the central party stands an African American woman—possibly Sarah, who resigned her position later that month. (Courtesy, Mount Vernon Ladies' Association)

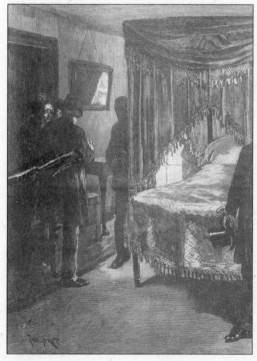

In the 1880s, an African American man stood guard over fashionable tourists in the room where Washington died. (Detail from drawing in *Harper's Weekly*, July 3, 1889; courtesy, the Winterthur Library: Printed Book and Periodical Collection)

Edmund Parker (1827–1898), Sarah's uncle and the guard at Washington's tomb from the 1870s until a few months before his death. (Courtesy, Mount Vernon Ladies' Association)

Formerly thought to be a portrait of Edmund Parker, this photograph depicts Thomas Bushrod (1825–1902), Parker's successor at Washington's tomb. (Courtesy, Mount Vernon Ladies' Association)

An MVLA employee serves milk in the well house behind the old kitchen, around the turn of the twentieth century. (Courtesy, Mount Vernon Ladies' Association)

Just outside Mount Vernon's gates, the electric railway opened a restaurant and souvenir shop at its depot, photographed between 1910 and 1920. (Library of Congress)

An African American child, probably the daughter of an MVLA employee, at the old porter's lodges—now marked "private entrance"—in the 1890s. (Courtesy, Mount Vernon Ladies' Association)

Since 1985, the Mount Vernon Ladies' Association and Black Women United for Action have sponsored an annual wreath-laying ceremony at the new slave memorial, dedicated in 1983. (Courtesy, Mount Vernon Ladies' Association)

coln democratized heroic leadership. The Civil War democratized patriotic death. Could George Washington and his estate remain something more than faded relics of a bygone past, aristocratic icons superseded by contemporary heroism?

Mount Vernon's furnished rooms and lovingly collected artifacts, linked to personal stories about George and Martha Washington, helped humanize the Father of His Country. In the East Parlor (or "music room"), visitors imagined the Washingtons as doting grandparents, listening and smiling while Nelly Custis played the ancient harpsichord. Better than the Bastille key, the Lafayette bedchamber conjured up the friendship between Washington and his French protégé. Washington's own room connected him to death scenes of more recent vintage, including Lincoln's excruciating final hours in a bed across the street from Ford's Theatre. Most of all, the pathetic tale of Martha's bedchamber was designed to endear George Washington to Victorian visitors. As Hollingsworth and his guides loved to recount, the widow chose the only room on the third floor with a view of Washington's grave. Her existence was spartan, for the room had no fireplace or other source of heat. A quarter-circle hole, cut from the bottom of the door, reinforced the image of Martha's lonely vigil. Through that aperture came and went her pet cat, the only companion of her declining years. Some visitors suspected Hollingsworth of embellishment, but the story had a purpose. This Martha was not the archaically titled "Consort of Washington," the words etched on her sarcophagus. Instead she was a bereft wife, a figure of sympathy to any American who had lost a loved one. Her grief made George Washington a beloved spouse.*[17]

At the same time, the mansion breathed life into a world that was meaningfully distant from the present day. In 1874, a year after she left Mount Vernon forever, Ann Pamela Cunningham had written a

---

*The skeptics were right. In the early 1980s architectural research located a stovepipe in another third-story bedchamber, one of the four that opened from the main stair landing. Martha Washington almost certainly lived in that room after her husband's death. Not only did it have a source of heat—essential for an old woman who had lived her entire life in comfort—but it also placed her nearer her beloved grandchildren. The MVLA has since altered its interpretation to make this "Martha Washington's garret bedchamber." The room Hollingsworth showed visitors is now the "South Lumber Room," off-limits to visitors.

farewell address to her MVLA comrades: "Ladies, the home of Washington is in your charge—see to it that you keep it the home of Washington." Americans demolished their past relentlessly, razing forests and old buildings to erect the new. In the rush of modernity, George Washington's home remained America's oasis of constancy, so long as "vandal hands" did not desecrate it. Let them see, Cunningham exhorted, that the MVLA resisted the "fingers of progress." Every antique or antique-looking bureau or chair set Mount Vernon, its inhabitants, and its style more firmly in the eighteenth century. To southerners, this Mount Vernon represented a world they had lost, a civilization obliterated by civil war and postwar industrialization. To northerners, it was a temporary respite from an economy and society regulated by the time clock and the train whistle. A fifty-year obsession for all things colonial began with the nation's centennial. The guests at Martha Washington Tea Parties were parvenu industrialists, and labor unrest brewed outside the banquet halls. But such festivities evoked a harmonious past when the *riches* were not *nouveaux* and the lower orders knew their place. Mount Vernon's period rooms similarly evoked a material world imaginatively removed from Gilded Age materialism.[18]

To many white Americans, the black people at Mount Vernon served a kindred purpose. Historical alchemy occurred as everyday excursionists ate their lunches in the old kitchen, near the large hearth with its giant crane. In some visitors' minds, a meal of sandwiches, fruit, ice cream, and coffee or milk became a latter-day immersion in George Washington's Virginia hospitality. The guidebook encouraged this impression; it was in that very kitchen, where visitors could now get "a good and reasonable lunch," that "the daily meals of the family, white and black, were prepared." Throughout the South old plantations were being remade as tourist resorts, with black people lending apparent authenticity to the picture of a bygone age. Even at the Centennial Exhibition in Philadelphia, a "Southern Restaurant" employed black men as waiters and performers, to transport visitors vicariously to antebellum times. Excursionists aboard the Potomac steamer to Mount Vernon saw the same thing, black men performing. These were often local fishermen taking the steamboat downriver to pursue the day's catch for the local market. Their singing earned a few extra dollars from a different market, appreciative tourists. Oblivious of their economic strategy, Homer Gage, a sixteen-year-old white schoolboy from Massachusetts, found the show an unsettling reminder of black people's lack of education, especially because Frederick Douglass, who represented "what all of his race may become through the acquisition of knowledge," was also on board the day Gage visited.[19]

Black people's performance at Mount Vernon needed to be subtler because visitors complained about anything that smacked of "catch-penny schemes." There was Thomas Mitchell, described by one correspondent as "a noisy colored man," shouting, "Bus to the mansion; 10 cents." Or young West Ford, the "unpicturesque darky" selling bouquets and potted plants, or "another uninteresting colored person who has canes to sell." Even Edmund Parker, "the labeled guide" at the tomb, annoyed a *New York Times* reporter by talking of Washington's resting place as if it were a dime museum marvel. Mitchell, Ford, and Parker all were doing their jobs, which included guard duty. Left unsupervised, some tourists took anything they could, from pebbles around the tomb to the pillow shams from Lafayette's bed. So Hollingsworth posted his uniformed employees around the grounds. Visitors liked watching black people but not being watched by them. One excursionist complained about the "impatience and insolence" of "a young colored policeman going by the name of Ford," one of West's sons. Hollingsworth responded with proper deference to white visitors: "This boy probably is not a bad fellow really, but does not yet know how to behave himself." Nathan and Sarah Johnson struck the right balance, taking visitors' money for lunches and photographs while appearing appropriately subservient.[20]

White people in motion romanticized black people seemingly fixed in place. One newspaper reporter imagined Sarah and other employees as "lineal descendants" of Washington's own slaves who possessed a hereditary right to remain at Mount Vernon forever. In reality, the men and women who worked there in the 1870s and 1880s did not descend from George Washington's "servants"; all of them had lived somewhere else during the Civil War years; and they lived on the premises only because they worked there as the MVLA's employees. Misreading everything he saw, this writer concluded that few families in America could "boast of living on the ground on which their ancestors lived nearly a century ago." This last line echoed Cunningham's farewell lament, that post–Civil War Americans migrated so frequently that "the hearth-stone seems to have no resting place."[21] African Americans were no exception, even though the vast majority of them remained in the agricultural South, place-bound by contract, debt, or family ties rather than by chattel slavery. Thousands of black people traversed the region immediately after the war in search of family members sold away or sought new homes and opportunities in towns and cities. Most of Sarah Johnson's brothers and sisters no longer lived nearby. West Ford's baby brother Andrew had gone as far as Iowa. Mount Vernon's remaining black people evoked America's past simply by staying in place, ostensibly resisting the fingers of progress on ground that neither they nor their ancestors had ever owned.

For a week in late spring every year George Washington's mansion became the living home to the women of the MVLA, a sorority in the business of reverence. They came from Summerville, Georgia; and Portland, Maine; Cincinnati and Milwaukee, elite women roughing it in a mansion without indoor plumbing. By day they assembled in council around a table in the small dining room, a portrait of Ann Pamela Cunningham watching over them. They reviewed Superintendent Hollingsworth's account books, reported on money and relics collected in their home states, deliberated about contracts with steamboat operators and photographers, and legislated policy for the coming year. Accompanied by Hollingsworth, they assessed for themselves the state of gardens, outbuildings, and livestock. For one day of each council, they were joined by a committee of men appointed by Virginia's governor and legislature in accordance with the MVLA's state charter. This largely ceremonial Board of Visitors heard reports about the women's work, enjoyed a feast prepared by Sarah, and helped the association respond to carping journalists. On the Sunday of council week the women decamped en masse to Pohick Church to worship in George Washington's pew. Every night each of the women retired to her bedchamber in the mansion, furnished with contributions from her own state. In the Virginia Room, Emma Reed Ball slept in the bed where Washington had supposedly died. Directly upstairs slept Wisconsin's Martha Mitchell in Martha Washington's bed, the recent product of a Milwaukee cabinetmaker. Living for a week within the hallowed walls, the MVLA's governing women dreamed of George Washington's world by night and worked to re-create it by day.[22]

Ever since Cunningham's departure, the MVLA had operated as both legislature and executive. Cunningham had relied on only a trusted few vice regents, but by the late 1870s and early 1880s more than a dozen women participated actively, forming committees to handle much of the business. These were "quiet business people," women of executive experience at home as well as Mount Vernon. Susan Hudson of Connecticut, a widow in her midfifties in 1880, managed a Fairfield household that included her octogenarian parents, a coachman-gardener, two Irish domestic servants, and an English butler. Georgia's Philoclea Eve lived in her son-in-law's household but also owned and ran five plantations. The vice regents' husbands were prominent in state and local affairs; they included several congressmen, the chief justice of Delaware, and the president of Florida's largest railroad company. These women maintained extensive social circles as well as amply staffed households.[23]

Their own experiences with servants, mostly Irish for the northern vice regents and black for the southerners, predisposed the women to take an interest in Mount Vernon's employees. Several vice regents developed a maternalistic sense of obligation toward the unlettered women, men, and children who lived on the grounds. Nancy Halsted, who taught Sunday school at home in New Jersey, asked Hollingsworth to inquire "among your colored people" whether each owned a Bible. She volunteered to send a half dozen, as well as hymnbooks for those who could read and sing. Three years later she went further, sending a crate filled with 167 books. Inside were infant and youth catechisms and other books for a Sunday school library, as well as arithmetics, grammars, spellers, readers, histories, and geographies for a "day school," plus paper and pens "for the little folk." Susan Hudson must have learned that Warner May led religious singing on the grounds, for she had seven copies of a hymnbook sent to him from New York. Desirous "that our people should have religious advantages," she encouraged Hollingsworth to pay an Alexandria preacher to come out to Mount Vernon at least one Sunday a month. "It will add to their social & moral status," she wrote.[24]

The residents' physical status proved a greater concern. Illness still plagued Mount Vernon every summer and fall. Sick employees worried the vice regents for business as well as benevolent reasons; lost workdays, especially when tourists were numerous, meant extra expenses for day laborers. When Sarah and Smith Johnson contracted diphtheria "again" in the summer of 1877, Hudson asked Hollingsworth about the drainage from their house. She had seen "the servants" throwing kitchen slops out their back doors, an incubator for illness. After consulting a physician, Hudson recommended spreading "disinfectants everywhere," using pails for slops, and whitewashing the employees' houses. Typhoid fever would come next, she feared. Halsted wrote in more measured tones, emphasizing the importance of good drainage. The following summer Hollingsworth had the old drainage tiles taken up from Sarah and Nathan's house and replaced with new terra-cotta pipe. In an early form of health insurance, the MVLA also authorized Hollingsworth to pay the employees' doctor bills with association funds.[25]

As Sarah and Nathan became more involved with the lunch business, they had less time for other work. In 1879 visitors complained about dust in the banquet hall, the library, and the small dining room. The vice regents for Illinois and Ohio, who constituted the mansion committee, prepared a seventeen-point list entitled "Nathan's Instructions." The particulars were exacting: sweep and dust so that not a cobweb was visible; use a brush instead of a broom; never clean the windows with soap; polish all the brass hinges and door handles every week, taking care not to deface the paint on the doors. The vice regents made two copies of the list, one for their illiterate butler and the other for Hollingsworth. But they also understood that Nathan was now as much a manager as a domestic servant. With the MVLA's approval, he hired a neighbor's daughter, a seventeen-year-old black woman, to help clean the mansion twice a week, for fifty cents a day plus board. The following year the council lamented that all the turkeys, chickens, and ducks had suffered from cholera. Because Sarah could not devote all her time to the poultry, it seemed "necessary to have a special person in charge of it" in order to reap any profits. In the mansion and the henhouse, the MVLA displayed both concern with the Johnsons' workload and an eye to the bottom line.[26]

By the mid-1870s, after nearly a decade's acquaintance, many of the vice regents had become friendly with Sarah, who attended to their needs during council meetings and visits throughout the year. Hollingsworth became a conduit for exchanges between Sarah and the Ladies, as when Georgia's Philoclea Eve asked him to read Sarah a list of prices: calico dresses for $2 to $3.50, "nice <u>tucked</u> underskirts" from $1.25 to $2, collars starting at 15 cents, a black alpaca suit for $11 or $12. Eve offered whatever summer and winter clothes Sarah desired if Sarah sent her money at once.[27] Not only had Sarah's ties to the vice regents strengthened, but her means and tastes had also risen since 1868, when Nancy Halsted sent raw cloth, not store-bought garments.

The vice regents' relations with their superintendent, however, were rarely maternalistic and sometimes prickly. After the 1876 council a few of the Ladies remained behind to look over his account books. They asked him about several charges for wine and brandy, which he testily attributed to the Board of Visitors' penchant for drink. When the vice regents told him they would return to complete business the next Monday, Hollingsworth replied, "<u>I shall not stay here to work on Sunday, and the servants will not</u>, either." He further informed them that they need not check his accounts, because the Board of Visitors was to do so. Comegys reminded him that the women were "sovereigns at Mount Vernon" and he was their employee. She and Philoclea Eve surmised that the superintendent had been drinking, but sober or not, Hollingsworth inhabited a difficult position.[28]

As the banner centennial year gave way to the perennial challenge of making ends meet, the close of each year's tourist season occasioned belt tightening. Housing and feeding the "old, faithful servants" were necessary, wrote Susan Hudson, but all unnecessary expenses should be cut. Lunchroom waiters, day laborers, and newer employees were furloughed during the off-season. Tensions rose in the fall of 1877, when a new figure took center stage among the vice regents. Cunningham's successor, Lily Berghmans, married a man named Laughton, planned a long European trip, and appointed Margaret Jane Mussey Sweat, the longtime vice regent for Maine, acting regent. Like Hudson, Halsted, and other vice regents, Sweat took "a personal interest" in the black employees' well-being, asking Hollingsworth whether the drainage on the Johnsons' house had been repaired and insisting that

Sarah be supplied with a coffee roaster for the lunch table. But soon Sweat also became Hollingsworth's nemesis. She asked him to forward every bill to her, from groceries to uniforms, and she reviewed his payroll with an accountant's eye.[29]

The gulf between superintendent and acting regent ran deeper. A published novelist, travel writer, and prolific contributor to newspapers, Sweat possessed a streak of cultural iconoclasm. She had championed the controversial writings of George Sand in the 1850s, and in 1890 she was to invite Susan B. Anthony to discuss women's suffrage before her Washington, D.C., women's study club. Sweat and Hollingsworth nominally shared a political affiliation. The superintendent was a Democrat, and Sweat's husband, a Democratic congressman during the war, served on the Democratic National Committee in the 1870s. But that allegiance meant something different in Maryland and Virginia than in Maine. In border states, Democratic politics connoted conservatism, especially in race relations, and Hollingsworth appears to have been no exception. Democrats in 1870s Virginia stood against a biracial coalition known as the Readjusters, whose electoral base lay in a rare alliance of ordinary white and black farmers and workers. When Mount Vernon's black male employees went to the polls in the late 1870s and early 1880s, they likely cast their ballots for Readjuster candidates, to Hollingsworth's chagrin.[30]

In an earlier era Hollingsworth might have displayed a planter's paternalism, taking care of his "people" enslaved and free. Now, to his mind, Mount Vernon's employees were only that, free laborers with no ancestral right to live there, merely the benefit of housing if they did their work. As Hollingsworth anticipated reducing expenses for the winter in 1881, he decided to fire some of the "old, faithful servants," the gardener, West Ford, and his family. West and Ellen Ford lived on the grounds with seven children, ages one to nineteen. Three of their sons came onto the MVLA's payroll intermittently. This large family had irked the superintendent for more than a year. The previous November Hollingsworth had dismissed one of the sons who had married a white woman and moved into the porter's lodges without permission. The Fords were constantly sick, he explained to the regent Lily Laughton (returned from her travels, widowed again, and back in charge). "They never provide anything for themselves," so others had to cut wood to keep them warm in winter. The family lived in "such a dirty, squalid manner" that Mount Vernon would be better off without them. Firing West Ford and his sons would save seventy dollars a month. Evicting the whole family would rid the place of a clan of dependents.[31]

But the Fords stayed. No evidence survives to explain whether Laughton overruled Hollingsworth's decision, the superintendent backed down, or West Ford himself appealed to the regent's authority. However, the outcome surely reminded Hollingsworth of his own place as an employee of the MVLA, a status that various small incidents reinforced. The vice regents caught bookkeeping errors in his ledgers at the 1881 council meeting. That year and the next, the council drafted lists of instructions for his coming year's work. Several items indicated the vice regents' concern for their employees, as well as the role Sarah Johnson played. In 1880 the council authorized Hollingsworth to buy a stove for Sarah's cellar and to take "every precaution against fire in putting it up" and appropriated $150 for repairs to West Ford's house. Although the council ended each session with a tribute to the superintendent's performance, Hollingsworth grew weary of their meddling.[32]

When the crisis finally came, the lunch business was the catalyst. The lunchroom remained profitable until 1882, despite the slow winter months. In 1882–83, however, its fortunes turned when a nationwide economic depression reduced tourism to Washington. Mount Vernon's expenses outran its revenues that year, and Laughton drew money from the endowment fund four times to cover everyday expenses. Poring over Hollingsworth's ledgers at the May 1883 council, the finance committee concluded that the lunch table was indeed losing money. The payroll had climbed from about $400 to nearly $500 a month since 1881, much of it for waiters. Food costs were by far the largest other expenditure. Hollingsworth challenged the MVLA's interpretation. If the lunchroom were discontinued, he argued, employees currently boarded by Mount Vernon would have to supply their own food and would require higher wages. Worse, the reduction of hospitality would displease visitors. The MVLA overruled him unanimously. As of June 9, visitors would no longer be able to purchase lunch on site, only milk and the dairy products of Mount Vernon's own cows and chickens. At the same meeting, confronted with a doctor's bill for $189, vice regents drew from their own household experiences to discuss the matter. The council voted to stop paying employees' doctor bills and instructed Hollingsworth to tell the workers that they should thenceforth expect to pay the physician themselves. Finally, the MVLA decided to trim the "extravagantly high" payroll by dismissing several employees and cutting the pay of several others.[33]

Visitors missed the lunch table, as Hollingsworth had predicted. Writing in *The Washington Post*, "Sybil" implored the MVLA to reverse its decision. On a recent visit Sybil and her adult companions, a young mother and an older lady, had brought only a few apples and some cake for the two children in their party. Adults and children divided this meager fare like "shipwrecked mariners" and returned to the boat exhausted. Washington's "home life" was evoked by more than the furnished mansion, Sybil wrote. Coffee and homemade bread served "in the old kitchen where they were formerly partaken" had become part of the hospitality that reminded visitors of olden days. Sarah Johnson and the black waiters were similarly imagined in the past, as faithful servants of slavery days rather than paid employees serving store-bought bread, a status that bore too much resemblance to modern commerce.[34]

For black people, the end of the lunch table brought not nostalgic regret but a real problem, lost jobs and opportunities. The night after the MVLA adjourned the fateful council meeting, the employees who were soon to leave Mount Vernon gathered in front of the mansion. Mournfully and then joyfully, they sang, beginning with "Whispering Hope" and concluding with "Always Be Cheerful." They had sung many of these hymns recently, at a benefit for their church nearby. While they sang "Ring the Bells," they tolled the large bell that had convened the council, briefly employing the MVLA's instrument for their own music. Over the following summer Hollingsworth reported "a great deal of trouble with the servants." Several quit rather than accept pay cuts, leaving a workforce barely sufficient to meet the summer rush.[35]

According to Hollingsworth, Nathan and Sarah Johnson gave him the most trouble of all. "In a bad humor & dissatisfied with <u>everything</u>, since the lunch table was abolished," they had lost the entrepreneurial responsibility they had enjoyed. Hollingsworth's accusations rubbed salt in the wound. To several vice regents and apparently within the local neighborhood, the superintendent claimed that Nathan and

Sarah's poor management and dishonesty had sunk the lunch business. Hollingsworth told Philoclea Eve in September that he was secretly pleased the lunch table had been abolished. "Properly conducted," it might have turned a profit. "But rest assured, my dear Madam, that nothing can ever prosper at Mt Vernon, while Nathan & Sara are there." Sarah complained of overwork. Nathan and Sarah talked about leaving, which Hollingsworth thought would be "a happy riddance." The following winter fell hard on Mount Vernon, as ice closed the river to steamboats for weeks. As receipts sank, Hollingsworth failed to make the payroll. Some employees received their monthly wages, but Nathan and Sarah Johnson waited months for back pay. Relations between them and the superintendent grew chillier than the Potomac air. Sarah refused to cook or clean for Hollingsworth any longer, perhaps at Nathan's insistence.[36]

For at least some vice regents, the controversy tarred everyone's standing. Wisconsin's Martha Mitchell placed blame on all sides. Hollingsworth had not been the same since suffering a stroke in 1880. He hired a nephew as clerk, bookkeeper, and mansion guide, but one of his closest friends, the captain of the Mount Vernon steamboat, "did not know where the money went." Nathan and Sarah also bore some responsibility, Mitchell believed. Nathan had run the lunch table, buying and dispensing food. "If our darkies are like all other darkies—they will take food or use it for their friends." Mitchell's comment referred to the widely accepted "service pan" practice; Irish or black, domestic servants commonly took home leftover food, with their employers' tacit or express permission. Mitchell believed that a "housekeeper"— implicitly a white woman—might have prevented the problems, by keeping better control of both the books and the food. At the same time and albeit in derogatory fashion, the vice regent accurately identified African Americans' communal ties. Sarah Johnson's refusal to do Hollingsworth's domestic work did not merely express her hostility. It also created a job for her half sister Milly Mitchell, whom the superintendent hired instead.[37]

By the time the Mount Vernon Ladies' Association prepared to reconvene in May 1884, the lunch business had found new life just outside

Mount Vernon's grounds. Edward Gibbs, the neighbor whose farm had supplied staples for Nathan's business, opened his own restaurant within a few hundred feet of the Mount Vernon gates, in partnership with Hollingsworth's nephew, the clerk. Visitors once again enjoyed a midday meal, now a purely commercial enterprise served by members of the white Gibbs family rather than by black Mount Vernon employees.

The steamboat excursionists had no inkling of a toxic atmosphere around Mount Vernon that spring. "All the colored people in the neighborhood" had become Hollingsworth's enemies, thanks to his charges against Nathan and Sarah. The superintendent resented not only the Johnsons but also perceived enemies in the MVLA. He stewed that two of his best employees, "white democrats," had left Mount Vernon after the previous year's cutbacks while longtime black servants had kept their jobs. Several vice regents sensed that the coming council would also test their own unity. Tensions between Laughton and Sweat, on one side, and Halsted and Hudson, on the other, had mounted for several years. On the eve of the 1884 council, the vice regent for New York, Justine Van Rensselaer Townsend, implored Halsted, whose husband had just died, to attend the meeting. "Can you lay aside personal sorrow just now, dear friend, for never will the old conservative advisers be more needed than at this Council when great changes will probably be made, & great judgment will be needed."[38]

The steamboat brought sixteen vice regents to Mount Vernon on Tuesday and Wednesday, May 20 and 21. Their deliberations began on Wednesday with the reading of Ann Pamela Cunningham's farewell address, reports of contributions from various states, and the superintendent's annual report. The problems came to the fore on Friday, when the council stopped taking minutes and commenced discussion of "the present defects in management." While that evening's *Washington Post* and *Alexandria Gazette* reported that Hollingsworth would probably resign, Sarah Johnson presented her "Book of Accounts of Sales" for the council's inspection at a five o'clock session. Later that night, apparently, several vice regents summoned her to their bedchambers. Sarah climbed the stairs quietly, so as not to disturb the women who had already retired or those unsympathetic to her purpose there. Margaret Sweat awaited her, along with probably Laughton, Wisconsin's Mitchell, and several others. Sarah had spent the day waiting on them, cooking and serving their meals. Now by candlelight she discussed Mount Vernon's management with her employers. Only a longtime, trusted female employee, not a man or a relative newcomer, could have entered the Ladies' rooms and their confidence in the dark of night. The white women continued their conversation after Sarah had retired to her own bed in the butler's house.[39]

Reassembled in council Saturday morning, the MVLA prepared a list of nineteen questions for Hollingsworth, many of them accusatory and clearly drafted after the conversation with Sarah. Had the superintendent, against the previous year's orders, continued the lunch business after the mandated closing date? Had he discharged the employees as directed by the council? What had happened to the remaining inventory of the lunchroom? Did Sarah do his cleaning and cooking? How did the sale of photographs work, and how were its receipts recorded? Next the women voted on a difficult question: Should Hollingsworth be required to answer the questions in writing? Voting yes implied a lack of trust, a breach in the relationship between employers and superintendent. Voting no suggested that matters could be handled as they had long been, with conversation. Counting proxies for absent vice regents, the ballot came out ten to ten, with Margaret Sweat casting four votes in favor of written answers. Laughton asked for time to consider her deciding vote, and here the record of any discussion was clipped out of the manuscript minutes the following year. The regent broke the tie by voting no.[40]

As Saturday's session continued into the night, the vice regents unanimously accepted a series of resolutions, all aimed at tighter control over their superintendent. The MVLA's Washington banker, not Hollingsworth, would henceforth settle accounts with the steamboat captain. The council would establish each year's payroll, and nobody else could be hired without the regent's express permission. Hollingsworth was to receive instructions about his duties and the limits of his authority between annual councils. Finally, he was always to make the payroll on time, on the last day of every month, and to report to the regent that he had done so. At Pohick Church on Sunday, the women no doubt prayed for comity, but financial accountability remained the subject as Monday's session opened. Hollingsworth was to deposit all receipts (greenhouse, photography, milk, canes) into the MVLA's bank account and present his accounts to the regent monthly. The "person in charge of the cows" was to keep a daily account of milking, and "the person in charge of the milk," Sarah, was to "note down the quantity of milk furnished her daily, keep an account of the manner in which it is disposed of, and give such report to the Superintendent at the end of each week."[41]

On Monday afternoon, notwithstanding the council's vote, Hollingsworth delivered written answers to Saturday's bill of indictment. He admitted selling lunch to tourists after June 9, 1883, but at his own expense. Visitors came to Mount Vernon expecting lunch, he had explained, so he had allowed sandwiches and ice cream to be sold through August. He had intended to give any proceeds to the MVLA, but the venture had lost money. As for dismissing the employees, he explained that he could not fire them as of June 9, because they had been hired at a monthly wage, but he had let them go at the end of June. The eighteenth question must have particularly rankled, for Hollingsworth answered, "Most Emphatically No! And I cannot believe that the ladies of the Council fully appreciate the nature of the imputation embodied in their question—that of theft or embezzlement, on my part." The margins of Hollingsworth's document reveal the MVLA's reactions: "Reply unsatisfactory"; "Question misunderstood"; "Very unsatisfactory." Rather than call the superintendent before the council, Laughton appointed a five-woman committee to visit him in his office and get better answers.[42]

Hollingsworth may have persuaded this "Committee of Inquiry" that the Johnsons had become insubordinate, for the entire council turned to the question of Nathan and Sarah on Tuesday morning, May 27. The Ladies voted unanimously to give "written instructions to Nathan and Sarah in regard to their work and duties" and that "these instructions be given to Nathan and Sarah by the Regent, and that she explain these orders in the clearest manner." However, this solution implied a desire to separate the warring parties, both of which were by 1884 part of Mount Vernon's resident management. The MVLA did not reaffirm that everybody at Mount Vernon was subject to the superintendent's bidding, as Betsey Mason had told Hollingsworth twelve years earlier. Instead it gave instructions directly to Nathan and Sarah, unfiltered through Hollingsworth, a dramatic show of respect for the Johnsons' position. Wednesday morning's session opened with a contrite Hollingsworth expressing his regret for disobeying the order to close the lunch table the previous June.[43]

Exhausted by a contentious week, seven vice regents departed on Wednesday afternoon's steamboat, while their colleagues persevered one more day. On Thursday morning at eleven Laughton reported that she had explained the council's instructions to Nathan and Sarah, who were "ready to obey, and to attend to their duties." Apparently the Johnsons responded with a request of their own. The council's next order of business was to vote that Hollingsworth, the gardener, and Hollingsworth's clerk take turns staying at Mount Vernon on weekends, beginning the following Sunday. With these men helping protect the place on the Sabbath, Hollingsworth must now "allow Nathan the privilege of going to Church one Sunday in each month" and make sure the other "colored servants should have a similar privilege." With Thursday afternoon's steamboat about to depart at two o'clock, the council adjourned. The MVLA's 1884 meeting was finally over.[44]

Eleven days later the *Washington Sunday Gazette* published an attack on the MVLA, under the title "Mount Vernon. Loose Financial System—Dotage and Imbecility—An Investigation Necessary." The correspondent claimed to unmask the discord beneath the recent council meeting. The employees all rejoiced, he wrote, when the last vice regent boarded the steamboat and "loud, quarrelsome, and unseemly sounds" ceased to emanate from "the mansion of historic memory." Hollingsworth had diligently pulled Mount Vernon from the chaos of 1872, but two or three women had conspired against him for years, doing their best to "annoy him in his duty." One was a tyrant, a thinly veiled reference to Laughton; another, a New England "atheist," undoubtedly Margaret Sweat. Even Hollingsworth and many of the vice regents, claimed the writer, did not know Mount Vernon's true financial status. An investigation needed to penetrate all the way to the regent's bank account. As Martha Mitchell realized, only Hollingsworth or someone close to him could have written this article. It revealed information only an insider could know.[45]

The "great changes" predicted by Justine Townsend had only begun. The 1884 council had revealed disturbingly sectional strains within the

MVLA. A "feeling of North & South" seemed to be "creeping" into the Ladies' deliberations, Mitchell wrote to Susan Hudson, who had missed the meeting. Hollingsworth agreed. In a letter to Hudson, his closest friend on the MVLA, he listed his supporters and detractors among the Ladies. His "friends," he believed, were predominantly the southern vice regents: Eve of Georgia, Ella Washington of West Virginia, Ella Herbert of Alabama, and Emma Ball of Virginia, as well as Delaware's Margaret Comegys and Ohio's Elizabeth Broadwell. His "bitter enemies" were Laughton, Sweat, Rhode Island's Abby Wheaton Chace, and—"the biggest traitor of them all"—Lucy Pickens of South Carolina. The "color line" was at work against him too, Hollingsworth thought. It was betrayal enough that Sarah Johnson went to the vice regents' rooms late at night to testify against him. More humiliating and disgraceful, "Mrs. Sweat has been in correspondence with Sarah, Nathan & Smith, & has employed them to act as spies upon my movements." The superintendent consulted with attorneys and made plans to resign.[46]

To the public, Mount Vernon's situation appeared to be deteriorating again, after all the progress made since the Civil War ended. Hollingsworth cataloged the woes: rotting fences, dying fruit trees, worn-out land, "the public made angry and embittered against us, and the Press ready to break out on us." He blamed the layoffs of the previous two years, which had left the grounds short-staffed. In contrast, the 1885 council read the situation as "a serious neglect of duty" by Hollingsworth and authorized Laughton to give him "every opportunity to justify himself." The superintendent's and the council's diagnoses differed, but not their remedy. On Thursday, May 28, 1885, Hollingsworth gave the MVLA an ultimatum: without a unanimous vote of confidence, he would resign. Only five women voted for him, against eight willing to "accede to his wish to retire." The council passed a resolution and presented Hollingsworth with one of the Mount Vernon cows as an expression of gratitude for his twelve years' service. Refusing their request that he stay until a successor could be appointed, he departed Mount Vernon immediately after Memorial Day.[47]

His enemies would come to regret impugning his character, Hollingsworth had hinted to Susan Hudson. Two days after his ultimatum a new weekly publication appeared in Washington, titled the *Trade, Traveler and Excursionists' Guide*. Devoted to "literature, railroads, steamboats, hotels, public resorts, real estate, and the people's rights," the newspaper was in fact a rant against the Mount Vernon Ladies' Association. It resurrected the charges of a decade earlier—that the MVLA was a secretive monopoly, that its admission fee effectively barred two-thirds of all Americans from visiting the shrine the people had purchased—and added a new claim to the familiar litany. By attempting to bar a railroad company from erecting a depot near Mount Vernon's gates, the MVLA had revealed yet again its "aristocratic" temperament as well as its fear that railway passengers would undermine its steamboat income. Couched in the language of democracy, the *Trade, Traveler and Excursionists' Guide* served two agendas: Hollingsworth's bitterness and railroad speculators' thirst for the Mount Vernon market. These messages had limited appeal; there is no evidence that the *Guide* outlived its first issue.[48]

Sarah Johnson could take only bittersweet satisfaction in Hollingsworth's downfall. At six in the morning on May 9, three weeks before the superintendent left, Nathan died of "rheumatism of the heart." The *Alexandria Gazette* noted his passing, but not in its whites-only obituaries section. Instead a little item appeared among the "Local Brevities," between the remodeling of a navy steamboat and the opera house's excellent turtle soup. Nathan Johnson's claim to fame was as "a much respected colored servant," who had once been Augustine Washington's "butler and head servant—a position which he retained for over thirty years."[49] As black people asserted their presence in America's and Virginia's public spaces, whether by celebrating Emancipation Day or voting for the Readjusters, conservative white people such as the *Gazette*'s editor romanticized slavery days. Presented as faithful servants before and after the war, figures like Nathan embodied a comforting continuity: three decades in the same job in the same place, in freedom as in slavery. The profound transformations in his life went unmentioned. So did those at Mount Vernon, where Nathan had done more than merely evoke an Old South past. In operating the first lunchroom at an American historic site, he helped create the New South's commerce of historic hospitality.

SEVEN

Sarah Johnson's Papers

Seven weeks after Hollingsworth's departure, Sarah Johnson and her fellow employees assembled to hear their new superintendent's "manifesto." Reading aloud from a large sheet of paper, Harrison Howell Dodge described their collective obligations, written in his straight, clear hand. The "dignity" and "Sacredness" of Mount Vernon must always remain foremost in their minds. Employees must always be neatly dressed, polite, and respectful in the presence of visitors. They should guard against relic hunters and correct anybody who jested or made light of General Washington, his memory, or his family. They should work together to preserve, protect, and improve Mount Vernon, so as to spare the women of the MVLA all possible anxiety. Finally, they must observe and obey Dodge's every command. He in turn promised to treat them fairly and honestly and to strive for the harmony that would benefit Mount Vernon's welfare. After Dodge had completed his reading, he asked each listener to sign the next page, testifying that he or she "cheerfully" agreed to follow his every requirement. The clerk John L. Nicholls and the gardener Franklin A. Whelan, the two white employees, signed first, followed by J. W. (West) Ford and his stepson George. The five others—Sarah, her stepfather Warner May, her brother-in-law Thomas Mitchell, her uncle Edmund Parker, and her half sister Milly Mitchell—each made an X, and Whelan inscribed their names below their marks. At thirty-three, Dodge was younger than every black person in the room except George Ford.[1]

Pens and pencils were Harrison Dodge's most powerful tools. Having spent the war years on his uncle's Maryland farm, he knew agriculture, horticulture, dairy farming, and the care of livestock. But his most recent experience, which equally commended him to the MVLA, was as a longtime clerk at Riggs Bank, where he kept meticulous accounts. Prominent Washingtonians recommended Dodge for the job, and his great-grandfather had served under General Washington in the Revolution, an appealing lineage. After their recent struggles with Hollingsworth and with one another, the vice regents foresaw better days. Martha Mitchell believed that the diverse women of the MVLA had "surmounted our worst difficulty." Now they needed to remain true to one another and not "let our employees get over us." Neither Harrison Dodge nor any of these women imagined in July 1885 that he would hold the reins for fifty-two years, longer than George Washington had, or that he would become Mount Vernon's firmest master since the Father of His Country. Dodge recorded each laborer's daily work in a little pocket diary. He kept account of every aspect of Mount Vernon's operation, from major restorations to the nickels Sarah Johnson collected for selling milk. He corresponded voluminously with regents and vice regents, finding with each woman just the right mix of deference, familiarity, and authority. His annual reports, delivered at the MVLA's council meetings and printed in its minutes, detailed the previous year's progress, forecast the coming year's needs, and explained the issues awaiting resolution, all with an accountant's precision and a practiced author's fluency and subtle wit.[2]

"Inspected Mansion with Sarah (servant in charge)," Dodge wrote in his diary on his first Friday at Mount Vernon. Sarah, who succeeded Nathan as keeper of the mansion, led the new superintendent through George Washington's house. Room by room, pencil and paper in hand, Dodge took inventory of every relic and article of furniture. In a dark corner of the old pantry, he found a letter-copying press, which Sarah told him had been gathering rust there since Upton Herbert's day. Dodge resurrected the little machine, to make copies of his correspondence.[3] By all appearances, their first prolonged encounter revealed the worlds of difference between Sarah Johnson and Harrison Dodge. The former slave and longtime employee had accumulated her expertise through experience, work, and word of mouth. The new superintendent was a man of facts and figures, a sense of command, and a belief in the written word. Despite these differences, Sarah and Dodge shared a commitment to hard work and to Mount Vernon. Each possessed a sphere of responsibility: the mansion for Sarah, the entire operation for Dodge. As he filled up diaries and pressed letter books, the superintendent came to respect Sarah as far more than an illiterate "servant in charge." All the while, even without signing her name, Sarah accumulated papers of her own, written documents that crafted a life apart from Mount Vernon. An enterprising new superintendent, new choices by the veteran employees, and new technologies all reshaped Mount Vernon's community over the next seven years.

More than any other black employee, Edmund Parker consciously played a role. The guard at Washington's tomb, Parker asked men to doff their hats out of respect to America's founding father. He requested that pilgrims not take pebbles from around the tomb, knowing all the while that they would ignore him. (Every few weeks one of the employees hauled a wheelbarrow full of new gravel, to dump there for mementos.) Parker figured in one of Harrison Dodge's very first decisions at Mount Vernon. On his second day on the job the superintendent walked down to the wharf to meet the visitors. Stopping at the tomb, he recoiled at the sight of Parker selling canes. Black men had engaged in that commerce on that spot for more than thirty years, but to Dodge it smacked of sacrilege. He relocated cane selling to the old kitchen and assigned it to the young man who had taken Nathan Johnson's place selling photographs. Segregating the marketplace from the shrine, the new superintendent did not yet realize that many visitors took Mount Vernon's relics home, pilfered or purchased, as proof of their reverence.[4]

Dodge was suspicious those early days when Parker asked for a week off at Christmastime, still months away. That was when "de sperits come back and make a turrible sturbance at de tomb," Parker explained. Dodge paid the request little heed until just before Christmas, when Parker reported that the spirits had come, moaning in the old slave cemetery near Washington's tomb. A "committee of investigation," including an unwilling Parker, ventured into the woods where many of the old slaves lay buried. No invisible hands snatched Parker to take him under the ground with his forefathers, and Dodge thought that he had proved that the moaning noise came from the wind in the trees. The superintendent found the entire incident incongruous. How had black people, who feared spirits in burying grounds, become the guardians of a tomb? Long-held folk beliefs, which existed alongside Christianity for many African Americans, probably helped explain Parker's anxiety.[5]

So did simple calculation: he wanted a Yuletide holiday. That first Christmas, Dodge went home to Washington to dine with his family. Returning to Mount Vernon the morning of December 26, he was chagrined to find that several employees had taken the day off without permission. By the next year, however, he appreciated their holiday spirit. He asked the regent to release the payroll money early, gave the men time off on December 22 to do their Christmas shopping in Alexandria, and gave everyone a holiday until December 28. Moreover, even as he challenged Edmund Parker's superstitions, he gave Parker's son a job, paying fifteen-year-old Harry two dollars a week to assist his father and do farmwork. Prodded by his employees, Dodge learned to accommodate their desires.[6]

He also learned Sarah's importance to the place and to the MVLA. She knew her work so well that he supervised it lightly, rarely mentioning her in his diaries. The superintendent respected her expertise and experience. Sarah could account for the historical placement of nearly every piece of furniture in the mansion. When Dodge came across an old high-post bed that might be useful for the Maine Room, she identified it as the property of Virginia's vice regent. She advised him about the Ladies' bedchambers and meals as he anticipated his first MVLA council meeting in May 1886. The Maryland Room lacked a slop jar and water bucket, Sarah noted; there was still enough English breakfast tea, but he needed to order another pound of oolong. Sometime between cooking the Ladies' meals and supervising the maids and waiters hired for that council meeting, Sarah importuned her friends in the MVLA about her own concerns. The mansion committee visited her house and found it damp, owing to poor drainage and a leaky roof. The MVLA voted to authorize immediate repairs, including a cement floor in the cellar. The Ladies had another reason to fix Sarah's house. When all the bedchambers in the mansion were occupied, Sarah's two second-story rooms could be pressed into service as vice regents' quarters. (Smith Johnson, now in his midtwenties, no longer lived with his mother at Mount Vernon, leaving Sarah's house an entirely female space suitable for white ladies' habitation.) Sarah must also have complained of overwork, because the MVLA allocated eight dollars a month for a "young assistant" to help her clean the mansion and cook the everyday meals.[7]

Sarah was not the only overburdened employee. The men tended the farm, gardens, and livestock until just before the steamboat arrived. Then they donned their navy blue shirts, black trousers, black hats, and silver badges to guard the property and attend to visitors. After the boat steamed away, they returned to their laboring clothes and to their farm and maintenance work.

Dodge saw from the start that his resident workforce was stretched too thin. Gutters were clogged with leaves and other rubbish. Weeds and undergrowth marred the walkway in front of the mansion. Walks and roads needed mending. All these eyesores had elicited complaints since Hollingsworth's last years. Although the regular employees did their best, visitors' hours interrupted their manual labor every day. Moreover, two of the black men, Tom Mitchell and Edmund Parker, were in their middle or late fifties, while Warner May had passed sixty. "Good picked men" could be hired from the neighborhood for seventy-five cents a day, Dodge told Laughton, who authorized him to hire several day laborers. He had miscalculated the local labor market. All the surrounding farmers paid ninety cents or more for a day's labor, and nobody would work for less. Laborers expected to be paid every Saturday, not monthly like the regular employees. Dodge hired six men at ninety cents a day—"the very best I could do"—and asked Laughton for a check for the first week's labor in early August. To complete the most urgent tasks a month later, he hired three additional men before the corn-harvesting season began and the prevailing wage increased.[8]

Dodge's day laborers came mostly from a four-mile radius around Mount Vernon, and several of them were landholders in their own right. A few belonged to families well known at Mount Vernon: James Quander, a descendant of people freed by George Washington, was married to a granddaughter of old West Ford. Among the local landowners who did day labor in 1885, Andrew Lee was typical. Lee owned ten acres and worked for Dodge for twenty days. Two of his sons also joined Mount Vernon's workforce: seventeen-year-old Jarvis for nearly four months and twenty-one-year-old William for a week. Given the Lees' modest acreage, they supplemented partial self-subsistence and limited truck farming with paid work for others, earning $101.17 at Mount Vernon that season. Several other men earned three dollars a day, rather than ninety cents, because they brought horses and wagons for hauling gravel. One of them, Sandy Alexander, owned 41 acres of what had been George Washington's River Farm, east of Mount Vernon between Little Hunting Creek and the Potomac. Another, Lovelace Brown, was amassing a small empire, beginning with a 13-acre plot near Gum Springs that he had bought for eight hundred dollars in 1870. Adding an entire 72-acre section of Augustine Washington's old land, another tract once owned by Bushrod Washington, and several more parcels, Lovelace Brown came to own more than 130 acres. Unlike Andrew Lee and several landless day laborers, Brown probably did not need the $31.50 he earned at Mount Vernon to make ends meet; perhaps it helped him expand his landholdings. Still, his presence on Dodge's labor roll reveals how permeable the boundaries were between landownership and day labor.[9]

Bit by bit, with an expanded workforce and the MVLA's approval, Dodge began to make Mount Vernon old again by making it new. Vice regents continued to adopt and furnish the remaining chambers of the mansion. The vice regent for Kansas spearheaded a fund-raising drive to restore the old greenhouse slave quarters, entirely with old bricks. On a visit to Massachusetts, Dodge located a set of spinning equipment of "ye olden time" and purchased it to re-create the spinning house. Sons of Missouri's deceased vice regent sent a check to restore George Washington's deer park, an innovation that Washington himself had abandoned after a buck injured one of his slaves. Dodge enclosed seven acres and ordered a Tennessee buck and six does. Unfortunately, the fast-multiplying herd exhausted the foliage in its pen and required extra feed, an unanticipated expense. Like Washington's unfortunate slave, Dodge found himself on the wrong side of antlers one February day when he tried to retrieve some litter a visitor had thrown into the paddock. The buck charged at him, leaving the superintendent with lacerated legs and an injured kneecap that kept him out of work for three weeks. But his young daughters enjoyed the creatures, and visitors found the deer park a picturesque reminder of Washington's own day.[10]

Visitors noticed the difference in Mount Vernon's appearance. Caroline Healey Dall, who had first seen George Washington's home when she was a twenty-year-old Boston schoolteacher in 1843, moved to Washington in 1878 and frequented Mount Vernon well into the 1890s. Dall knew the place familiarly enough to act as a guide whenever she brought guests, drawing in other visitors to listen to her narration. Having witnessed the deterioration of the grounds in Hollingsworth's later years, she welcomed Dodge's "improvements." To her satisfaction, the new superintendent found a way to keep the hens and dogs penned up, in fact a concession to modern sensibilities more than an accurate depiction of an eighteenth-century plantation. Dall thought the grounds looked better in 1887 than ever before, unwitting testimony to the happy effects of hiring day laborers to supplement the overburdened regular workforce. Sophie Bledsoe Herrick, a prolific author and editor, visited that same year to write a magazine article. For a nationwide audience, Herrick emphasized the spell of bygone days that Mount Vernon cast, from the eighteenth-century furnishings in the mansion to the boxwood-bordered old gardens. The present intruded on the past here and there, in the shape of "tawdry" modern furniture in one mansion room, blue bottles of fire-extinguishing solution in another, and various traces of destruction by "vandal hands." Nonetheless, any visitor motivated by more than "idle curiosity" could easily be transported to a simpler time.[11]

Sophie Herrick and Caroline Dall were pilgrims of an earlier sort, genteel travelers inclined toward pensive, reverent reflection. By 1887, the centennial of America's Constitution, another sort of visitor was far outnumbering the Herricks and Dalls. As professions and trades created national associations and as fraternal organizations such as the Knights Templar spread across the Union, Washington enjoyed burgeoning popularity as a convention site. A trip to Mount Vernon became a standard part of these tourists' itinerary, usually with a ceremony at Washington's tomb. Pilgrimage had long coexisted and overlapped with tourism, and "idle" sightseeing had always been less newfangled than its critics implied. Back in the 1850s self-styled pilgrims had complained about the similar effects of twice-weekly steamboat traffic to Mount Vernon. But assemblages of the 1880s dwarfed their antebellum predecessors, whether it was a hotel proprietors' convention in 1887 or Republicans converging on the capital for Benjamin Harrison's inauguration as president two years later. Compared with many of these visitors, Herrick and Dall had much in common with each other: strong early education; a lifelong intellectual bent; even children to raise alone when their minister husbands left them.[12]

On the subject of Mount Vernon's black workers, however, these two women's impressions diverged. Dall, an early acolyte of transcendentalism, a onetime abolitionist, and a leading advocate of women's rights, embodied New England's Unitarian, reformist spirit. As a regular visitor to Mount Vernon, she noted happily that "all the colored people remembered me." West Ford, Edmund Parker, and Sarah Johnson seemed like her own contemporaries, fellow conduits to earlier times. Herrick imagined them instead as part of the illusion, throwbacks to slavery days. The daughter of a diehard Virginia secessionist, she had imbibed her father's nostalgia for an Old South remembered through rose-colored glasses. Herrick fixed upon the way the black mansion guide introduced himself. He had "b'longed to de fam'ly," born at Mount Vernon, as his father had been before him. Herrick rhapsodized about the ex-slaves' connection to days gone by and about slavery itself. Emancipation was far from Sophie Herrick's mind as she toured the mansion and grounds. As resurgent Democratic governments began to impose Jim Crow segregation on southern law and society, white southerners' and many northerners' image of antebellum slavery came to reflect a southern, white mythology of benevolent masters and contented slaves. White Americans, North and South, rewrote the Civil War as a struggle between equally valiant, equally praiseworthy white Yankees and white Confederates. They relegated the conflict over slavery to the memory of African Americans and white ex-abolitionists such as Caroline Dall. Herrick extended the Old South backward in time, all the way back to George Washington's 1790s. The "relation of master and servant in its perfection," the "beautiful and redeeming feature" of the peculiar institution, seemed reincarnate in the reverent, loving way Mount Vernon's contemporary servants described General and Mrs. Washington.[13]

It survived too in the "handsome mulatto woman" of sweet voice, gentle demeanor, and perfect courtesy in the family kitchen—Sarah Johnson. A sign on the door indicated that milk was sold for the benefit of the MVLA. Herrick asked for a glass and inquired the price. With a slight curtsy, Sarah replied, "Fi' cents a glass, *onless*, ladies, you will kindly accept it from the 'sociation." Sarah likely knew or suspected that these ladies included a magazine writer. But her generous, ostensibly ordinary response prompted another of Herrick's nostalgic effusions. Mount Vernon had escaped the "sordid quality" that made most "show-places" offensive. More than this, everyone from the lowliest Negro to Dodge himself made visitors feel welcome to a home. Their services did not seem like "mere perfunctory offices, performed for pay." Wage labor, thought Herrick, would be misplaced at Mount Vernon, at odds with the affection that ought to inspire workers and visitors alike. True appreciation required vicarious, reverent absorption into a bygone domestic sphere, a process best accomplished if the setting were authentic and the workers comported themselves appropriately.

In fact Sarah Johnson handled visitors' money every day but Sunday, because most had to pay for their glasses of milk. Just as the sign on the door said, their nickels, recorded by Dodge in a little ledger, went into the MVLA's coffers. When tradesmen and their laborers boarded at Mount Vernon, Sarah pocketed twenty to sixty cents a day for each man she fed. She also earned commissions of three or five cents for selling Mount Vernon's authorized guidebook and Benson Lossing's history of Mount Vernon. Despite Sophie Herrick's nostalgia for a world of service free from commerce, Sarah Johnson knew Mount Vernon as not only her home but also her place of business.[14]

Herrick was unknowingly describing a script, the way black workers presented the past and themselves to colonial revival visitors on nostalgic quests. "Belonged to the family," a phrase African Americans at Mount Vernon had used with visitors for fifty years, fudged the essential fact that their ancestors had never belonged to George Washington, only to his brother's descendants. It sustained the illusion of these black people's own authenticity. Part of the script was official. Most of the furniture was "antique, but not original," said the black mansion guide, the sort of distinction that appealed to collectors and connoisseurs such as Herrick and the MVLA women. He also retold Hollingsworth's old story about Martha Washington's bedchamber, complete with the cut-away corner in the door and the grief-stricken widow's feline companion. But part of the script was also the guide's own, in content or inflection. He volunteered "in a tone of genuine and reverent affection" that his favorite room was the one in which Washington had died.[15]

The guide's spirit may have been as authentic as Sophie Herrick imagined. Presenting Washington's death chamber to the public six days a week, he could have imbibed a reverence for the man or at least a fascination with the objects he explained to (and protected from) visitors. Like his predecessors of slavery days, he could also believe that association with the Father of His Country in some sense ennobled him. It certainly distinguished him from the typical black sharecropper or farm laborer. Uniformed in blue and black, he commanded white people's respectful attention. Yet he might also simultaneously remember the direct consequence of George Washington's death in that room: it freed slaves. Drawing his monthly pay at Mount Vernon, he could imagine a Washington more congenial to his memory than the longtime slaveholder.

At the same time, Sarah Johnson and her compatriots were not immune to the historic associations of the place. One December day a ragged old tramp appeared at Mount Vernon. To Dodge he seemed "crazy & irresponsible." Sarah recognized his condition too but accorded him the grace and sensitivity with which she treated all visitors. At the mansion door the old man politely asked, "Is General Washington in? I have a message for him." Sarah answered that the general had just stepped out, that she would send for him, and that the stranger should have a seat and rest. After she had summoned Dodge, together the housekeeper and superintendent supplied the man with food, shoes, and socks. The tramp escaped Dodge's attempt to put him on the boat to Washington and disappeared, but he lived on in the employees' memory. The men greeted one another by asking whether they had seen "your friend, the tramp" lately, and they mock-ceremoniously asked Sarah, "Is General Washington at home?" The old man returned several months later, his hair matted, his face emaciated, his feet frostbitten, not unlike Washington's soldiers at Valley Forge, the ordinary men who had helped win American independence.[16] There must have been thousands of moments like this, when Sarah and the other workers treated visitors with dignity, found humor in their peccadilloes and their variety, and imagined *them* into the past that Mount Vernon evoked for its employees no less than for its guests.

Visitors in the 1880s could find young West Ford in George Washington's gardens, selling flowers and telling stories. He recounted how Thomas Jefferson had planted the sweet-smelling shrub alongside the path to the old schoolhouse, where Martha Washington's grandchildren had once learned their lessons—a legend without a grain of truth. His favorite story, probably just as fictitious, involved the Nelly Custis rosebush, so named by General Washington because it was the spot where Lawrence Lewis had proposed marriage to Nelly. This tale circulated so widely that the bush became known as the Wishing Rose, a romantic landmark for young couples visiting Mount Vernon. Unlike Oliver Smith fifty years earlier, Ford made no pretense to have seen the long-ago events. The stories were his heirlooms, passed down from two generations of Fords before him. In turn, Ford himself seemed like an heirloom of Mount Vernon, a relic of the past even though he was only in his forties.[17]

West Ford came by his stories through his family, a clan formerly divided by slavery. He had been on the slave side. His father, most likely old West's son William Ford, had been free from birth. His mother, however, remained enslaved to Washingtons all her life, passed down from Bushrod to John Augustine to Jane Charlotte to Augustine, and her condition dictated her children's servitude. When old West divided his Gum Springs land among his four free children, William had received his share. But when William died in 1874, those acres went to the four children he had fathered with his wife, free Henrietta Bruce, the children who had never been slaves.[18] Young West's inheritance amounted to stories, not land.

West's half brother George W. Ford may have wanted to correct their father's omission. William and Henrietta's eldest son, George Ford had joined the United States Tenth Colored Cavalry after the Civil War and headed west. He trained at Fort Leavenworth, Kansas, terrain as far from Mount Vernon as the Missouri River from the Potomac. Sent into battle against Plains Indians, Comanche and Arapaho and Cheyenne, Ford was among America's first buffalo soldiers, black troops in a white man's army, fighting "red" men. After a decade, two tours of duty, and a bullet in the leg, he had earned the rank of quartermaster sergeant and an honorable discharge. He moved to Beaufort,

South Carolina, his wife's family home, and became superintendent of the United States military cemetery there. He had no plans to return to Gum Springs. After his father died, George W. Ford considered what to do with his share of the family land. Rather than leave it in his full siblings' safekeeping, he virtually gave it to a Ford who had not shared in the family bounty. He sold West Ford twenty-three acres for twenty-five dollars. This was West's wage for a month's work at Mount Vernon and far less than the market value of the land.[19]

When West Ford told visitors his stories of olden times, he did not mention his own place in a new Virginia. He did not tell them how much he prized education or that he and his children could read and write. In this way, he played along with visitors' fantasies of old-time black people. Nor did Ford say where else he employed his oratorical talents. Like his brother Andrew in Iowa, West performed marriages and preached the gospel, within Fairfax County and occasionally across the Potomac in Maryland. On those occasions he was known as the Reverend John West Ford. A leader within the Gum Springs community, he sold one of his twenty-three acres to the local school trustees to erect a new colored school.[20]

Like many of Harrison Dodge's day laborers, Ford belonged to Virginia's growing number of black landholders, even as white supremacist Democrats reclaimed the reins of state government in the mid-1880s. Within Fairfax County's Mount Vernon District, a territory that sprawled across forty-seven thousand acres (six times the size of George Washington's original property), about eighty African Americans owned land. At Mason Neck, about five miles southwest of Mount Vernon, a black enclave occupied part of the Gunston Hall plantation once owned by Washington's compatriot George Mason. One black farmer, who had been free before the Civil War, now owned fifty-six acres there. Around him lived eighteen other black families, most renting land or working as farm laborers. Together they purchased land for their Shiloh Baptist Church and established a colored school, the way residents of Gum Springs had done in the 1860s. In the opposite direction from Mount Vernon, five miles north en route to Alexandria, another Mason heir sold several tracts to African Americans in the 1880s. Other black landholdings, mostly parcels of ten acres or less, were scattered around the district. Typical of African Americans across Virginia, their average holdings were considerably smaller than white people's, and blacks owned less than 2 percent of the district's land. Still, like black people throughout the South, they prized even a few acres. A farm of one's own testified to a stake in the society. It also afforded the opportunity to grow some of one's own sufficiency—as many of them had done on their garden plots in slavery—and now to sell some produce in the local market, a pursuit formerly subject to the master's sufferance. It did not, however, make a farmer self-sufficient, and that helps explain why West Ford and his stepson George still lived and worked at Mount Vernon.[21]

Across the United States white and black small landowners had much in common, including working for others to make ends meet. At Mount Vernon the distinction between white and black workers was clearer. For all his experience there, West was only the assistant to Franklin A. Whelan, the white gardener hired in the early 1880s. John Nicholls, the clerk Dodge inherited from the previous regime, was also Hollingsworth's nephew and a partner in the new lunch business just outside the Mount Vernon grounds, facts that practically ensured conflict. In September 1886 Dodge fired Nicholls, who protested to the regent and several vice regents. Dodge had treated him like a servant. For his part, Dodge told the Ladies that Nicholls had been repeatedly insubordinate, setting a perilous example to other employees. With a small workforce, Dodge expected everybody on the estate, himself included, to pitch in at any menial task. Nicholls countered that his genteel status shielded him from "the work of a laborer." As Dodge and Nicholls's relationship approached the breach, the superintendent hired another white man—a fact he pointedly noted to the MVLA—as a jack-of-all-trades. Frank Harding proved adept at pruning trees, doing carpentry, laying bricks, and guarding the mansion during visitors' hours. He worked alongside the black employees and day laborers, and Dodge paid him the same wage that black regular employees got. But Dodge believed that Harding deserved more and persuaded the MVLA to raise the new man's monthly wage from twenty to thirty dollars. Harding minded Dodge's authority better than Nicholls had, but he bedeviled Dodge's new clerk and second-in-command when the superintendent went on vacation. Harding resigned after two years; even at thirty dollars a month, it was difficult to keep white employees.[22]

Turnover also occurred within the ranks of the longtime black workers. Tom and Milly Mitchell announced their intention to leave near the end of 1887. Milly, born at Mount Vernon in 1850, cleaned the superintendent's rooms and sometimes, bedecked regally in a bandanna turban and spotless calico dress, took Sarah's place selling milk. Tom had worked at Mount Vernon since he was six years old, an indentured free black child. For nearly twenty years he had tended the horses and driven the coach that ferried visitors between the wharf and the mansion. Now fifty-two, he wanted to retire. On December 16 the Mitchells vacated their house across the lawn from Sarah's. Dodge hired Warner May's wife, Dolly, to do Milly's work, and West Ford's son-in-law Ben Carter to do Tom's. Hardworking but ill suited to caring for horses, Carter lasted only five months and was replaced by one of the dependable day laborers, Richard Broadus.[23]

On May 26, 1888, at three-thirty in the afternoon, Sarah's stepfather, Warner May, died. May had farmed Mount Vernon's land since Augustine Washington had purchased him forty-two years earlier. To Dodge, the old man seemed a relic of traditional farming, not scientific agriculture. How much lime did the soil take per acre? asked the superintendent. May stuttered that he had not applied lime to the depleted land in years but that (in Dodge's transliteration) "if yer want to p-p-put it on 'bout thick nuf to t-t-track a rabbit, one bushel to de acre w-w-would do de trick." When Dodge seemed incredulous, May adjusted the amount downward to three pecks. But as he had with Sarah Johnson, Dodge came to respect Warner May's dedication to even the most degrading tasks, like cleaning the outhouses. He mourned the loss of "one of the best servants" and attended the funeral with all the employees, who remembered a patriarch and devoted friend.[24]

With her stepfather's death, Sarah and her uncle Edmund were the last of her family on the Mount Vernon payroll, but she was soon to join a new family. Among the nearby black landowners, William Robinson possessed an unusual secondhand connection to American history. Born in Berkeley County (now in West Virginia), he had somehow ended up in a freedmen's or contraband camp in Civil War Louisiana. There he met Harriet Newby, a widow with several children and a historic past. Harriet had been married to Dangerfield Newby, whose white father had flouted antebellum convention by freeing and marrying the enslaved mother of his children and emancipating them all.

The Newbys moved to Ohio, but Harriet remained the property of another Virginia slaveowner, who refused to sell her or her children to Dangerfield. Angry and desperate, Dangerfield Newby joined John Brown's army, imagining an opportunity to rescue Harriet and their family. Instead he met his death early in the raid, possibly at the hands of Augustine Washington's sharpshooter brother Dick. Rather than migrating to Ohio, Harriet and their children were sold south, ending up in Louisiana. William Robinson and Harriet Newby married, had four daughters of their own, and returned to Virginia shortly after the war, when former slaves were congregating in freedmen's villages near Washington. By 1870 the Robinsons were living in Fairfax County; a decade later William bought ten acres of Mason family land, halfway between Mount Vernon and Alexandria. Harriet Robinson died in the early 1880s. With one of their daughters, William had purchased nearly forty acres more by decade's end, placing him among the district's most substantial black landholders.[25]

When and how Sarah Johnson met William Robinson is lost to history, but they must have quickly discovered their similar experiences. Berkeley County, William's birthplace, was immediately northwest of Jefferson County, where Sarah's Parker relatives had lived and worked at Blakeley. Historic associations connected William and Sarah to the nation's storied past, even if Harpers Ferry represented disunion and radicalism, the very antithesis of Mount Vernon. Just as likely, they got to talking about what they shared as Baptists, parents of grown children, and upwardly mobile African Americans. As they became acquainted, they could find in each other the compatibility of contemporaries after first marriages to much older people. Harriet Newby had been more than a decade William Robinson's senior, Nathan Johnson fourteen years Sarah's. Early in 1888 Sarah Johnson and William Robinson became engaged.

With assistance from Sarah's friends among the MVLA, they planned the kind of wedding neither had enjoyed the first time. The vice regent for Illinois, who inhabited one of the grandest mansions in Washington, D.C., promised Sarah a yellow dress. The bride-to-be postponed the wedding several times waiting for it to arrive. Harrison Dodge complained that William Robinson was not good enough and that Sarah seemed to value the gown and other gifts more than the marriage itself, but he missed the point. This wedding was to symbolize more than merely freedom, the newfound prospect of legal marriage that emancipated couples had seized back in 1865. This wedding also bespoke respectability and gentility. Over two decades of hard work, William and Sarah had made places for themselves in the local black community. Sarah had also earned the respect of some of America's wealthiest white women.[26]

"The pleasure of your company is requested at the marriage of Sarah Johnson to William Robinson": the engraved invitation followed time-honored principles of etiquette. Neither Sarah nor William could read in 1880, but twenty years later Sarah would be able to say she could. To arrange for the printing, Sarah and William could have taken their desired wording to a local printer and paid for his services, or the invitation, like Sarah's gown, may have been the gift of a generous vice regent. Recipients of the invitations were not confined to family. Margaret Sweat, the Maine vice regent who had supposedly hired Sarah and her family to spy on Superintendent Hollingsworth four years earlier, preserved hers in a scrapbook of Mount Vernon memorabilia. The bride and groom's neighbors probably received them as well, even if they already knew about the event by word of mouth at church or market. Sarah also had relatives beyond the neighborhood, beyond even the boundaries of Fairfax County, people who had once worked at Blakeley or Mount Vernon and had not returned after the Civil War.[27]

On Wednesday, October 24, William Robinson traveled the twenty miles west to the Fairfax County courthouse. He carried the deed that finalized his most recent land purchase, to have it notarized and filed with the county, but his main mission that day was to obtain a marriage license. The longtime clerk of the court filled out and signed the decorative form, a document that bore witness to the couple's past even as it legalized their future. In the spaces designated for the bride's and groom's parents, the clerk wrote: "   & Jane Robinson" and "   & Hannah May." Where the bride's and groom's fathers should have been named, white space attested to the white fathers African Americans did not identify in the public legal documents archived in courthouses that white elected officials controlled.[28]

The next evening, shortly before six o'clock, neighbors and relatives and friends gathered in Sarah Johnson's house at Mount Vernon. The steamboat tourists had departed for the day, leaving the grounds to the celebrants. At Lily Laughton's request, there had been no announcement in the newspapers—either because the regent did not want to advertise Mount Vernon as a potential wedding site or because she did not want the public to know that African Americans were getting married there. The Reverend Samuel Madden, pastor of Alexandria's Alfred Street Baptist Church, performed a simple ceremony, and the guests reveled until nine that night. The newlyweds' friends may have prepared a festive meal, to spare Mount Vernon's longtime cook the burden of making her own wedding supper. According to Dodge, Sarah looked radiant in her yellow dress.[29]

The newlyweds lived apart at first, as Sarah returned to work and William to his farm. William came to Mount Vernon only occasionally. Their arrangement resembled those that "abroad" spouses had made in slavery. But now the Robinsons could devise an alternative: make William one of Mount Vernon's day laborers, like the other black landholders who worked there sporadically. Dodge hired him on probation and tested his abilities. Robinson proved to be an efficient guard in the mansion and a knowledgeable, careful farmer, especially in the orchards. At its council that spring, the MVLA voted to employ him "on his own terms": a dollar a day, now the going rate for day labor, rather than a regular employee's monthly wage. Under this arrangement, if he worked six days a week, William Robinson could make as much as he would in a regular position but without the responsibility of guarding the grounds on Sundays. He could take additional days off to tend his own farm. Also in 1889, the Robinsons deepened their ties to the local community of black landholders when William's daughter Louisa married Ulysses Grant Brown, the son of the well-to-do Lovelace Brown.[30]

On April 16, 1889, Sarah became a landowner in her own right. Her four-acre plot was on the land once owned by Augustine Washington, about two miles north of the MVLA's property. When Augustine's land had been divided among his orphaned children, his daughter Eleanor got the 133¾-acre parcel just south of the one Lovelace Brown eventually bought. Eleanor Washington Howard sold twenty acres to Lloyd Washington, a black farmer (and no relation to the white Washingtons). Sarah paid Lloyd Washington $350 for her triangle-shaped plot, considerably more per acre than the average Fairfax County property. A small farmhouse, valued at fifty dollars, accounted for part of the difference. The location mattered more. Sarah's land lay at the intersection of two roads, one of them a major access route to Mount Vernon. That intersection in turn lay along a proposed railroad route from Alexandria to Mount Vernon. Sarah bought prime real estate, with ease of access to markets, the potential to open her own business along the thoroughfare to Mount Vernon, and good resale value. Despite her recent marriage, she bought it as Sarah Johnson, not Sarah Robinson. She may have initiated the transaction before October 1888, or this may have been a way to keep her property distinct from her new husband's (and his children's). Given the price she paid, Sarah and Nathan could well have been saving for years to buy land of their own. Purchasing in his last name honored that dream.[31]

In the Mount Vernon District of Fairfax County, Sarah's purchase was extraordinary. Other black women owned land, but most had inherited it. Portions of the Gum Springs tract, for example, became the property of old West Ford's daughters and granddaughters. Other women landholders were the widows of men who had purchased the property. Like the Fords, a number of the women landholders belonged to families that had been free long before the Civil War, some of them descendants of people George Washington had emancipated.[32] Sarah possessed neither those decades' head start nor any landed forebears, only the hard, dedicated work that she and Nathan Johnson had done since 1865.

Between 1889 and 1892 change came to Mount Vernon in yards, not inches. Many of the longtime employees were weary in the fall of 1889. Hobbled by rheumatism, Edmund Parker performed less and less maintenance work. His son Harry, now nineteen, resigned in early November. Sarah felt overworked and underpaid, her twenty dollars a month incommensurate with the tasks of managing the mansion (for which Nathan had received thirty), doing the cooking, keeping the chickens, and serving and selling to visitors. West and George Ford were building a double house on West's Gum Springs land. When it was completed around Christmas, they told Dodge that they wanted their families to live closer to the children's school and that the three miles between Mount Vernon and Gum Springs had become increasingly inconvenient. Dodge tried in vain to coax the men to stay, offering rooms and furniture to use during the week if they preferred not to commute daily. But the suddenness of their departure—they resigned on December 30 and left the next day—angered the superintendent. Other family considerations may also have led West Ford to desire a change. One of his sons had died a few years earlier, and a second had become violently insane at Mount Vernon in the fall of 1888. Ford's wife was likely ailing by December 1889, prompting him to move his family closer to their community and to doctors' care in Alexandria. Six months after the move, she died of kidney disease. Within a few years, West Ford remarried, embarked on an itinerant preacher's life, and left Virginia. In a last act of generosity to the local community, he sold his land to the trustees of the Joint Stock Club of Gum Springs, established to sell small parcels to aspiring black landowners. Among the purchasers was Sarah's half sister Milly Mitchell, the former Mount Vernon employee.[33]

The remaining employees, especially Sarah, became more valuable as their number dwindled. At the 1890 MVLA council, Laughton announced that Sarah Robinson planned to leave as well and move to her husband's farm. Sarah claimed ill health; she had been to the doctor in Alexandria that March. She desired rest, a change of climate, and a residence closer to her church. But the Ladies were loath to lose her. They voted unanimously to provide nearly everything Sarah wanted: a substantial raise to thirty dollars a month, the use of a "conveyance" (at Dodge's discretion) to go to church, two months' vacation, a raise for her assistant from eight to fifteen dollars a month, and extra pay for any extra work she performed. That last perk yielded small sums like the pennies she received as commission on book sales, the sort of money slaves had received for working beyond their assigned tasks or during their holidays. Around the same time, Sarah began to pay Dodge for lamp oil. These little financial exchanges in both directions implied that Sarah possessed an entrepreneurial existence beyond her monthly wage as well as a lamp to illuminate her house in the evenings. Sarah stayed, and William Robinson continued to do day labor at Mount Vernon, six days a week, most of the year. Taken together, the MVLA's concessions to keep Sarah were an extraordinary testament to her value.[34]

Edmund Parker likewise assumed added significance as other veteran black workers departed. During the 1891 council the *Evening Star* of Washington, D.C., sent a reporter to profile the MVLA women and their work. The correspondent turned his attention to the servants. At Washington's tomb, he kept Parker talking about his own life while the paper's sketch artist drew the old guard's picture. Augustine Washington, explained Parker, had been "a good massa, as they went in dose days." Back then, he continued, nobody thought to put black people's pictures in the newspaper. But "nowadays somebody makes a picture out of me ebery day. Dat is, dey say so; I never sees any of dem. Dey all carries dem little boxes with a hole in one end." Despite his language, Parker had been familiar with cameras for at least thirty years, ever since professional photographers first frequented Mount Vernon. In 1891 Mount Vernon employed photographer Luke Dillon to take and sell pictures of the site, as well as of visitors who wanted images of themselves standing next to the mansion. But Parker was describing a new phenomenon, tourists' own handheld cameras. Amateur photography had become an American obsession in just the past three years, soon after Kodak had introduced the first of these devices. The "little boxes" measured about six by three by three inches, and came with the film already loaded. When the reel was finished, the photographer sent the whole camera back to Kodak, which developed the pictures and returned the camera reloaded. In a concession to modernity, the MVLA grudgingly permitted visitors to take their own photographs, relinquishing a monopoly that had helped finance Mount Vernon's upkeep. Edmund Parker's deliberate quaintness reinforced the appearance of antiquity even as newfangled technology captured his image for posterity.[35]

Other technological changes propelled Mount Vernon and its neighborhood toward the twentieth century. Connecticut's vice regent sent Dodge a typewriter. Telephone poles were installed, and the first phone calls from Mount Vernon were made on May 4, 1891. Most important, Dodge continually searched for the most up-to-date fire prevention system. "Hand grenades," the little blue bottles of liquid extinguisher that Sophie Herrick noticed, were an ineffective stopgap.

A system of underground cisterns and pumps, installed in the 1870s, needed updating. At Dodge's recommendation, the MVLA purchased the Holloway fire extinguisher, a system complex enough to require a resident engineer. Dodge hired a white man, J. B. Clark, who earned sixty dollars a month, lived on the grounds with his wife and children, and got a plot of land to raise his own vegetables.[36]

The steamboat remained a barrier to many visitors (who could not afford an entire day's excursion from Washington) and to year-round traffic to and from Mount Vernon. Two ideas to facilitate the journey gathered momentum in the early 1890s. Prominent citizens of Alexandria won a state charter to create a wide highway between Washington and Mount Vernon and sought the federal government's backing. Dodge recognized the speculators' hands behind this ostensibly patriotic proposal but applauded it nevertheless. It would attract visitors and, even more important, "be a Godsend" to residents in Mount Vernon's vicinity, landlocked in winter whenever the Potomac froze. The Mount Vernon Avenue Association was a decade before its time, the automobile age. More successful were the Philadelphia investors behind the Washington, Alexandria & Mount Vernon Railway Company. From Virginia to California electric railways became a transportation phenomenon in the 1890s. They promised cleaner, more efficient local travel than horse-drawn carriages. For years potential investors had imagined the financial rewards of a railway to America's shrine. For years too the MVLA had dreaded losing its steamboat revenues and fiscal solvency to private speculators and its sacred aura to motley mass tourism. Now, wrote Laughton, "we must accept the inevitable."[37]

But only with "great regret." Dodge and the MVLA fretted about the implications. More Americans than ever would be able to afford the time and expense of sightseeing, once the railroad reduced the trip from Washington to less than an hour. The time for farming and groundskeeping would dwindle, as trains brought visitors all day long. Mount Vernon would need two workforces, one to guard the premises and guide visitors, the other to perform the daily routine maintenance. Laughton would not be the one to lead Mount Vernon into this new era; she died in November 1891, before the electric railway became a reality. However, her successor as regent, New York's Justine Van Rens-

selaer Townsend, shared her misgivings. Convening the MVLA council in June 1892, Townsend grudgingly welcomed representatives of
the railway company. The railroad men proposed to build their terminal near the Gibbs lunchroom just off the Mount Vernon grounds.
Streetcars would run every hour from ten to five-thirty, with the fare
from Washington ten cents. On Sundays, when Mount Vernon was
closed, the route would end at an earlier stop. The railroad would not
allow the sale of alcoholic beverages on its property, would police its
terminal at Mount Vernon, and would forbid any "pavilion for dancing"
on its grounds there. Trying to make the best of unwelcome necessity,
the MVLA responded that its grounds would be open only from eleven
to four and stipulated that the railroad company must find a way to
prevent crowds from descending upon Mount Vernon just before closing time. Mount Vernon, Townsend wrote, "has but little (if anything)
to gain and much to lose by this railroad enterprise."[38]

Residents of Gum Springs thought they had something to lose from
a different road project that season. The Alexandria and Accotink
Turnpike, built by private investors in the 1850s to improve travel between Alexandria and the Quakers' commercial village at Accotink, had
never been completed—because of old West Ford's land. In Gum
Springs the two major sections of the turnpike were connected by a
country road, which had several bends and poor drainage. Now, forty
years later, the Fairfax County government had assumed responsibility
for the turnpike. Fifty citizens petitioned the county to straighten it by
cutting through eight Gum Springs farms. The signers included numerous commercial farmers and descendants of the original Quaker
inhabitants, as well as prosperous African American farmers who had
relatives in Gum Springs but did not live there themselves. They also
included Joseph Gibbs and Harrison Dodge. For the restaurateur and
the superintendent, an improved road would encourage land visitors
and make their own frequent travel to Alexandria more convenient.
The men and women of Gum Springs had other concerns. The division
and damage to individual farms were bad enough; West Ford and his
neighbors had built outlets from their farms to the country road, which
would become useless. Worse, the new road would disrupt their community's life. Black residents had erected Bethlehem Baptist Church
and their new schoolhouse along the country road. The new turnpike

section would leave these institutions and their post office off the main thoroughfare. Thirty-four men and five women signed a petition opposing the project. The opponents included white and black people, many of them residents of Gum Springs. Young West Ford's stepson George, until recently employed at Mount Vernon, signed, as did several descendants of the original West Ford.[39]

Unlike the MVLA, Gum Springs' residents won their skirmish in the unending contest between commercial development and local communities. Their petition revealed the political consciousness and sense of potential efficacy that black people had developed over the past three decades. They had recently petitioned for, and won, an election precinct in their own neighborhood, so that they no longer had to travel five miles to vote at Accotink. Every election day Mount Vernon's male employees took time off to go to the polls at the Gum Springs schoolhouse. Harrison Dodge cast his first vote as a resident of Virginia there, surrounded by black and white fellow citizens.[40]

Hired labor, swelling numbers of visitors, new technologies, new independence among the longtime workforce: all the strands of change at Mount Vernon converged in September 1892. The Grand Army of the Republic, the resurgent fraternity of Union veterans, was planning a mass meeting in Washington in midmonth. Anticipating unprecedented throngs, Dodge advertised for extra guards. On Monday, September 5, he returned from a weekend with his family to find "a lot of applicants" and hired twenty-seven of them, white and black men from the surrounding countryside and from Alexandria. He also hired several "colored women," one to work in the spinning house and three to help Sarah sell milk and do other domestic chores. The superintendent extended visitors' hours from ten to five and declared that the second and third floors of the mansion would be closed during the GAR convention. Even if "unreasonable people" objected, Dodge was determined to protect the MVLA's property at all costs.[41]

On September 16 the extra employees were on the grounds by nine, two and a half hours before the first steamboat brought the advance guard of veterans. The next day, Saturday, more than eleven hundred people visited. Dodge remained on the premises on Sunday, the eighteenth, when Mount Vernon was closed. No steamboats landed there that day, but GAR men came all day by road and had to be turned away. On Monday boats started arriving at ten and kept coming until late afternoon, but everything went smoothly: "Great day!!" Dodge wrote. More than seven thousand people visited, the largest number Mount Vernon had ever welcomed in one day. That record survived only until Wednesday, a rainy day that Dodge apologetically described to the regent as "a veritable hell." The employees labored to keep more than ten thousand "dirty, bedragled [sic], common people" in good spirits. All those muddy feet, trudging through the mansion and across the grounds, left Mount Vernon a "hog-pen" that would take days to clean up. In all, nearly thirty thousand people came to Mount Vernon during the GAR convention, by far the busiest week ever.[42]

The same week the Washington, Alexandria & Mount Vernon Railway opened for business. The first streetcar made its trial run on Tuesday evening, and the hourly schedule (from Alexandria, not yet Washington) commenced the next afternoon. The onslaught of steamboat visitors dwarfed the two hundred streetcar passengers that day, but by week's end Dodge was writing about "crowds by boat & rail." The MVLA's fears appeared to be realized when the cars kept bringing passengers as late as six, forcing Dodge to turn them away with all the tact he could muster. "The class of people that patronize the road," he wrote, were exactly what cheap rates attracted: "a good many negroes and the commoner sort of whites." They required more supervision than the "more refined class that we have long been used to." The superintendent canvassed the neighborhood for several new employees, including a gatekeeper to man the railroad entrance and a night watchman to eject after-hours trespassers.[43]

He also needed a new housekeeper.

Sarah Robinson had determined to leave two years earlier. Higher wages, little perks, and opportunities for extra income had postponed her departure but not changed her decision. By now she was a grandmother. Her son, Smith, had married a woman named Mary, and their son, Nathan, named for his grandfather, had been born on October 21, 1891. Exactly five months later Smith Johnson had purchased 2.2 acres adjacent to his mother's property. William Robinson continued to commute on weekends between Mount Vernon, where Sarah lived and where they both worked, and his own property, where his daughter, son-in-law, and grandson lived.[44]

Overwork and family may not have been Sarah's only motivations for departure. The Washington reporter who interviewed Edmund Parker in 1891 also met Sarah, whose picture appeared in the newspaper too. The correspondent described Sarah's "smiling manner," which made the milk she sold into "a veritable nectar." After noting that her second husband lived with her in the Mount Vernon "butler's house," he described the dwelling: "It is as neat and attractive as tasteful hands can make it, and visitors enjoy peeping past its hospitable threshold as much as they do any other glimpse to be secured of life at Mount Vernon." However complimentary, these words revealed how fully Sarah had become part of Mount Vernon's spectacle. Visitors' prying eyes thwarted any desire for domestic privacy. Like Jane Charlotte Washington a half century before, she may have grown weary of people who considered her part of the show. Along with her managerial responsibilities and her nice clothes, Sarah had over the years adopted notions of gentility and privacy more in keeping with the late-nineteenth-century middle class than with the role that visitors imagined her playing. No less than Dodge and the MVLA, Sarah may have dreaded the new age of streetcar crowds at Mount Vernon. By the spring of 1892 she was talking about when, not whether, she would depart. As Dodge described the new engineer to the MVLA council, he noted also that the man's wife could assume Sarah's duties, "in case Sarah left Mount Vernon, as she now proposes doing in the autumn."[45]

On September 30, the week after the GAR left and the electric railway arrived, Sarah Robinson resigned her position at Mount Vernon, followed by her husband and her assistant. The next day she turned over her keys to Mrs. Clark, the engineer's wife. Mount Vernon's new housekeeper was a white woman, and its new cook would be as well. Later that year Dodge sought recommendations for "a good man (& his wife) for service at Mount Vernon." He wanted a man who could care for cows, tend the vegetable garden, guard the mansion, and occasionally act as night watchman. The woman would supervise the kitchen and dining room and cook for ten or twelve people but not wash or iron anything except the table linens. Above the phrase "(& his wife)," Dodge added the word "white."[46]

By the time the MVLA convened the following May, the engineer and his wife had already resigned; a guard's wife was serving as the temporary housekeeper. Another couple, the watchman-gardener and cook for whom Dodge had advertised, had worked out no better. The wife had quit and departed, and the superintendent had not yet found another cook. In Sarah's absence, Dodge and the Ladies recognized her value more than ever before. Townsend wrote in her annual report that everyone on the estate felt the departure of Sarah, "our valued servant and friend." Visitors from Washington had "expressed their loss of her cheerful welcome and deferential manner." The regent hoped that the MVLA would provide some testimonial to Sarah's long, faithful, efficient service, for Sarah's sake and as "an incentive to fidelity" among the remaining employees.[47]

And so the MVLA did, in a unanimous resolution. The first version, drafted by North Carolina's Letitia Walker, echoed the sort of mistake visitors made about Sarah: "Being a descendant of the Washington family of slaves, she came to us by inheritance with the place where she was born & had lived so long." Other vice regents excised the unwitting suggestion that Sarah had been their property:

> When this Council assembled at Mount Vernon the ladies missed the familiar face and pleasant greeting of Sarah Johnson, their old servant who after a service of thirty years at Mount Vernon has voluntarily severed this long existing connection with the old place and gone to her farm near by, much to the regret of her employers. A descendant of the family servants of General Washington's household she was a fitting head to the Mount Vernon servants of to-day, and as housekeeper of its venerable Mansion was most efficient and most valuable in ministering to the comfort of the ladies when at Council. She obeyed to the letter during the interim of Council all instructions given for the care of the various rooms, the linen, silver, brasses, etc. The ladies in Council offer this tribute to her fidelity and integrity with many good wishes for her prosperity.[48]

The MVLA's encomium still got Sarah's lineage wrong, evidence of how well she had played her part. It ignored her new married name, perhaps because the Ladies had known her so long by another. But it expressed the affection and respect Sarah had won for her work and her character. Within the boundaries of contemporary racial relations, she had developed friendships with many of the Ladies.

The MVLA ordered a copy of its resolution sent to Sarah. A wedding invitation, a marriage license, a deed, and a tribute from her longtime employers: safeguarded in her little house on her own land, Sarah Johnson's papers attested to remarkable achievement.

EIGHT

Edmund Parker's Performances

Tall and dignified, his hair and beard gone gray, his shoulders slightly stooped, Sarah's uncle Edmund Parker seemed to have guarded George Washington's tomb forever by 1893. He wore Mount Vernon's blue uniform and silver badge, totems of his solemn responsibility. On sunny days he sat in a chair by the iron railing that protected the sarcophagi of the "old General" and Martha Washington. When it rained, he took shelter in a little sentry box a few feet away. Rain or shine, he kept one eye on the Virginia ivy that grew up the tomb's brickwork, and the other on potential relic hunters angling for cuttings of the leafy vine. When visitors crowded around to hear his tales of bygone days, Parker stood beside an old tree and orated, in a dialect that white people associated with native black Virginians.[1]

His narrative mixed anecdotes of the Washington family with stories from his own life. He had come to Mount Vernon in 1841, he explained, a fourteen-year-old boy brought by John Augustine Washington. In 1855 he had helped entomb his master's mother, Jane Charlotte, the last Washington interred there. He had watched her sons throw the key into the Potomac, locking the family vault for all eternity. Stationed at the tomb since 1874, Parker told of the notables he had seen: the emperor of Brazil and the princess of Spain; retired generals of the Union and Confederate armies; presidents and first ladies. Like Oliver Smith, Phil Smith, Jim Mitchell, and both West Fords before him, Edmund Parker appeared to visitors as fully a relic of the place as the pebbles he asked them not to pocket. A reporter for *The Washington Post*, a frequent visitor who had witnessed Mount Vernon's changes over the years, preferred to dwell on its continuities: the same old buildings overlooking the broad Potomac, the same ancient trees and paths conjuring up memories of olden times, and "the same old Virginia darky" keeping watch over the sacred tomb.[2]

By the 1890s, when Sarah left and Edmund Parker was the last of their family still employed there, three histories were on display at Mount Vernon. The first lived again in the mansion, where the MVLA sought to re-create George Washington's eighteenth-century surroundings, relic by relic. Parker made no pretense of personal acquaintance with General Washington, unlike a few elderly black people in and around Washington, D.C., who still claimed to have been his cook during the Revolution.[3] Instead Parker drew his anecdotes and his own authenticity from the second history, the years after Washington's death when the family still owned Mount Vernon. At the tomb a pair of obelisks commemorated the later owners: Bushrod Washington and his wife; John Augustine and Jane Charlotte and their son Augustine, the master Edmund Parker remembered best. To white people who romanticized "slavery days," those antebellum years now seemed part of one long stretch from George Washington to Robert E. Lee. But at Mount Vernon the two were distinctly presented, an age of Washington's life and an age of his memory. As Edmund Parker narrated it, the second period had ended thirty years earlier, with the sale of two hundred acres to the MVLA. He did not say—because most of his listeners did not want to be reminded—that it had also ended with the Civil War and the abolition of slavery, which forged new sacred memories for him, of the rebirth of freedom Lincoln envisioned at Gettysburg.

Those events begat the third history, in which Edmund Parker was a salaried employee and Americans supposedly revered Washington less. Self-described pilgrims at Mount Vernon had decried the encroachments of commerce and tourism ever since the 1830s, but now their lament had a new context. African American citizenship, massive immigration from eastern and southern Europe, and industrialization were transforming the nation's population, politics, economy, and culture. To some observers, Ulysses Grant's enormous, expensive, ostentatious mausoleum in New York City seemed to exemplify the new America better than Washington's tomb did. Parker's performance at the tomb, like the refurnishing of the mansion and the restoration of George Washington's deer park, echoed the MVLA's gospel of historic preservation as patriotic education. All sought to hold the modern world at bay, outside Mount Vernon's gates with the electric railway depot.[4]

But Edmund Parker belonged to this new world as well, in ways he did not mention to visitors. He did not live at Mount Vernon, nor had he and his wife, Susan, raised their family there. After the war they had lived in Alexandria. In the late 1870s they had left Virginia and moved to Pennsylvania. They may have relocated temporarily to help Susan's aged father there, or they may have imagined a different life altogether as farmers not far from Gettysburg, already an American shrine to a more recent past. They returned in 1882, Edmund to Washington's tomb and the family to Washington, D.C. Every other Monday morning Edmund took the steamboat, and later the electric streetcar, to Mount Vernon, bringing two weeks' groceries. He resided in the old laundry building there, with a little bed and an oil stove to cook his meals and warm his nights. He returned home to his family every other Saturday afternoon, an arrangement that resembled plantation slavery's "abroad" marriages. His children spent their adult lives in the nation's capital. Like hundreds of thousands of rural black people who migrated to cities in the 1880s and 1890s, they labored like urban folk aspiring to better things for themselves and their own children. One of Parker's sons worked as a private watchman, another as a janitor in Congress; one daughter as a seamstress, another as a cleaning woman. While Parker became a folk figure, old "Uncle Edmund" familiar to white tourists at Mount Vernon, he became a grandfather at home in Washington. There, quietly, proudly, he and Susan watched their progeny carving out new lives.[5]

In May 1893, while the MVLA honored Sarah Robinson for her long service and Edmund Parker held forth at Washington's tomb, American and international visitors entered a replica of Mount Vernon seven hundred miles away. At the World's Columbian Exposition in Chicago, thirty-nine states and three American territories erected buildings to display their native agricultural, mineral, and artistic products. The

Virginia Building, a perfect likeness of George Washington's mansion, embodied the Old Dominion's history according to the state's exhibition managers. Mimicking the MVLA's quest for original Washington furnishings, white Virginians from old families sent heirlooms for display, all to represent "an old Virginia home of the Colonial period." Lucy Preston Beale, the woman of distinguished lineage who presided over the building, had visited the real Mount Vernon the previous summer as she planned its reproduction. Beale lent an aura of southern domesticity to the Chicago premises. So did the building's attendants, "old Virginia negroes," performing (for pay) both the daily labors of hospitality and the imaginary roles of slavery days.[6]

The most prominent of these workers was Sarah Washington, an "old colored woman" of gravity, dignity, and courtesy. A Wisconsin newspaper described her as "a typical survival of the servant of the old school" and "a direct descendant of the old Washington house servants," proud of her exalted last name. Proclaiming that the "Janitress of the Building Has a Past," the *Chicago Tribune* identified her more specifically: she had been "the wife of the cook of John A. Washington." "Sarah Washington" might have been Sarah Robinson, once the wife of Nathan Johnson, John Augustine Washington's butler. While inspecting the original Mount Vernon mansion with Harrison Dodge, Lucy Preston Beale had likely encountered Sarah, who kept it in proper order and knew its interior history better than anyone else. Sarah Robinson's history and demeanor would have made her Beale's ideal for an authentic re-creation, a servant of the old school with decades of experience catering to elite white women and modern tourists. A newspaper writer who met her as "Sarah" and learned she had once belonged to the Washingtons could easily assume she shared her former masters' last name, a common misperception then and since.[7]

Sarah Robinson's whereabouts in May 1893, when the World's Columbian Exposition opened, are unknown. Revealingly, she was *not* at the MVLA's council meeting, cooking for her former employers. That spring, nine months after resigning her position at Mount Vernon, Sarah may simply have preferred not to return yet. But the following year and nearly every year afterward until 1906, Sarah spent council week at Mount Vernon, working for the Ladies. Possibly she was in Chicago in 1893, reprising the role she had perfected at the real

Mount Vernon on a new stage and for larger audiences. Or possibly
Sarah Washington was somebody else, portraying not just a servant of
"Old Virginia" but also a version of Sarah Robinson, the present-day
employee who attended to visitors at a historic house museum. Robinson or Washington, the Sarah in the Virginia Building saw black waiters and janitors around the exposition, as well as finely dressed visitors
of the black elite and middling classes. She could also have encountered, or at least heard about, the most famous black woman there:
"Aunt Jemima," formerly a minstrel show character and brand name,
now reinvented as a historical character and portrayed by a Chicago
servant and former Kentucky slave named Nancy Green. This Sarah
might have heard too that prominent African Americans protested
both the color line that barred blacks from most exposition jobs and
the stereotypes that exhibits such as Aunt Jemima fostered. Unlike
Mount Vernon, the Columbian Exposition was a theater where white
Americans' racial fantasies and black Americans' critique of racism and
inequality shared the stage.[8]

Four years later, at the original Mount Vernon, Sarah Robinson was
working for the MVLA council when a newspaper reporter arrived to
profile the Ladies' proceedings. The correspondent found her in the
old kitchen, an irresistible subject for picturesque description. Sarah
became "a colored mammy of extreme respectability," who prepared
scrumptious bread and other old Virginia delicacies without any newfangled technique. Born at Mount Vernon, descended from "one of the
old Washington servants," Sarah returned annually to cook for the
MVLA even though she was married and had "a cozy little farm of her
own." Consciously or not, this reporter wrote Sarah's life as a cousin of
Aunt Jemima's now familiar history, in which old-fashioned cooking,
loyalty to her old master, and a timely encounter with northern capital-
ists provided a faithful servant with financial independence. Sarah
Robinson's less dramatic story got just two paragraphs, but its ca-
dences were similar: the cook and mammy forever faithful to her longtime employers, even after establishing a life of her own off the
plantation.[9]

Fifty weeks a year Sarah Robinson lived more prosaically, a middling farmer's wife. She resided not on her own "cozy" four-acre farm
near Mount Vernon, but on her husband William's larger acreage

closer to Alexandria. William's daughter Elizabeth, son-in-law, and grandchildren inhabited the neighboring ten acres. Sarah's son, Smith Johnson, who waited tables at the Gibbs restaurant outside the Mount Vernon gate, probably managed her farm along with his own two acres. The Robinsons owned a modest farmstead: a horse or two, cattle, a wagon, and various tools. Hogs were likely for slaughter and home consumption, but William's accumulation of cattle—two in 1892, four by 1899, seven by 1908—may have signaled commercial production, in a vicinity that sent dairy products into Washington once the electric railroad ran all the way there in 1896. Most revealing, at the turn of the century Sarah acquired a sewing machine and William wrote a will. Sarah's experience at Mount Vernon and with the women of the MVLA had schooled her in refined clothing and linens. Now she could sew tighter seams and higher-quality garments, bedding, and towels for her adopted family than she ever could by hand and perhaps parlay the new machine into an additional source of income, taking in work for neighbors and friends. William Robinson's will, witnessed by two white attorneys who lived nearby, named Sarah his executrix and bequeathed his estate to his children after her death. It testified at once to his accumulation of property and to his trust in Sarah's integrity and legal ability.[10]

Living nearer Alexandria allowed the Robinsons frequent contact with a larger African American community and a shopping district. Another of William's daughters, Louisa Brown, worked in the city as a white woman's domestic servant, as did Dolly May, the widow of Sarah's stepfather, Warner. On Saturdays Sarah went into the city, where she bought groceries and picked up her mail from an elderly white storekeeper. William belonged to the black R. H. Lancaster Lodge of the Odd Fellows, a nationwide fraternal organization. The Robinsons may have worshipped at Alfred Street Baptist Church, the Alexandria congregation that dated back to the early nineteenth century. Every September 22, black Alexandrians welcomed compatriots from Washington and all over eastern Virginia for the Emancipation Day parade and festivities, commemorating the anniversary of Lincoln's preliminary emancipation proclamation as black people did in cities across the United States. Farmers from Gum Springs marched in the parade several years, and in 1894 Dandridge Smith—Sarah's contemporary, the grandson of old West Ford, and now a leader in the Gum Springs community—was its grand marshal. Two years later Sarah's son, Smith, was among the marshal's staff.[11]

Work for the MVLA, ten or twelve days each spring, enabled Sarah to maintain ties to the elite white women she had known for decades. Earning two dollars a day plus a "special gift" when the Ladies adjourned, Sarah made nearly what her monthly salary had been in 1892. Council work became a family endeavor. Sarah's new stepdaughter, Louisa, earned 75 cents a day as a maid, Smith Johnson $1.50 a day as a waiter. Dodge did not like Smith but continued to employ him for council because he knew the routine and because Sarah was there. The MVLA women welcomed Sarah back, learning of her activities and renewing an old acquaintance. In 1894, when the farmhouse on Sarah's property burned, they voted a hundred-dollar gift to help her rebuild and to add monetary value to the previous year's resolution of gratitude. Many of the Ladies continued to trust their old employee's judgment, particularly in matters of service. When in her midfifties Sarah reduced her participation at council and assumed the title of special assistant or kitchen consultant for a dollar a day, Dodge and the MVLA asked her advice about possible successors as head chef. One vice regent apparently sought her recommendation for a personal cook.[12]

Dodge also solicited Sarah's recollections about the interior of the Mount Vernon mansion. In 1896, as the ceiling in the central hallway sagged, the superintendent planned to reinforce it with the historically appropriate support. But had that been a straight beam or an arch? His predecessor, Hollingsworth, now dead, had installed an iron girder with round columns, clearly an innovation. Dodge consulted everyone likely to remember: the Civil War superintendent Upton Herbert, Augustine Washington's son Lawrence (who had been a small boy when the family sold the mansion to the MVLA), and the longtime employee. "Sarah says she remembers perfectly," he wrote to Herbert, that it had been a straight timber "when she was a child here," and she recollected that an arch had been installed later. Dodge considered memories from a slave childhood valuable clues to the authentic architectural past, even though Sarah had been born at Mount Vernon almost half a century after George Washington had died.[13]

While Sarah Robinson pursued her new life, her old Virginia home was being reshaped anew. Ever visionary, Harrison Dodge worked constantly to restore the eighteenth-century appearance of the mansion and grounds while applying modern engineering to perennial problems like fire prevention and drainage. Former quarters for white servants were refitted as rooms for the vice regents in council, and California's new vice regent, Phoebe Apperson Hearst, donated money to begin draining Hell Hole, the swampy area near the Potomac that caused the employees' annual malaria. Equally important were the external forces that had gathered momentum in Sarah's last years on the payroll, especially white Americans' burgeoning nostalgia for an Old South peopled by "old-time Negroes" and the massive increase in visitors resulting from the arrival of the electric railway. Mount Vernon was being remade along the color line, a historic site in the new world of Jim Crow—a development Harrison Dodge had anticipated when he hired a white woman to replace Sarah.

Clanging streetcars making hourly runs, the electric railway transformed Mount Vernon. Dodge had predicted one of the fundamental results. No longer could one force of employees work the farm and grounds from seven until ten-thirty in the morning, attend to visitors from eleven to two-thirty, then return to maintenance work until five or six. Now, depending on the season, the grounds were open from ten or eleven to five o'clock. Work began as early as ever, but without the time to clean the mansion and walkways, prune the shrubbery, mow the lawns, care for the animals, tend the farm, and do other needed maintenance. Dodge's solution: employ two workforces all year.[14]

The permanent or regular force, paid by the month and mostly resident on the estate, included white and black men and women with specific duties. At the head of these employees were the staff: Dodge; his assistant, James Young; the veteran gardener, Franklin Whelan; the engineer who tended the increasingly sophisticated fire apparatus and other mechanical systems; and the housekeeper, Victoria Vickers, Sarah's German-born successor in charge of the kitchen and mansion. Then came a corps of white men, the gatekeeper and guards. During visitors' hours the gatekeeper sold tickets at Mount Vernon's new primary entrance north of the mansion and near the railway depot.

Steamboat passengers, who still landed at the wharf downhill from the tomb, could purchase tickets aboard ship and walk or take a coach up to the mansion area. The guards, stationed in the most trafficked rooms of the mansion, protected against relic hunters and provided historical information. Before and after visitors' hours, these men pitched in at the daily maintenance. For example, gatekeeper William Vickers, the housekeeper's husband, had charge of the cows, and coach driver Christian Stout tended the horses. At the bottom of the regular work-force were the servants, all black: gardener's assistant William Harrison; his wife, Agnes, who cleaned Dodge's and Young's offices and bed-rooms; an ever-changing procession of cooks who reported to Mrs. Vickers; and a housemaid for the mansion hired out of Mrs. Vickers's own pocket. Edmund Parker, now in his late sixties, performed light la-bor around the tomb but earned his monthly wage primarily as its keeper. Parker was not the only regular employee who made his home elsewhere. Several of the white guards, whose families did not reside on the grounds, lived dormitory style in the old buildings and spent alter-nate weekends in Washington, as did Dodge and Young. As a courtesy to Mount Vernon, the steamboat and railway companies provided passes for their travel, as well as for the full-time residents' transporta-tion to Alexandria for shopping and other activities in town.[15]

Day laborers constituted the other workforce. Two were white men, hired as extra guards for the mansion. The rest, usually six in all, were black men whose labors included "repairing roads & walks, mowing lawns, hauling & handling leaves in winter, cutting dead timber, grub-bing volunteer growth along fences, transplanting young trees, cutting & laying sod, mixing & laying concrete when needed beside the varied work in connection with the farm."[16] The black day laborers were not paid to talk with, guard against, or sell souvenirs to visitors. Their me-nial work made it possible for the white regular employees to do so.

Only two black employees, Edmund Parker and the cook who sold milk behind the kitchen, interacted with visitors. Each could be mis-taken for an "old-time Negro." Parker, the elderly storyteller of bygone days, could be imagined as the "uncle" made nationally popular in Joel Chandler Harris's Uncle Remus stories. The cook, described by one visitor as a "portly Negress who is the presiding genius" of the kitchen, was Aunt Jemima reincarnate. In this era when mainstream journals described a national "Negro problem" and state legislatures devised ways to segregate white and "colored" citizens, Parker and the cook suited white Americans' conceptions of the "good Negro." The day laborers, decades younger than Edmund Parker, could not be mistaken for old-time Negroes, so they were seen but rarely heard.

In part, the employees who attended to visitors were mostly white because the longtime black employees had retired or resigned, several of them like Sarah Johnson and West Ford to become landholders in their own right. But Dodge had also chosen not to replace them with black people, transforming the century-old complexion of Mount Vernon's workforce.

That decision resulted largely from the other great change the electric railway had wrought. As the number of visitors exploded, breaking a hundred thousand a year early in the twentieth century, the bulk seemed to hail from the common classes, more inclined to excursion than to pilgrimage. The cheaper streetcar fare, now fifty cents for the round trip from Washington, beckoned locals and out-of-towners alike. Many visited Mount Vernon to escape the city, not to honor America's greatest hero. The frequent pilgrim Caroline Dall took the steamboat on the Monday after Easter 1893. Instead of her accustomed "delightful repose," she found a "rowdy crowd," including "many negroes," who had come by streetcar. When Dall tried the electric road herself the following year, it ran late, and she saw far less scenery than she expected. She took the boat home, but that was full of noisy children. Even steamboat excursionists were different from before. Many of them also spent a few hours at Marshall Hall, the amusement park across the Potomac where the *Charles Macalester* also landed. In cities across the United States, including Washington, more and more working-class Americans—white and black, native- and foreign-born—had the spending money for a day's excursion or a night on the town.[17]

New crowds posed new challenges. At the old well behind the kitchen, visitors had long used a chain and bucket to draw glasses of water. Now this "crude method" seemed undesirable as well as difficult to operate. "All manner of people—black as well as white—handle the chain which passes down into the water, necessarily polluting it." Dodge could have been referring simply to sanitation—more visitors, more dirty hands on the chain, more germs in the water—but the nature

of the crowds, economically and socially more mixed than before, both-
ered him too. They required firmer control than the smaller, contained
gatherings of earlier days. Ticket takers, guards, and other officers needed
to command visible authority. Uniforms and badges alone would not
suffice. No less than Edmund Parker at the tomb, mansion guards had
to look the part. Well-spoken white men equally at ease correcting the
genteel relic thief, conversing with affluent white women, and handling the occasional young ruffian white or black, they also had to
sound the part. Some visitors thought Mount Vernon should hire only
"Americans" and complained if they heard an employee whose speech
patterns seemed foreign.[18]

Dall and Dodge both alluded to the presence of black visitors, but
most of the tourists were white, as Mount Vernon's pilgrims had always
been. If black people had come in greater numbers, and certainly if they
had come in large groups, Dodge would have mentioned it in his regular missives to the MVLA regent. The "commoner sort of whites," more
than the occasional African American visitor, concerned Dodge most.[19]

To Susan J. Hudson, longtime vice regent for Connecticut and the
MVLA's recording secretary, George Washington and his home offered
the appropriate education for a polyglot America. For several years
Hudson concluded the association's annual reports with pointed com-
mentary on Mount Vernon's patriotic responsibility. "Is the United
States to remain American or is it to become foreign?" she asked in
1894, a year of nationwide depression and labor unrest. The MVLA's
mission became all the more vital as hundreds of thousands of immigrants arrived from Europe, knowing nothing of America's history.
Schools were the place to begin. Because inculcating a love of Washington among children would help "counteract the influence of the
ever-increasing foreign element in our country," the MVLA sponsored
contests around the United States for the best student essay on his
character. Pilgrims traveled to Mount Vernon from across the nation
and around the world. The "more reflective" of them lingered at the
tomb, while the "lighter-hearted" strolled through the grounds and
mansion, admiring the old-fashioned furnishings. At Washington's
bed, in his library, amid the trees, they all communed with the Father
of His Country, and they departed with greater knowledge and height-
ened reverence. In 1896 Hudson hoped that "in time the various na-

tionalities of which our population is composed might be united in a sentiment of patriotism whose inspiration is born at Mount Vernon." Her rhetoric softened, from forebodings of a foreign menace to hopes that new immigrants would assimilate into traditional Americanism. By then white people around the United States imagined Old Virginia, with its tranquil plantation households and faithful black retainers, to be part of that traditional America. Mount Vernon embodied this idealized history, frozen in mythic time.[20]

In the summer of 1898 Edmund Parker knew he was dying. His wife had perished late that spring, and cancer ravaged his stomach. He took sick leave in June, under a physician's care at his daughter's home in Washington. On July 6 one of his sons brought his beloved uniform back to Harrison Dodge at Mount Vernon, with the message that Edmund might never return for duty. Regular visitors missed his presence at the tomb. One of them, a writer for *The Washington Post*, learned of his whereabouts and went to talk with him. Finding the old man "in a half stupor in a clean, comfortable bed in a cool room," the reporter learned a different story from that which most visitors to Mount Vernon ever had. Parker's oratory had lost its energy, but not its eloquence.[21]

He told of his life in slavery, a narrative that little resembled Old South fantasies. He and Susan had been married forty years earlier, in the library of the Mount Vernon mansion. A white parson had officiated, unusual for Augustine Washington's slaves. But mostly slavery meant "mighty hard work. Had more put onto me than I could perform, 'cept as I took care of myself. There was mighty heavy timber on that Mount Vernon farm, and we slave folks was pulled and hauled. Altogether, as far as kindness was concerned, I reckon they meant well enough, although life is a burden to a slave person; indeed it is—left without eddication and the mind terrified all the time." When the Civil War broke out, he cooked for Union troops, first the Zouaves in Alexandria and later in the Capitol Prison and at Fort Washington across the Potomac from Mount Vernon. Perhaps because the reporter was white, Parker did not say how he had come to work for Union armies: by escaping, as so many slaves had done in that unsettled time. He emphasized instead his pride in what came after the war: his exalted work at Washington's tomb, wearing a uniform with nickel-plated but-tons "jest like the army's." He also praised the kindness of Dodge and the MVLA, "the very finest ladies in the land." This was not merely the gratitude that black people knew how to affect for supposed white benefactors and for white audiences. Parker's employers indeed as-sisted him during his illness. Exhibiting the maternalistic concern they had shown their longtime employees since the 1870s, the MVLA con-tinued to pay his monthly wage as a pension. Dodge visited him in his sickroom, bringing both the money and the MVLA's promise to pay for his funeral.[22]

Parker also offered a brief glimpse into his family's life. He and Su-san had had nineteen children; nine of them were still alive, married, and living in Washington. He did not explain, or the reporter did not recognize, the ways his family's experience reflected more recent trans-formations in African American lives. His children had joined the ur-ban black working class and left farm labor behind forever. In the city too, Parker's children could care for him in his last months.

Edmund Parker died there on December 30, 1898. An Australian-born physician of Scottish descent attested to his umbilical cancer, while Parker's children listed their father's occupation as "Watchman at Washington's Tomb Mt Vernon." They ordered a casket and hired carriages to take the mourners and the body from the black-owned un-dertaker's parlor to Columbian Harmony Cemetery, an African Ameri-can burial ground just outside the city. Dodge, who attended the funeral, thought the arrangements unduly elaborate, at $130 far more costly than if the Parkers had to foot the bill themselves. But he paid the expenses, sent flowers, and kept his complaints between himself and a few of the MVLA women.[23]

Parker's obituary, which appeared in *The Washington Post* the day after he died, revealed Mount Vernon's continuing place in the na-tional imagination, the old guard's modest celebrity, and contemporary white fantasies about slavery. It also made national news. *The Sun* (New York) reported it in mid-January under the headline "A Faithful Guardian of Washington's Tomb," and local papers from Ohio to Nevada ran versions over the subsequent months. From the details and errors in the original three-paragraph article, the writer probably drew upon the August interview and a conversation with Harrison

Dodge. Parker could tell more of Mount Vernon's early history than anyone else alive because he had spent his whole life there. "Born a slave," he had lived to see freedom, but "such changes had few charms for him. He preferred to spend his days as they had begun, within the beautiful and historic enclosure of Mount Vernon." In fact his days had not begun there, and he had been happy not to have spent his later Mount Vernon years as he had the early ones. One oft-reprinted variation gave just a single detail from Parker's life in slavery, his wedding, and noted that the MVLA had pensioned him, made him comfortable in his final days, and paid for his funeral. Ignoring the rest of his testimony about slave life, ignorant of the family that had sustained Edmund Parker as surely as the MVLA ever had, the newspapers cast him instead as the favored slave and faithful, honored servant. It was at once a role Parker had honed through decades of performance and a testament to the imagination of turn-of-the-century white Americans north, south, and west.[24]

Edmund Parker had created a role and a job at Mount Vernon. Even before his death, his absence from the tomb left an enormous void. One of the day laborers, a good-looking, polite middle-aged black man, replaced him temporarily, but Dodge knew that this part required precisely the right person. To maintain "as long as we can the time-honored spirit of the place," he explained to the regent, Justine Townsend, they must hire a successor "as typical of 'ye olden time'" as Edmund. Esau Parker, who had been born at Mount Vernon as Augustine Washington's slave and had worked as a waiter there in the lunch table years, applied for his father's job. But Dodge rejected him as too short and too young.[25]

Dodge found his man close to home, but not in the Parker family or among Mount Vernon's veteran employees. The superintendent had his eye on Thomas Bushrod, the sexton at Pohick Church, six miles away, where George Washington had worshipped and where the women of the MVLA attended Sunday services during the annual council meetings. In "character and type," Dodge believed, Bushrod surpassed even Edmund Parker. He looked the part: in his midseventies; tall; "black with white wool and beard, an attractive combination." His manner was "especially deferential." He possessed an attractive lineage, having been the slave of two fine Virginia families, the Fitzhughs and the Lees. His ancestors had probably belonged to Bushrod Washington's maternal grandfather, a distant but meaningful connection to Mount Vernon. Because Bushrod was loath to relinquish his weekly duties at Pohick, Dodge offered him fifteen dollars a month, five dollars less than Parker's wage, to take the position without any responsibility between Saturday afternoon and Monday morning. Thomas Bushrod started work a few months before Edmund Parker died, but only after the superintendent had "drilled" the new keeper of the tomb. Maintaining Parker's role, not merely filling his duties, was essential regardless of, or precisely because of, black people's changing roles and lives outside Mount Vernon's gates.[26]

By all accounts—which, like Parker's obituary, appeared in newspapers around the nation—Bushrod learned fast and well. He doffed his hat in the presence of ladies and waved it for emphasis as he spoke in exaggerated, drawling dialect, less oratorical but no less effective than his predecessor. Having inherited Parker's anecdotes about the history of the tomb, Bushrod added his own. If someone asked whether he had seen George Washington, he obligingly but cleverly let them do the math: "I's only a po' ole slave man. I kin neither read nor write. I was bo'n in the year 1825, now wasn't I? An' nex' year'll be 1900, won't it, an' how old'll that make me? . . . Gen'l Washington'll be dead a hund-ed yea's nex' yea', won't he?" Explaining that he had never belonged to the Washingtons as his predecessor had, Bushrod expressed pride in his own provenance; he had known the hero of the Confederacy when he was still just Captain Robert E. Lee. Bushrod admitted the horrors of slavery, including the sight of a man forced to whip his own half-white wife, but he attested that his own masters had always treated their slaves kindly. Fitzhughs, Lees, Washingtons: Virginia's first families had all been model slaveowners, as Bushrod told it. By the centennial of Washington's death, guarding his tomb had become both employment and theater. Thomas Bushrod seemed to embody the old-time Negro of Uncle Remus tales and plantation fiction, comforting to most white Americans, and despised by many black Americans, in the dawning era of Jim Crow.[27]

Half a century earlier the presence of black people at Mount Vernon had been controversial, to some visitors a troubling blot on a national shrine. By 1899 the faces and bodies and words of old black people had come to define old-time southern domestic life. In the words of *The Washington Post*, Thomas Bushrod was "a regular old down-South plantation darky," his black skin, snow-white hair, and "soft, droning plantation voice" combining to perfectly authentic effect. Other visitors commented on the mammylike black woman selling milk in the old kitchen. Mount Vernon was hardly alone in hiring and featuring such characters. Other southern sites had their own versions. When Virginia preservationists began the historic interpretation of Jamestown and Williamsburg at the turn of the century, they hired black custodians to convey the white organizers' version of colonial times. Tennessee women organized to purchase the Hermitage using the MVLA as their model. There Andrew Jackson's ancient body servant, "Uncle Alfred," guided visitors around and grew misty-eyed at his old master's grave.[28]

In the first months of 1900, while Thomas Bushrod testified to the greatness of Washington and the beneficence of the Old Dominion's past, the state legislature was crafting a new Virginia in the image of Jim Crow already enacted farther south. The General Assembly authorized a new constitutional convention, which two years later produced a state constitution that disenfranchised virtually every African American and many illiterate whites. When Sarah's son, Smith Johnson, registered to vote at Gum Springs in 1902, it was the last time he or his neighbors were able to do so. The 1900 Assembly also began the process of legally segregating the state's commercial transportation. At least since the 1880s most Potomac steamboats had separated white and colored passengers, confining black people to the lower decks and barring them from the dining rooms. The Supreme Court's 1896 decision in *Plessy v. Ferguson* affirmed such practices, as long as the spaces provided for blacks were not inferior to those for whites. On that basis Virginia passed its turn-of-the-century laws requiring steam railroad companies to furnish separate coaches and steamboats to provide separate accommodations. Technically, neither law applied to the vehicles that served Mount Vernon. The Potomac was not within Virginia's jurisdiction, and the Washington, Alexandria, & Mount Vernon Railway ran on electricity, not steam. In 1901, citing the latter loophole, Alexandria's city council declined to mandate "Jim Crow cars." Its distinction survived only a year, for soon the General Assembly specifically author-

ized electric railways in Alexandria and Fairfax County to segregate
their coaches, made it a crime to sit in the wrong section, and empow-
ered conductors to enforce the statute. The Alexandria streetcars were
segregated on May 1, 1902.[29]

The first arrest occurred the next day. A black schoolteacher from
Washington refused to take the seat indicated by the conductor and
was turned over to the police in Alexandria. She most likely intended
to test the new law, for when the mayor issued a five-dollar fine, she
replied that he would have to lock her up until her lawyer in Washington was contacted. White as well as black people were arrested for
violations, most prominently Robert E. Lee's daughter. Laden with
packages, Mary Custis Lee took a seat close to the exit, which happened to be in the colored section. The conductor insisted that Lee
move when a black man boarded, she refused, and to everyone's em-
barrassment she found herself in police custody when she disembarked in Alexandria. A few local Confederate veterans mobilized in
her support and momentarily threatened to seek the law's repeal, but
this ill will among whites soon cooled. White passengers came to see
segregation as natural, if they saw it at all. Black people's misgivings
and resentment persisted, but arrests were few. The Washington,
Alexandria, & Mount Vernon Railway experienced little overt resistance, unlike in Norfolk and Richmond, where African Americans boy-
cotted the segregated streetcars.[30]

By 1904 most visitors' experience of Mount Vernon began on a segregated vehicle, either steamboat or streetcar. Boarding the railway in
Washington, passengers sped through a historic landscape in transition. They glimpsed the Smithsonian Institution and the U.S. Botanic
Garden on the left and the 555-foot Washington Monument on the
right, then crossed the bridge into Alexandria County. High on a hill to
the right appeared Arlington House, once the home of George Washington Parke Custis, Robert E. Lee, and Mary Custis Lee, later the
grounds of Freedmen's Village, now Arlington National Cemetery. Farther on could be seen the dry bed of an old canal, which George Washington had imagined would connect tidewater Virginia to the Ohio
country. Beyond Four Mile Run, the streetcar passed undulating, fertile fields, which "suburban improvement is invading and gradually
dotting with handsome residences," according to a guidebook. Seven

miles below Washington was commercial, historic Alexandria, and soon came the lands that had once been George Washington's River Farm plantation, the easternmost section of greater Mount Vernon. River Farm was now divided into smaller holdings, including dairy farms that supplied the Washington market. The guidebook writer rhapsodized that the railway had made this idyllic countryside easily accessible to those in search of "charming suburban homes."[31]

In an hour the streetcar reached Mount Vernon, the twenty-second stop, the end of the line, and except for Washington and Alexandria the busiest depot on the route. Near the twenty-year-old Gibbs restaurant, another entrepreneur operated a lunchroom and souvenir stand in the railway station. It was as tawdry as Niagara Falls and "other public resorts," Harrison Dodge complained. The smell of frying chicken lingered in the air. A large sign in the depot falsely advertised the "Official Mount Vernon Spoon, Approved by the Lady Regents." Shouting his wares, the vendor employed "every trick of the trade, every catch-penny device" to part pilgrims and their money. Equally troubling to Mount Vernon's superintendent, the enterprise outside the gates interfered with legitimate souvenir sales within, the guidebooks, photographs, and wooden items that the MVLA authorized for sale in the garden and the kitchen.[32]

After paying the gatekeeper their quarters and entering the estate, visitors saw two labor forces, the speaking workers, largely white with a few African Americans in familiar and stereotypical roles, and the anonymous black day laborers. A quarter century earlier Nathan and Sarah Johnson, West Ford, and Warner May had taken visitors' money, sold them souvenirs and food, spoken with them in the mansion, and showed them the gardens. Now, in the garden, Franklin Whelan dispensed the anecdotes and the souvenirs. Whelan told West Ford's old story about Nellie Custis's "wishing rose," without Ford's dialect but with the detail that black lovers had long believed in the rosebush's romantic power. He also sold flowers, plants, and objects made from Mount Vernon wood, including a little hatchet that evoked Parson Weems's mythical tale of Washington and the cherry tree. Across the oval bowling green, the old family kitchen where Nathan and Sarah had once run the lunch business now served as historic and commercial space. Dodge had relocated eighteenth-century kitchen equipment from another old Virginia plantation house, to make the building appear more authentic. Victoria Vickers ran a sales table there, offering guidebooks, photographs, and more of the wooden souvenirs. The chambers of the mansion, more fully appointed every year as vice regents collected furniture and accoutrements, exhibited familiar pieces along with the new, for the Bastille key and the marble mantelpiece remained the focal points they had been ever since Bushrod Washington's day.[33]

Visitors of 1904 saw a new guard at Washington's tomb, with a message rather different from Edmund Parker's or Thomas Bushrod's. After Bushrod died late in 1902, Dodge hired a series of similar black men to fill the role, for hiring the elderly meant hiring often. Alfred Jasper, the "quaint old darkie" who came next, died in March 1904. "So one by one do the faithful old servants pass to their rest," Dodge sighed as he sought another "old style negro." He hired Edon Hammond, a Methodist preacher who was appropriately polite but more "grandiloquent" than Parker, Bushrod, or Jasper. One visitor encouraged Hammond to have his "remarkable effusion" published to distribute at the tomb. The eight-page pamphlet featured pictures of the Father of His Country, the Washington family crest, and the American flag on its front cover—and Hammond's own photograph on the back. Like his predecessors, Hammond described the history of Mount Vernon's ownership and the people and organizations who had planted each tree near the tomb. The original tree planted by the prince of Wales back in 1860 had died, and an iron mourning band had been placed around it when another was planted in 1889. "Now, ladies and gentlemen," Hammond proclaimed, "you can plainly see . . . the Iron representing the union and strength of American institutions, and the British Oak the perpetuity of the brotherhood between the King of England and the President of the United States of America." Hammond's oration seemed perfectly suited to turn-of-the-century Anglophilia. Many native-born white Americans emphasized the ties that bound England and America rather than the revolution that had split them, a conservative response to economic and social change, particularly immigration from eastern and southern Europe.[34]

Amazingly, however, Hammond also lauded George Washington as the father of a diverse nation. Washington had bequeathed freedom and union not only "to be distributed among the sons and daughters of the United States of America" but also to everyone who came "from distant lands and beyond seas. All of whom were made welcome participants, without discrimination or preventation." In one sense, Hammond echoed familiar American pieties. Most visitors could nod their heads in assent as the Methodist minister preached the national gospel. But black visitors, and anyone else who paused to consider Hammond's words, might have heard a question more than an assertion: Was every American in 1904 indeed welcome to enjoy Washington's legacy of freedom?[35]

Black men and women experienced the journey to Mount Vernon quite differently from whites, starting when they boarded the streetcars from the rear and took seats in the colored section. Notwithstanding the obligatory provision that accommodations for white and black passengers be equal, the ride to Mount Vernon was an exercise in second-class citizenship. The railway schedule, which described the trip from Washington to Mount Vernon through "Ole Virginny," compounded the insult by pointing out the " 'nigger-head' cobble stones" and the old slave pen to be seen in Alexandria. Faced with the injustice and humiliation of segregated steamboats and streetcars, often unavoidable in everyday work life, many black people chose other modes of transportation and different destinations for their leisure hours. Lodges, fraternal organizations, church groups, and other societies chartered steamboats, including several owned and operated by black entrepreneurs. Perhaps most significant, African Americans had found or made sites for their own enjoyment by the early twentieth century. "As Mount Vernon is the Mecca of the whites," one entrepreneur advertised, Harpers Ferry became a resort for blacks, particularly those of the Washington elite and middling classes. They spent a summer weekend or longer near the site of John Brown's raid, encouraged by black-owned and friendly businesses and accommodations. For a briefer, less expensive trip, there was Notley Hall, a Potomac amusement park owned by Lewis Jefferson, a black millionaire in the nation's capital. Sarah and William Robinson may have participated in this world of black excursions, for in 1905 William's Odd Fellows lodge chartered the *River Queen* to spend a summer day at Glymont, another popular resort and amusement park.[36]

Between 1904 and 1906 Harrison Dodge received and refused several requests to land the *River Queen* at Mount Vernon. Although the boat was owned by the same company that ran the *Charles Macalester* to Mount Vernon and other Potomac sites, the MVLA's contract with the Mount Vernon and Marshall Hall Steamboat Company stipulated that only the *Macalester* was permitted to land at Mount Vernon's wharf. This was not the only problem. The *River Queen* had been used "for negro excursions," and the MVLA was "opposed to the use (for its Mt. Vernon visitors) of boats" employed for such traffic. In white people's parlance, "negro excursions" were dens of violence and vice, even if the travelers belonged to the middling and elite classes. When the steamboat contract was up for renewal in 1905, the MVLA vetoed the boat company's attempt to add a clause permitting the use of the *River Queen* when the *Macalester* was booked elsewhere. The following year the National Negro Young People's Christian and Educational Congress planned a Washington convention of African American college students and instructors from around the nation. The organizers chartered the *River Queen* for several excursions and asked Dodge's permission to include Mount Vernon. Again the superintendent refused, citing the contract with the boat company. According to Dodge, the MVLA harbored no intention "to <u>exclude</u> negro excursionists, but simply insist on their coming by the <u>regular</u> means of transit, the steamer Macalester or the Electric Railway, both of which routes are just as much open to them as to others." About 250 convention-goers visited, far fewer than anticipated. Dodge did not recognize the stigma that black people—particularly "the higher classes of Negroes" attending a conference devoted to racial equality—associated with the segregated boats and streetcars. Jim Crow had arrived at Mount Vernon.[37]

Edon Hammond's time there lasted less than two years. By one account, ill health forced the seventy-nine-year-old to resign, after his doctor had forbidden his standing by the tomb in all weather. By another, the old man took offense when he was not permitted to distribute his little pamphlet to his listeners, the sort of commerce that Dodge had forbidden ever since cutting off cane sales at the tomb back in 1885. The MVLA voted Hammond a fifty-dollar gift to assist him in his final illness; he died on June 24, 1906. Over the next seven years Dodge was to hire three more elderly black men to guard Washington's tomb. It was becoming difficult, he lamented, to find "any of the 'ancient & honorable' class. Their like has forever passed."[38]

The spring of 1906 also marked Sarah Robinson's last appearance working for the annual MVLA council. Now sixty-one, Sarah likely wanted to retire at last. Many old vice regents, the women she had known for years, had died or would soon breathe their last: South Carolina's Lucy Pickens in 1899; Wisconsin's Martha Mitchell in 1902; Maine's Margaret Sweat and North Carolina's Letitia Walker in 1908. Justine Townsend resigned as regent in 1909 and died three years later. At each woman's demise, Dodge flew Mount Vernon's flag at half-mast. Himself now among the old-timers, the superintendent fretted about modernizing tendencies contrary to the "true Washington spirit" as a new coterie of women, led by the new regent, Harriet Clayton Comegys (who had succeeded her mother as vice regent for Delaware), came to the fore. Over the next years Dodge and the MVLA apparently lost touch with their longtime employee and housekeeper. Sarah's husband, William, was ill in the winter and spring of 1908, receiving sick dues from his Odd Fellows lodge. When he died late that fall, the lodge paid Sarah the widow's fifty-dollar death benefit, but the MVLA did not take notice. Nor did the association acknowledge the death of her son, Smith Johnson, around the same time. Sarah continued to live on William's land, joined there by her grandson, Nathan, who turned eighteen in 1909.[39]

Other elderly black employees and even the relatives of former employees continued to receive the MVLA's maternalistic attention. After Richard Broadus, the black coachman, suffered a stroke at Mount Vernon, the association allowed him and his children to remain on the estate and paid his monthly salary as a sort of pension until he died seven years later. Matilda Taylor, the maid Mrs. Vickers hired to clean the mansion and kitchen, received a monthly stipend in her final illness. And when Dodge learned late in 1911 that Thomas Bushrod's widow was confined to an Alexandria almshouse, the MVLA sent five dollars to assist in her support. Dodge dispensed the MVLA's benevolence with a dose of his own paternalism. He placed the MVLA's small bequest to Broadus's children into a bank account, so that the eldest would not squander it, and he withheld part of Taylor's stipend, figuring that she did not need the whole sum and that her family would seek additional support for her funeral. When they did, he used the money he had set aside.[40]

Harrison Dodge's relationships with Mount Vernon's employees had always been complicated. He had arrived at Mount Vernon a thirty-three-year-old bank clerk, determined to take command of a workforce that had been there for decades. As he got to know longtime "servants" such as Sarah Johnson and Edmund Parker, he appreciated the kindnesses that the women of the MVLA extended to them. Now, after a quarter century at the helm, he had adopted many of the same attitudes, including their sense that the "old Negroes" were a responsibility to be borne. This view prevented Dodge and most of the Ladies from seeing their employees whole, from recognizing how they took care of themselves and their families. At the same time, unlike the Ladies, Dodge supervised the employees every day. He knew their individual work habits and something of their family lives. He cared about them, even if that feeling often took the form of thinking he knew what was best for them. This paternalism owed a great deal to long-standing white attitudes toward "our" black people but also to his own identity by 1910. Nearing sixty, Dodge was now among the oldest people at Mount Vernon, not one of the youngest.

As Mount Vernon's regular workforce was transformed, white employees won a share of the MVLA's concern as well. Black or white, each regular and day worker received an annual Christmas gift from Phoebe Apperson Hearst, the vice regent for California. After Cassie Thomas, the long-serving white gatekeeper, contracted tuberculosis and moved to a sanatorium in the central Virginia mountains, the MVLA continued to pay his salary as well as the medical expenses. By the 1910s employment at Mount Vernon was becoming for white people what it had been for blacks thirty years earlier, a family endeavor. White children grew up on the estate. Some joined their parents on the payroll.[41]

Unlike the Johnsons and Fords of an earlier time, these white employees did not live in the historic buildings on the bowling green. Beginning in the 1890s, Dodge advocated the construction of new cottages, down by the old porter's lodges and out of sight of visitors.

Preventing fire was partly the issue; the superintendent and the MVLA wanted to discontinue the use of oil stoves and fireplaces in the historic structures. Privacy mattered too; white families could not be expected to live under the microscope of curious pilgrims' peeping. Finally, authenticity was at stake. When black people had lived in the old buildings near George Washington's mansion, visitors could assume mistakenly that these had once been slave quarters and that their contemporary inhabitants were descendants of Washington's slaves. White employees possessed no such historic associations, even though many of the old buildings had actually housed white servants and employees in the eighteenth century. Finally, in 1907, the MVLA authorized the construction of four five-room cottages, intended for white employees with families. William and Agnes Harrison, the elderly black couple who had been at Mount Vernon longer than any of the white workforce, kept their old cabin, and the cook and her daughters still lived in the attic above the old kitchen. Meanwhile, the white Rouses and Clarks and Permars moved into the new bungalows. There they could maintain little vegetable gardens and entertain friends from the neighborhood out of visitors' sight and Dodge's immediate supervision.[42]

While some resident employees got new housing, wages fell far behind prevailing local rates. Dodge had paid his day laborers $1 a day since 1887, even as nearby farmers came to pay as much as $1.50. He managed to keep his laborers because he offered year-round employment rather than the seasonal work that farmers hired. Now, however, the streetcars were transforming once remote farm country into suburbs of the nation's capital. Army posts in Fairfax County and public works projects in the District of Columbia needed laborers, and the going rate rose to $2 a day. When Dodge's day laborers came to him in 1903 with a "pathetic" but effective appeal, the MVLA had forestalled the problem by increasing their wage by 25 percent. But when they "struck for higher wages" in 1907, Dodge was compelled to raise their rate to $1.50 a day, enough to keep most of them.[43]

Resident and day laborers alike felt pinched, and Dodge and the MVLA confronted a real crisis nine years later. The problems began when rampant inflation left Mount Vernon's monthly and daily wages utterly deficient to meet the cost of living. On October 28, 1916, all the guards and day laborers, black and white together, pleaded with

Dodge for help. The price of food and other necessities had doubled in a year. Day laborers, who had to heat their homes and buy heavier clothing in winter, would no longer work a ten-hour day for $1.50, especially when unskilled workers in Washington and at nearby munitions plants could earn twice as much for eight hours' labor. The regular employees could not make ends meet either. It was "unquestionably an emergency," Dodge wrote to the regent as he beseeched the MVLA's help. Comegys approved raising the day wage to twenty cents an hour, a decision she largely left to the superintendent, who knew the day laborers and the market best.[44]

Resident employees were another matter. Their monthly wages were determined at the MVLA's council each spring and could not be altered by the regent alone. Moreover, Comegys and the vice regents considered these employees the way they thought about their own household staffs. Maternalistic feelings produced acts of kindness such as Mrs. Hearst's Christmas gift. The same instincts led the Ladies to pry into the resident employees' lives, not unlike the way Mount Vernon's proprietors ever since the Washingtons had monitored the daily lives of black workers, enslaved and later free. Unaccustomed to scrimping for everyday expenses, wondering whether the distress was exaggerated, Comegys visited Mount Vernon to learn "more about the actual condition of the Regular Employees" and asked Dodge for information about their living expenses. She proposed giving most of the regular employees an extra five dollars each month while the inflation persisted. Others, depending on their needs, would receive less. (The elderly Harrisons would get nothing because Dodge estimated that their combined fifty dollars a month met their needs.) Dodge thought this solution too parsimonious, especially for employees with families. To buttress his case, he asked to see their monthly bills. W. L. Rouse, who had four children ages three to ten, itemized his expenses. Meat had increased from 11 to 20 cents a pound in the past eighteen months, a bushel of potatoes from 60 cents to $1.50, children's shoes from $1.25 to $2 a pair. The proposed gift, added to Rouse's $55 monthly wage, would not keep up with inflation, although everyone would appreciate any increase at all. All the employees "are most economical, and stint themselves in every way possible to 'make ends meet,'" Dodge told Comegys.[45]

War revealed once more Mount Vernon's triple identity as home, work-place, and enduring, malleable national symbol. The little resident community felt the impact even before the United States declared war on Germany in April 1917. Harrison Dodge's son-in-law, an army offi-cer, was killed on a tour of observation at the Italian front that Febru-ary. Soon the sons of Mount Vernon employees registered for the draft, several of them went off to war, and Dodge's grandson entered West Point. As inflation kept spiraling upward and war-related job opportu-nities abounded nearby, keeping day laborers and resident employees grew even more difficult than in the previous year. The housekeeper's assistant, a black woman, quit because her husband and sons earned enough money building roads to support the family. For hardworking black women, leaving the workforce, not entering it, signified a family's achievement. Month after month the cost of day labor rose. Local farmers could not get help at $3 a day by October 1917; government contractors paid $3.50 in January 1918 and $5 just three months later. Dodge tried to keep up, raising Mount Vernon's hourly wage to twenty-five cents, but by early 1918 he had lost all but two day laborers to the draft or to government jobs. Obtaining skilled or unskilled laborers became hopelessly uncertain, and the superintendent postponed all plans for forestry work, architectural restoration, and other inessential projects. When even the gardens, lawns, and farm suffered, he in-creased the hourly wage again, to thirty cents. The regular employees' monthly wages bought even less than they had during the 1916 crisis, so they tried to make the most of their family vegetable gardens, did without meat, and weighed other opportunities. In January 1918 they submitted a "round-robin" letter to the superintendent, describing their plight and asking for additional help. Ultimately the MVLA gave most of them a 10 percent raise, and Dodge paid them overtime at the new hourly rate to perform the tasks he could not find day laborers to do.[46]

Routine maintenance became all the more important as crowds swelled. Contrary to expectations, war brought more visitors than ever before, more than 120,000 from May to November 1917 alone. Amer-icans poured into Washington for war-related business and govern-ment jobs. Thousands of soldiers, sailors, and marines made local training camps and forts into small cities. In April 1918 a community service division of the War and Navy departments' Commissions on Training Camp Activities requested that Mount Vernon be opened on Sundays and holidays, virtually the only days when government employees and military men could visit the place with the deepest "patriotic appeal to American citizens." Seconding the plea, the commander of nearby Camp Humphreys argued that Mount Vernon's aura of patriotic worship could cultivate new soldiers' morale—if servicemen alone were admitted on Sundays. If Washington's home were to become "a mere place of public amusement, a resort for the idle and curious, a picnic place for Sunday excursionists," its value to the nation's fighting men would be lost. Better that soldiers be kept away than that they perceive Americans' irreverence for "the tomb of their greatest soldier." The MVLA responded to these entreaties, which echoed six decades of the association's own rhetoric. For the summer of 1918 visitors' hours were extended until six o'clock during the week and until eight on Saturdays. Men in military uniform were admitted free and were permitted to visit the grounds (but not the mansion) on Sunday afternoons, a temporary suspension of the Sabbath closure that dated back to Bushrod Washington's day.[47]

July 4 had always been a popular day to visit Mount Vernon, but in wartime 1918 it offered another attraction, a major address by President Woodrow Wilson. With the typical summer heat leavened by a light breeze and a cloudless sky, crowds began arriving when the gates opened at ten o'clock that Thursday. More than two thousand people were there by noon, crowding the streetcars and the steamboat. Some came by automobile, increasingly the transportation of choice as military mobilization brought improved roads to the vicinity. By midafternoon perhaps ten thousand people were thronging Mount Vernon, including more than a thousand men in uniform who came in motor trucks and on foot as well as by streetcar. A hydroplane hovered above, keeping watch against trouble from air or river. Around 3:10, the government ship *Mayflower* was sighted on the Potomac. The president brought an unusually diverse party, for this Independence Day was to honor foreign-born American citizens whose wartime devotion to the United States had eclipsed "all distinctions of race," as he had put it a few weeks earlier. Americans of thirty-three different nationalities joined Wilson, each bearing a wreath or other floral tribute to lay at Washington's tomb. They represented America's immigrant origins, old and new: English and French, Hungarian and Ukrainian, Italian and Chinese, Venezuelan and Filipino.[48]

When the *Mayflower* landed at Mount Vernon's wharf, the president and his guests disembarked and walked uphill to Washington's tomb. Wilson took his place in front of the iron railing, where most days an elderly black man stood. The president squared his shoulders, standing rigidly at attention as the Belgian American representative spoke for all the assembled immigrant citizens. One hundred and forty-two years earlier, said Felix J. Stryckmans, a group of men declared independence in the name of free government. People from "the uttermost ends of the earth, already Americans in soul" even if they knew not a word of English, had come to the United States ever since. "We are the latest manifestation of that American soul," Stryckmans declared, now fighting the forces of autocracy with the soul of George Washington leading the way. Tomorrow's casualty lists would include "Slavic names, Teutonic names, Latin names,. Oriental names"— Americans all.[49]

Wilson took the stage at four o'clock, to cheering crowds behind a khaki wall of marines. Amid the roiling of war, he said, Mount Vernon seemed as "serene and untouched by the hurry of the world" as when the Father of His Country planned a new nation from the gentle slopes before the Potomac. Washington and his comrades acted "not for a class" that shared their own landed interests but for a people and "all mankind." Even at Washington's tomb, this was a place not of death but of achievement, full of inspiration for an idealistic American people. Echoing Lincoln's words at Gettysburg, Wilson proclaimed that Americans could "conceive anew the purpose that must set men free." The mission was international now, but America's revolutionary heroes would have done the same had they been present in July 1918. Mount Vernon, symbol of American nationhood for more than a century, had become the setting to avow a new global resolve. The principles wafted in the very air at Washington's home, Wilson concluded. Beginning here at Mount Vernon, revolt had led to liberation. Now, on the same ground, America's leader announced the spread of that revolt and liberation "to the great stage of the world itself!"[50]

Others challenged Wilson's history and his message. As an Indiana editorialist reminded readers, the founding fathers may have heralded a new era of freedom, but they also owned thousands of slaves, "human beings enduring the status of cattle." It took a Civil War and another president to create a real republic. Half a century later, he might have noted, that second American revolution remained incomplete. The crucible of war had not eradicated all distinctions of race. American citizens of African descent were not among the thirty-three nationalities that joined the president aboard the *Mayflower* and at the tomb. Wilson's Democratic Party had crafted Jim Crow regimes throughout the South, his administration had segregated much of the federal workforce, and he himself had declined to meet with black newspaper editors two weeks before his Mount Vernon address. Black soldiers fought in Negro units, as they had done since Andrew Ford's days in Union blue. None of this went without protest. African Americans called upon the president to end discrimination in the federal service, abolish Jim Crow cars on the railroads that carried American soldiers, and act forcefully against the lynchings that mocked his words about international respect for law. Closer to home, black people in Fairfax County had established a branch of the National Association for the Advancement of Colored People, to protest ordinances that drew the color line between white and black neighborhoods.[51]

The day after the president's address Mount Vernon returned to normal. Visitors arrived by segregated streetcar, partaking perhaps of the greasy fried chicken at the restaurant just outside the grounds. White men collected their admission fees, told them about the relics in the mansion, sold them souvenirs in the garden. At Washington's tomb they heard a familiar oration by a sixty-three-year-old black man named Charles Simms, the latest successor to the role Edmund Parker had created. Up the Potomac in Washington, however, a different house commemorated another history. The National Association of Colored Women had recently launched a fund-raising campaign to preserve Cedar Hill, the home of Frederick Douglass. They took their inspiration from Sojourner Truth and Harriet Tubman and their model from "the white women [who] saved the home of George Washington." On the afternoon of July 8 black people in the nation's capital made a pilgrimage of their own. For ten cents each, men and women and children assembled at Cedar Hill to enjoy refreshments, music, and a series of addresses on Douglass's life and work. All the speakers, including Douglass's last surviving son, agreed that "our hero . . . had aided in laying the foundation of the present freedom for which the world is fighting." As black newspapers from Pittsburgh to New Orleans put it, his home should be preserved reverently for "future generations of our race," just as Mount Vernon "is held in sacred honor by the white race." Like the much larger gathering at Washington's home four days earlier, these patriotic Americans embraced the cause of global liberation that the Great War represented. But far from white people's attention they celebrated a different hero and a struggle as unfinished at home as abroad. In the summer of 1918 the color line divided Americans' mythic past no less than their present.[52]

Old Negroes, New Memorials

On January 8, 1920, several of Sarah Robinson's friends visited Harrison Dodge at Mount Vernon. Sarah was ailing, they told the superintendent, and she was indigent. Friends had given her temporary shelter
the past several years, as rheumatism and old age prevented her from
working. Now she had been taken to Freedmen's Hospital, a medical
facility in Washington for black people. Friends were collecting money
to provide Sarah with the bare necessities, to make her more comfortable in what would likely be her final illness. They appealed to Dodge,
who conveyed their entreaty to the regent, Harriet Comegys. Could
the MVLA contribute something to help "one of the most faithful servants Mount Vernon ever had"?[1]

Sarah's situation had deteriorated over the past decade, since her
husband and son died. Her grandson, Nathan, married an Alexandria
woman in 1915 and established a household of his own. Piece by piece
Sarah sold the land she had purchased nearly thirty years before.
When Fairfax County widened the road from Gum Springs to Mount
Vernon in 1915, it bought half an acre by eminent domain. Three years
later, probably pressed by the same wartime inflation that afflicted
Mount Vernon's employees, Sarah sold the rest to a contractor who
boasted of having introduced cement and brick sidewalks to Alexandria. And in July 1919 she joined William Robinson's daughter and
grandson and their spouses to sell his land, on which her late husband's will had entitled her to live the rest of her days.[2]

By the beginning of 1920 Sarah was one of 291 inmates of the

Home for the Aged and Infirm in Washington. Created by the federal government in 1906 as a progressive alternative to the old almshouse, the home was designed to shelter the virtuous poor. On a 280-acre tract overlooking the Potomac, it boasted a professional staff, benevolent support from local churches and missionary societies, and such modern improvements as electric lighting. But like other government institutions in Washington and throughout the South, the Home for the Aged and Infirm practiced Jim Crow progressivism. White and black men and women lived in separate dormitories and ate at separate tables in the communal dining room. The home's superintendent claimed that this was no "manifestation of race prejudice" but rather an attempt to "let these distinctions fall along the lines of natural cleavage." Blacks and whites were free to attend meetings or services in each other's wards, but in practice they did not. Sarah Robinson lived among eighty-nine inmates in the black women's wing. On January 7, 1920, however, she was moved to Freedmen's Hospital, another federal institution, established for African Americans after the Civil War and staffed primarily by black doctors, nurses, and Howard University medical students.[3]

Sarah died there less than three weeks later, on January 25, 1920. She was seventy-five. The longtime superintendent paid Mount Vernon's respects. On January 27 and 28, while Sarah's body lay at an Alexandria funeral home operated by and for African Americans, Mount Vernon's flag flew at half-mast, the same tribute accorded to regents, vice regents, and American presidents. The next day it flew at half-mast again, this time for Lawrence Washington, the son of Sarah's former master Augustine and reputedly the last child ever born in the storied mansion.[4]

In contrast with the lengthy obituaries for Lawrence Washington, Sarah's name was merely listed among "deaths reported" in *The Washington Post*, and a brief obituary in the *Alexandria Gazette* said nothing about her far longer connection with George Washington's home:

ROBINSON. At Freedman's Hospital, Washington, Sunday, January 25, 1920, at 6 o'clock, Sarah Robinson, widow of William Robinson. Funeral Wednesday, January 28, from Alfred Street Baptist Church Alexandria, Va. Remains at Arnold's Chapel.

Services began at Alexandria's oldest black Baptist church and ended at Snowden & Bethlehem Cemetery in Gum Springs. There many of Sarah's longtime neighbors were buried: people she had known in slavery and in freedom, the revered minister of Bethlehem Baptist Church, the man who had sold Sarah her four acres. William Robinson's gravestone, now almost a dozen years old, read, "Loved in life, remembered in death," and carried the Odd Fellows emblem. Sarah was laid to rest beside him. Under her name, Sarah's stone read, "Faithful servant, well done."[5]

To the friends who buried her, Sarah had been a faithful servant of the Lord. To many white Americans, the same phrase meant something different when applied to black people. The image of loyal Negro servitude, comforting to white people ever since emancipation, loomed large after the Great War. Hundreds of thousands of wartime emigrants from the rural South found employment and discrimination in cities across the United States, while black servicemen who had fought to make the world "safe for democracy" returned to a segregated America that mocked President Wilson's idealistic words. A new generation of black Americans appeared ready to challenge second-class citizenship. Many white Americans wished to retreat into an imaginary past or to brandish it as a cultural and political weapon against the self-confident, politically and culturally assertive "New Negroes" who would confront Jim Crow. In 1922 the United Daughters of the Confederacy proposed a monument to the "faithful slave," a statue of a black mammy, to be erected in Washington on land set aside by Congress. As the Senate passed the authorizing legislation, black newspapers decried the hypocrisy of white people's honoring a racist fantasy while winking at the exploitation of actual domestic laborers past and present. The monument bill died in the House of Representatives, but the nationwide controversy over it revealed opposing forces unequally matched. With or without the mammy memorial, America's symbolic landscape was being painted white, from plantation house museums to roadside markers.[6]

By decade's end the MVLA had created its own faithful-servant memorial. In 1928 its tomb committee reported that the graveyard

where many of George Washington's slaves were buried was unmarked. A simple, permanent stone was to be placed on this conse-
crated ground before every trace of the graves disappeared. The
following year, after their annual council pilgrimage from the mansion
to Washington's tomb, the regent and vice regents walked the fifty
yards southwest to the new slab at the old slave cemetery. It bore the
phrase familiar to most Americans by then: IN MEMORY OF THE MANY
FAITHFUL COLORED SERVANTS OF THE WASHINGTON FAMILY BURIED AT
MOUNT VERNON FROM 1760 TO 1860, THEIR UNIDENTIFIED GRAVES SUR-
ROUND THIS SPOT. The area around George Washington's tomb offered
a unified picture of faithful servitude. George Ford, stepson of the
younger West Ford (and himself a Mount Vernon employee back in the
1880s), now held Edmund Parker's former job. As Dodge described,
Ford filled the old part perfectly: "George upholds the tradition of the
old servants in that he was born at Mount Vernon and the blood of
the old slaves is in him."[7]

Dodge wrote these words in his 1932 memoirs, published during
the bicentennial of George Washington's birth. In that nationwide,
federally funded celebration, historical pageants and re-creations featured black people only in the roles of happy, faithful slaves, the successors of Uncle Remus and forerunners of *Gone with the Wind*. The
civil rights leader and Harvard-educated historian W.E.B. Du Bois dis-
sented. "George Washington and Black Folk," a pageant he wrote for
the NAACP's *Crisis* magazine, imagined scenes from Washington's life
within a larger Afrocentric history of America: Crispus Attucks's mar-
tyrdom at the Boston Massacre, Toussaint L'Ouverture's leadership of
the Haitian Revolution, and ultimately a procession of black historical
characters and children marching and singing to the music of drums
and trumpets. A visual and aural celebration of African American race
pride, Du Bois's pageant was utterly removed from anything visitors in
1932 saw or heard at Mount Vernon. There Superintendent Dodge,
not any African American man or woman, was now the chief repository
of historical memory. His memoir described Washington's management and his own forty-seven years there. Among its main characters
were "The Old Negroes," the black people who had been there when
Dodge first arrived. He wrote of Sarah Johnson, Warner May, Edmund
Parker, and others with respect, acknowledging their command of
Mount Vernon's history and their dedicated labor. Even as he drew

them from firsthand memory, they became virtual folk figures of bygone days: Parker fearing Christmas ghosts, Milly Mitchell wearing her
turbans, West Ford telling stories about "Mars Tom Jefferson" planting
the sweet-smelling shrub. In Dodge's hands, Mount Vernon's Old Negroes were the very antithesis of the New Negro.[8]

Dodge had come to Mount Vernon too late, and by 1932 had been
on the job too long, to understand that Sarah and her predecessors, all
the way back to Oliver Smith, had always been New Negroes. Not,
certainly, in the terms of the Harlem Renaissance or the generation of
the 1920s and 1930s: Mount Vernon was not a place where people vo-
cally celebrated African American heritage or actively resisted white
supremacy. W.E.B. Du Bois was unlikely ever to claim West Ford or
Edmund Parker as a forefather or pioneer alongside Crispus Attucks or
Toussaint L'Ouverture. Nor would the ladies of the National Association of Colored Women, the elite black women who preserved Frederick Douglass's house in Washington, have claimed Sarah Johnson as a
foremother.[9] But from the moment Sarah, Edmund, or their parents
arrived at Mount Vernon, they had been pioneers in other senses.

First, of course, they were not George Washington's slaves, no matter what they let visitors think. They manufactured their own authenticity, assisted by white people's preconceptions. Second, in the roles
they performed on the job, they represented America's most cherished
shrine to thousands of people who would never have conceded their
full humanity. We can never know exactly what Sarah thought as she
sold that next glass of milk or answered the same question with unfail-
ing politeness for the hundredth time. Surely some days it was just a
job, a well-paying, respectable one at that. But on days when she sold
copies of George Washington's will along with the guidebooks and the
dairy products, she might have believed she was disseminating a document of emancipation and thus a different Washington from the one
visitors expected. More commonly, she could well have imagined that
she shared a mission with the women of the MVLA, to re-create the
idealized domestic world of the Father of His Country. Later generations of African Americans and scholars might interpret this as self-
delusion, a worker all too willingly identifying with her employers. Seen
another way, it would have been a breathtaking act of self-assertion, a
sense of belonging and ownership in that place and its legacy.

Third, and most important of all, their lives when the visitors were not there placed them squarely in a new world, even at this old place. Their aspirations to respectability and even a touch of gentility; their embrace of suffrage, church, and education; their financial enterprise, sporadic protests for higher wages, and land purchases; ultimately their resignations from Mount Vernon to pursue other lives and callings: all these marked Sarah and her contemporaries as avatars of new times. In this, they resembled millions of other former slaves whose daily assertions of individuality and community white people did not recognize and whose occasional confrontations white people preferred to quash and then forget. Imagining them as faithful servants, which they also were and for which they had gained their employers' real respect and in some instances even friendship, was safer and simpler.

In 1955 the last African American guard at George Washington's tomb told his story to *Ebony* magazine. Destiny had assigned Will Holland this humble position, he believed, because the magic of Washington's legend had enthralled him since childhood. Millions of visitors had heard him speak about the tomb and its inhabitants. Holland had chatted with every president from McKinley to Franklin D. Roosevelt, an unlikely tale given that McKinley had been assassinated in 1901. But the magazine's article reflected the larger integrationist enterprise of the early civil rights era. "We, too, are America," *Ebony* fairly shouted as it photographed Will Holland in uniform, lecturing to white visitors at Washington's tomb and standing beside the Stars and Stripes. Holland echoed that rhetoric. The sixty-eight-year-old guard wove inextricable links between past and present, the nation's history and his own autobiography. Raised near Mount Vernon, he said he had been a teenage waiter at the restaurant outside the grounds and a guide in the mansion before succeeding his father-in-law, George Ford, at the tomb in 1936. He had read extensively about Washington and conversed with historians. George Washington had "come alive for me" so often, reported Holland, that his death seemed recent. Will Holland retired a decade later, and the MVLA did not replace him. Thus ended a ninety-year job and with it a tradition. But Holland had created a lasting, utilitarian place on the sacred landscape. He designed the sentry booth, equipped with telephone, heating, and windows on all four sides—the better to watch for disrespectful visitors—that stands there to this day.[10]

Nearby, the "faithful colored servants" marker languished in obscurity for half a century. Overgrown with bushes, it was largely forgotten, merely a hazard to clumsy visitors who wandered into the woods. On a rainy Wednesday in early 1982, the *Washington Post* writer Dorothy Gilliam left the brick and gravel paths to walk in the slaves' own footsteps. Gilliam found the old slab and wrote a column criticizing its neglect. Much as word of Mount Vernon's decay had once spurred Ann Pamela Cunningham to action, so the Fairfax County chapter of the NAACP and African American community leaders raised the cry of sacred memory. The MVLA quickly cleared the overgrowth, installed two park benches, laid a path, and reopened the site. On George Washington's 250th birthday in 1982, the day President Ronald Reagan laid a wreath and hundreds of visitors paid homage at Washington's tomb, about thirty people gathered at the 1929 marker. Dr. Judith Saunders Burton of Gum Springs, a descendant of the first West Ford, laid a wreath at the slaves' burial ground. But the old stone retained its Jim Crow connotations, and the celebrants that day vowed to do more.[11]

African American women and men fueled the drive for a new slave memorial. That fall the MVLA, the local NAACP, and the Howard University School of Architecture and Planning sponsored a design competition. Howard's architecture school suspended classes for three days while thirty teams of students frenziedly sketched proposals. The winning submission invited visitors through a brick archway that echoed the brickwork at Washington's tomb. A tree-lined path would lead to a brick circle, where a broken granite column would be surrounded by concentric circles representing faith, hope, and love. These were the "qualities no one could take from these people," said the successful designer. Atop the column was this inscription: IN MEMORY OF THE AFRO AMERICANS WHO SERVED AS SLAVES AT MOUNT VERNON, THIS MONUMENT MARKING THEIR BURIAL GROUND DEDICATED SEPTEMBER 21, 1983, MOUNT VERNON LADIES' ASSOCIATION. The new memorial bespoke transformations in America's social and political landscape and not merely in replacing "faithful colored servants" with "Afro Americans" and "slaves." Legal victories and social progress had given black people, such as Dorothy Gilliam and the local NAACP leaders, platforms and influence to bring to the table with the MVLA. The contribution of Howard's students testified to a century of black higher education. And an interest in black history, nurtured in segregated classrooms of the Jim Crow South and brought into academic and popular currency in the 1970s, gave them all a rhetoric about histories erased by a dominant white culture.[12]

Yet divergent histories persisted, as the dedication ceremony revealed. The regent of the Mount Vernon Ladies' Association, Helen Sharp Anderson, described George Washington as an opponent of slavery who eventually freed his own people even though the nation was not ready for emancipation until sixty years and one civil war later. In words reminiscent of the 1929 marker, Anderson said that Washington, entombed close by, was "joined now to those faithful ones who served him and Mount Vernon so well." Inclusion and remembrance were Governor Charles Robb's watchwords that day, an echo of *Ebony*'s language of the 1950s. "The history of America must be the history of all Americans," Robb intoned, because the nation would not have become what it did without black slaves' contribution. Judith Saunders Burton saw it differently: "Here lie my ancestors. Thank God Almighty this day has finally arrived!" As members of the Howard University Choir sang softly, Burton read a poem she had written, full of the violence of slavery, "a people raped" of a country, a homeland, a tradition, a heritage, and a culture. Her celebration of black heritage and survival, long familiar to African Americans, had exploded onto white Americans' consciousness in the 1960s and 1970s. Burton and the new memorial reclaimed this spot on the nation's sacred landscape in the name of African Americans past and present.[13]

Every September since 1990, several hundred women, men, and children have gathered in the nearby grove to celebrate their African and American heritage and Mount Vernon's African American past. Many wearing colorful African robes, they pray, sing, and listen to oratory about the rituals that helped slaves survive. Then all rise to make their way to the new slave memorial. As the procession files through the brick archway and surrounds the circle, George Washington's 1799 slave inventory is read over a loudspeaker: all 316 names, adults identified by occupation, children by age. A single drumbeat follows each name. Distinguished guests, such as members of the Tuskegee Airmen

or the Senegalese ambassador to the United States, place a wreath on
the memorial, accompanied by more singing and chanting. The pilgrims file out, each person laying a sprig of boxwood near the wreath.
Sponsored jointly by the local service organization Black Women
United for Action (BWUFA) and the MVLA, the ceremony partakes
deeply of African American traditions of celebration and commemoration, from the singing of the "black national anthem," "Lift Ev'ry Voice
and Sing," to the recounting of scenes from a people's history. At the
same time, it echoes rituals that white people have performed at
George Washington's tomb for two centuries, especially the laying of
wreaths made from his ubiquitous boxwood.[14]

The somber reading of those 316 names is the center of this annual
event. It registers participants' physical and emotional passage from heritage ceremony to memorial service. It evokes the human history and the
legacy of slavery for all in attendance, whether or not they are descended
from George Washington's slaves. It links the horror and the magnitude
of American slavery to the community that once existed at Mount Vernon. It does not, however, identify who is actually buried there. Like so
many other particulars of enslaved people's lives, that information is lost
to history. Most of the individuals on the 1799 inventory did not stay long
at Mount Vernon after Washington listed them. Freed by the terms of
his will, some lived out their days on the grounds, but others departed for
Alexandria and more distant places. More were taken away in 1802, still
enslaved to Martha's grandchildren, and eventually laid to rest some-
place else. In death, as in life, dispersal was as characteristic of slavery as
a communal graveyard. But the point of reading all those names is not to
reconstruct an unwritten list of unmarked graves. It is to recollect the
community and the individuality of people trapped in an institution designed to strip them of both. Like the slave memorial, the ceremony honors the people who built families, cultivated traditions, and buried some
of their loved ones on ground that they shared with the Washingtons. For
the MVLA, it is an annual testament to the association's broadened vision, as well as to George Washington's foresight in freeing his slaves. For
BWUFA and the black people in attendance, it is a ritual of communal
solidarity across generations and centuries and a lesson for children and
grandchildren, an Afrocentric version of the way the MVLA has always
described a pilgrimage to Mount Vernon itself.

In recent decades Mount Vernon has also taken strides toward acknowledging its African American past and reversing its—and America's—history of omissions and distortions. Gladys Quander Tancil, a descendant of George Washington's slaves and a longtime ladies' maid during the MVLA's council meetings, volunteered to join Mount Vernon's first cohort of professionally trained interpreters in the 1970s. Rather than quietly allow her presence to imply newfound inclusiveness (or, depending on the visitor, age-old servitude), Tancil advocated adding African American history to the tours. Today archaeology at Mount Vernon has unearthed the material dimensions of slaves' existence. Members of the scholarly staff research and write on African American life, while the education department introduces every visiting school group to the lives and work of George Washington's bondspeople. A Slave Life Tour encourages visitors to imagine the grounds from the perspective of African American laborers. Slave habitations no longer bear the euphemism "servants' quarters," as they did into the 1980s. Interpretive placards at the outbuildings refer explicitly to the work of enslaved people, some of them mentioned by name, a far cry from the faceless "dinner was prepared" style of earlier decades.[15]

Some things have changed less. Like many other plantation house museums across the South, Mount Vernon still tends to divide its presentation of black and white lives. Slaves have their own, separate space in the education center. The Slave Life Tour provides an optional way to see the grounds but does not remap the landscape for every visitor. Also, slavery largely stops at the mansion house door, although even here a fuller picture is emerging. On the second-floor landing, interpreters mention the enslaved women who catered to the Washingtons' overnight guests. Soon, one can hope, similar details will find their way from everyday domestic spaces into the spots where historic events occurred: the large dining room where Washington planned the Yorktown campaign and learned of his election to the presidency and the bedchamber where Washington died, attended by Martha and his doctors and several slaves. It will always be George Washington's Mount Vernon. Without the Father of His Country, it would not be a national shrine. But as Washington well knew, his livelihood and his household depended every day upon unfree labor.[16]

So did his descendants at Mount Vernon, for six decades after he died. Enslaved laborers continued to work the land, serve its white proprietors and visitors, and bury their own dead in the slave cemetery, a fact acknowledged on the 1929 granite slab and a placard near the new slave memorial. But otherwise they go unmentioned—by the MVLA and by BWUFA.

Stirring and chilling, the roll call of Washington's slaves is also incomplete. Like the furnishing of the mansion and the restoration of the grounds, it freezes Mount Vernon in 1799. Naming the slaves brought there after his death would violate the chronology essential to Mount Vernon's historic preservation. It would also jar the overriding narrative of the place and its heroic proprietor. George Washington's manumission did not make his home a beacon of liberty. The persistence of slavery there contradicts the story of Washington the visionary emancipator. Just as striking, BWUFA does not claim Mount Vernon's nineteenth-century African American history either. This omission surely arises because that history has not been told. At the same time, the new slave memorial and BWUFA's version of the past, like Mount Vernon itself, owe their power to the historic association with George Washington. On America's revised mythic landscape, slavery and freedom are juxtaposed nowhere more starkly than at the Virginia plantations that America's founding fathers and their African American slaves shared.[17]

Great and small, today's monuments to the nineteenth-century African American past mainly celebrate resistance: the underground railroad; the vision of leaders such as Frederick Douglass; the freedom struggles of ordinary black folk. One such unsung memorial was erected a thousand miles from Mount Vernon in 2005. A curator at the African American Historical Museum and Cultural Center of Iowa uncovered the service records of Andrew Ford, the Mount Vernon slave of Sarah's generation who moved to the Midwest during the Civil War and joined the 102nd Regiment of the United States Colored Infantry. On Ford's long-unmarked grave in Cedar Rapids, the United States Department of Veterans Affairs has now erected a regulation white marble military headstone, identifying his unit and his dates of birth and death: ANDREW FORD PVT CO H 102 USCT JUN 30 1843 DEC 30 1928. Like the annual service at Mount Vernon's slave memorial, Andrew Ford's new marker could not exist outside the contemporary historical imagination. From a memorial plaza in Washington to cemeteries across the United States, black soldiers in Civil War blue have won places on the nation's historic landscape.[18]

Not so the ordinary black people whose work helped make George Washington's home, and their own, into America's shrine. Today traces of Sarah Johnson and her compatriots are difficult to find on the landscapes they once knew.[19] At Mount Vernon, the stand where Sarah served milk behind the kitchen is gone, leaving just the ancient water pump. The house where she lived for twenty-seven years as the MVLA's employee looks the same on the outside. Inside, however, historic architectural restoration has turned a free black family's home back into the storehouse and clerk's quarters of Washington's day. Even the flag that flew at half-mast in Sarah's memory is gone, removed from the lawn overlooking the Potomac because George Washington never had a flagpole there. Suburban growth has transformed the surrounding countryside. Two miles outside the MVLA's property, the land Sarah purchased has long since been subdivided. Lying at the intersection of state route 235 (Mount Vernon Highway) and county route 623 (Old Mount Vernon Road), it boasts large, expensive houses near a private academy. Meanwhile Sarah Johnson remains where she has lain since January 28, 1920: in an African American cemetery, four miles from Mount Vernon, her worn gray granite headstone sinking into the earth.

Sarah's disappearance is not unusual. No historic markers commemorate the former homes of the ordinary black people, husbands and wives and parents and workers, who built new lives after emancipation and persevered in the face of Jim Crow. But without their persistence, there would be no new slave memorial at Mount Vernon. Sarah Johnson and her contemporaries were the indispensable link between George Washington's slaves and the people who commemorate them today, even though Sarah had blood ties to none of them. Washington's slaves were remembered first, their memories told and retold, by the people who succeeded them long after 1799. The act of commemoration itself, the work of organizations such as Black Women United for Action and the Mount Vernon Ladies' Association, would not be possible without the work of black women and men more than a century ago. Their daily labors maintained Mount Vernon no less than the MVLA's fund-raising and governance did. Their carefully honed performances shaped the Father of His Country whom visitors saw as well as the image of slavery days. Their quiet devotion to family and community laid the foundations for later generations and new, more assertive African American memories. Sarah Johnson's name appears nowhere on George Washington's hallowed grounds. But it will always be her Mount Vernon too.

NOTES

ABBREVIATIONS

Individuals

APC	Ann Pamela Cunningham
BW	Bushrod Washington
ESW	Eleanor Selden Washington
HCC	Harriet Clayton Comegys
HHD	Harrison Howell Dodge
JAW	John Augustine Washington (III)
JCW	Jane Charlotte Washington
JMcHH	J. McHenry Hollingsworth
JVRT	Justine Van Rensselaer Townsend
LML	Lily Macalester (Berghmans) Laughton
MAC	Margaret A. Comegys
MJMS	Margaret Jane Mussey Sweat
NMH	Nancy Marsh Halsted
SCT	Sarah C. Tracy
SEJH	Susan E. Johnson Hudson

Collections

APL-SC	Alexandria (Virginia) Public Library, Special Collections
BFRAL	Records of the Bureau of Freedmen, Refugees, and Abandoned Lands, Record Group 105, National Archives and Records Administration
ED-MVL	Early Descriptions Binders, Mount Vernon Library
ER-MVLA	Early Records of the Mount Vernon Ladies' Association, Mount Vernon Archives
FqCCA	Fauquier County Courthouse Archives, Warrenton, Virginia
FxCCA	Fairfax County Courthouse Archives, Fairfax, Virginia
HHD-D	Harrison Howell Dodge Diaries, Mount Vernon Archives
HHD-L	Harrison Howell Dodge Letter Books, Mount Vernon Archives

JAW-D   John Augustine Washington (III) Diaries, Mount Vernon Archives
JCCA   Jefferson County Courthouse Archives, Charles Town, West Virginia
LMLP   Lily Macalester Laughton Papers, Mount Vernon Archives
LVA   Library of Virginia, Richmond
MHS   Massachusetts Historical Society, Boston
MOC   *Minutes of Council*, Mount Vernon Ladies' Association (with year of council)
MVA   Mount Vernon Archives, Mount Vernon Ladies' Association
MVL   Mount Vernon Library, Mount Vernon Ladies' Association
NARA   National Archives and Records Administration, Washington, D.C.
NJHS   New Jersey Historical Society, Newark
VHS   Virginia Historical Society, Richmond

INTRODUCTION: FOREVER OLD, FOREVER NEW

1. HHD-D, January 27 and 28, 1920.
2. Peter R. Henriques, *He Died as He Lived: The Death of George Washington* (Mount Vernon, Va., 2000), 54–63; Gerald Edward Kahler, "Washington in Glory, America in Tears: The Nation Mourns the Death of George Washington, 1799–1800" (Ph.D. diss., College of William and Mary, 2003); Gary Laderman, *The Sacred Remains: American Attitudes Toward Death, 1799–1883* (New Haven, Conn., 1996), 15–18; Sarah J. Purcell, *Sealed with Blood: War, Sacrifice, and Memory in Revolutionary America* (Philadelphia, 2002), 126–31. The quotation is from *The Fashionable Tour: An Excursion to the Springs, Niagara, Quebec, and Through the New England States* (Saratoga Springs, N.Y., 1828), 25. Reenactments of Washington's funeral, based on newspaper accounts of the Mount Vernon procession, at once translated national tragedy into local experience and served to forge a national community of feeling. On the connections between local and national commemoration, see David Waldstreicher, *In the Midst of Perpetual Fetes: The Making of American Nationalism, 1776–1820* (Chapel Hill, N.C., 1997).
3. W. W. Abbot, ed., *The Papers of George Washington, Retirement Series*, vol. 4, *April–December 1799* (Charlottesville, Va., 1999), 527–40 (list of slaves), 477–92 (will); Mary V. Thompson, "To Follow Her Departed Friend: The Last Years of Martha Washington," *Virginia Cavalcade* 51 (Spring 2002): 52–61; Abigail Adams to Mrs. Richard Cranch, December 21, 1800 (typescript, MVL); George Washington Parke Custis, *Recollections and Private Memoirs of Washington* (New York, 1860), 157; *Alexandria Gazette*, November 14, 1835; Edna Greene Medford, "Beyond Mount Vernon: George Washington's Emancipated Laborers and Their Descendants," in *Slavery at the Home of George Washington*, ed. Philip J. Schwarz (Mount Vernon, Va., 2001), 137–57.
4. U.S. census, 1820, Alexandria, D.C., p. 214; Karen Byrne, "The Remarkable Legacy of Selina Gray," *Cultural Resource Management (CRM)* 21 (1998): 20–22; Henry Wiencek, *An Imperfect God: George Washington, His Slaves, and the Creation of America* (New York, 2003), 335–43.

5. In all, nearly two hundred slaves lived at Mount Vernon at some time between 1815 and 1860. I have compiled a census of this community by drawing upon several sources: lists, diaries, and records kept by Mount Vernon's owners from Bushrod Washington to Augustine Washington; U.S. census enumerations; and estate inventories in county archives. This census, which elaborates place of origin and familial relationships as best as can be determined, is available at www.unr.edu/cla/history/casper.html.

6. More than thirty of these travelers' descriptions are collected in Jean B. Lee, ed., *Experiencing Mount Vernon: Eyewitness Accounts, 1783–1865* (Charlottesville, Va., 2006). Anthropologists, sociologists, literary critics, and historians have long studied the ways tourists imagine distance between their everyday lives and the sacred landscape. More recently, scholarship on cultural performance has emphasized how nonwhite interpreters and employees connote an "authentic" past for mostly white tourist audiences; examples include Erve Chambers, *Native Tours: The Anthropology of Travel and Tourism* (Prospect Heights, Ill., 2000), and Jane Desmond, *Staging Tourism: Bodies on Display from Waikiki to Sea World* (Chicago, 1999). A growing literature examines how ostensibly "native" guides imagine their own roles; see, for instance, Laura Peers, " 'Playing Ourselves': First Nations and Native American Interpreters at Living History Sites," *Public Historian* 21 (Fall 1999): 39–59, and Paige Raibmon, *Authentic Indians: Episodes of Encounter from the Late-Nineteenth-Century Northwest Coast* (Durham, N.C., 2005).

7. [Fanny A. Doughty], *Days at Mount Vernon: A Collection of Authentic Incidents in Modern Times* (Boston, 1879), 26. Mount Vernon is not alone: American sacred places have possessed changeable, often contested meanings that reflect, rather than transcend, historical context. Three collections provide a range of examples and approaches to studying them: Paul A. Shackel, ed., *Myth, Memory, and the Making of the American Landscape* (Gainesville, Fla., 2001); W. Fitzhugh Brundage, ed., *Where These Memories Grow: History, Memory, and Southern Identity* (Chapel Hill, N.C., 2000); and David Chidester and Edward T. Linenthal, eds., *American Sacred Space* (Bloomington, Ind., 1995). Richard Handler and Eric Gable, in *The New History in an Old Museum: Creating the Past at Colonial Williamsburg* (Durham, N.C., 1997), examine the difficult balances between preservation and erasure, museum and theater, scholarship and interpretation—especially when historians seek to transform the fundamental stories that a place tells.

ONE: OLIVER SMITH'S MEMORIES

1. "An Hour at Mount Vernon," *New-England Magazine* 7 (November 1834): 400; "A Visit to Mount Vernon," *Parley's Magazine* 4 (October 1836): 295; "Mount Vernon," *Alexandria Gazette*, July 16, 1834 (republished from *Boston Mercantile Journal*); "Mount Vernon," *Pennsylvanian*, January 18, 1836, ED-MVL.

2. "A Tour at the South," *Liberator* 4 (November 22, 1834): 186.

3. John W. Wayland, *The Washingtons and Their Homes* (Staunton, Va., 1944), 111–26; Division of John A. Washington's Slaves, c. 1787, George Washington

Masonic National Memorial, Alexandria, Va., photocopy in MVL; BW, "List of my Negroes, July 24, 1815" and "Meal Allowance for 1814," in John Augustine Washington (III), Mount Vernon Farm Book, MVA; "List of John Auge. Washington's Negroes 3d March 1783," from John A. Washington (I)'s Ledger C, MVA; John Augustine Washington (II) estate inventory, 1832–33, Jefferson County (W.Va.) Will Book 7, p. 148, JCCA.

4. William Faux, *Faux's Memorable Days in America, November 27, 1818–July 21, 1820* (London, 1823; repr., Cleveland, Ohio, 1905), 126; [George Watterston], "Letters from Washington . . . by a Foreigner," *National Register* 5 (May 30, 1818): 338, republished as *Letters from Washington, on the Constitution and Laws* (Washington, D.C., 1818), 121–22; James Jackson to John P. Jackson, March 4, 1825, John P. Jackson Papers (MG 47), NJHS. The best biography, David Leslie Annis, "Mr. Bushrod Washington, Supreme Court Justice on the Marshall Court" (Ph.D. diss., University of Notre Dame, 1974), describes the justice's family life; on the loss of his eye, see p. 60.

5. BW estate inventory, admitted January 28, 1830, Fairfax County Will Book Q-1, pp. 1–10, FxCCA; Annis, "Mr. Bushrod Washington," 103–104.

6. Wiencek, *An Imperfect God*, 88–91; Annis, "Mr. Bushrod Washington," 103–104; Janice Artemel, "1800–1840," in *Fairfax County, Virginia: A History*, by Nan Netherton et al. (Fairfax, Va., 1978), 152–64. From 1810 to 1820, Fairfax County's population declined by 13 percent, from 13,111 to 11,404. But its enslaved population fell by nearly one-third, from 6,485 to 4,433.

7. Adam Hodgson, *Letters from North America, Written During a Tour in the United States and Canada* . . . (London: Hurst, Robinson, & Co., 1824), 219; [Watterston], "Letters from Washington," 338. On the transformation within the Virginia gentry's worldview and daily life, see Jan Lewis, *The Pursuit of Happiness: Family and Values in Jefferson's Virginia* (Cambridge, U.K., 1983); Philip Hamilton, *The Making and Unmaking of a Revolutionary Family: The Tuckers of Virginia, 1752–1830* (Charlottesville, Va., 2003).

8. Robert F. Dalzell and Lee Baldwin Dalzell, *George Washington's Mount Vernon: At Home in Revolutionary America* (New York, 1998), 196–97; Francis Hall, *Travels in Canada, and the United States, in 1816 and 1817* (London, 1818), 336–37; David Hosford, "Exile in Yankeeland: The Journal of Mary Bagot, 1816–1819," in *Records of the Columbia Historical Society of Washington, D.C.* 51 (Charlottesville, Va., 1984): 38–39; A. Mary Eaves to Anne Price, December 17, 1812, ED-MVL; Faux, *Faux's Memorable Days*, 124.

9. "The Tomb of Washington," *New-England Galaxy, and Masonic Magazine* 3 (March 10, 1820): 85; Eliza Cope Harrison, ed., *Philadelphia Merchant: The Diary of Thomas P. Cope, 1800–1851* (South Bend, Ind., 1978), 111, 114; C. J. Jeronimus, ed., *Travels by His Highness Duke Bernhard of Saxe-Weimar-Eisenach Through North America in the Years 1825 and 1826* (Lanham, Md., 2001), 238; James Jackson to John P. Jackson, March 4, 1825; "Sunday Visit to the Tomb of Washington," *Religious Intelligencer* 11 (June 3, 1826): 13–14; Faux, *Faux's Memorable Days*, 123–25.

10. Marie Tyler McGraw, "The American Colonization Society in Virginia 1816–1832: A Case Study in Southern Liberalism" (Ph.D. diss., George Washington University, 1980); Eric Burin, *Slavery and the Peculiar Solution: A History of the American Colonization Society* (Gainesville, Fla., 2005), 6–19; Douglas R. Egerton, " 'Its Origin Is Not a Little Curious': A New Look at the American Colonization Society," in *Rebels, Reformers, and Revolutionaries: Collected Essays and Second Thoughts* (New York, 2002), 107–19.

11. Bushrod Washington, "The People of Color," *Niles' Weekly Register* 11 (January 25, 1817): 355–56; Hodgson, *Letters from North America*, 15–17.

12. Hodgson, *Letters from North America*, 15–17.

13. Alton S. Wallace, *I Once Was Young: History of the Alfred Street Baptist Church, 1803–2003* (Littleton, Mass., 2003), 10–18.

14. *Alexandria Gazette and Daily Advertiser*, advertisements beginning March 5, April 21, and June 14, 1821; "Judge Washington," *Niles' Weekly Register* 1 (September 29, 1821): 72.

15. *Niles' Weekly Register* 21 (September 1, 1821): 1–2. I have identified Sprigg and Williams through the 1820 U.S. census. To ascertain which slaves Washington sold, I compared the people in his 1815 list with those in his 1830 estate inventory. Certainly some people died in those fifteen years, but the absence of entire extended families suggests powerfully that they were sold away.

There is reason to believe that Bushrod Washington had sold substantial numbers of slaves before. His share of his father's estate in 1787 included forty-two Bushfield slaves. Many of them probably remained there through the 1790s, when Bushrod possessed no plantation of his own. He sold Bushfield three years after his mother's death in 1801 (Westmoreland County [Va.] Deeds & Wills, Book 22 [1809–1813], pp. 52–56, microfilm at LVA). Yet only two slaves from his Bushfield inheritance, Oliver and Doll Smith, appeared on his 1815 list, plus five or six people who were allotted to his mother, then to Bushrod after her death. It is improbable that 95 percent of his human inheritance died between 1787 and 1815 or—given his later actions—that he manumitted a sizable part of his Bushfield inheritance. Division of John A. Washington's Slaves, c. 1787; BW, "List of My Negroes, July 24, 1815"; inventory and division of Hannah Lee Washington estate, February 19, 1810, Fairfax County Will Book J-1, pp. 258–59, FxCCA.

16. *Morning Chronicle and Baltimore Advertiser*, August 24, 1821, p. 2; "Judge Washington" and "Notes and Remarks by the Editor," *Genius of Universal Emancipation* 1 (October 1821): 52–55; "Urbain Batrery" to BW, August 12, 1822, Bushrod Washington Family Papers (DMS 2005.4), John D. Rockefeller Library, Colonial Williamsburg Foundation, Williamsburg, Va. For a brief sketch of the episode, see Gerald T. Dunne, "Bushrod Washington and the Mount Vernon Slaves," *Supreme Court Historical Society Yearbook* 1980 (Washington, D.C., 1980): 25–29.

17. Quotations here and in the following two paragraphs appear in "Judge Washington," *Niles' Weekly Register* 1 (September 29, 1821): 70–72. Originally published in a Baltimore paper, this article was also reprinted in the *New York Spectator* on September 28 and other papers thereafter, as well as in the abolitionist *Genius of*

Universal Emancipation so that its editor could respond to Judge Washington's rationalizations.

18. Herbert Gutman, *The Black Family in Slavery and Freedom, 1750–1925* (New York, 1976), details the extensive nature of slaves' kin networks, as well as slaves' use of surnames that often went unacknowledged by masters.

19. Donald M. Sweig, "Northern Virginia Slavery: A Statistical and Demographic Investigation" (Ph.D. diss., College of William and Mary, 1982), 110–11.

20. *Alexandria Gazette*, June 1822, repr. in *Philadelphia Union*, July 29, 1822; *Niles' Weekly Register* 22 (July 13, 1822): 320.

21. Record of the Trial of Hannah, a Slave the property of Bushrod Washington (1821–1822), Governor's Office, Thomas Mann Randolph, Executive Papers, Acc. #41887, LVA.

22. Philip J. Schwarz, *Twice Condemned: Slaves and the Criminal Laws of Virginia, 1705–1865* (Baton Rouge, La., 1988), 94–99, 112, 200–205; on poisoning in African culture, particularly its relation to the murder of James Madison's grandfather, see Douglas B. Chambers, *Murder at Montpelier: Igbo Africans in Virginia* (Jackson, Miss., 2004).

23. *Alexandria Gazette and Daily Advertiser,* October 12, 1821; *National Intelligencer*, October 12, 1821. The conclusion that George and Ned were recaptured is based on their appearance in BW's estate inventory nine years later.

24. Record of the Trial of Hannah; letter of B. Harrison, attorney, in "Petition for pardon of slave Hannah," received February 18, 1822, Governor's Office, Thomas Mann Randolph, Executive Papers: 1822 Pardons & Undated, Acc. #41887, LVA. Hezekiah Scott, Hannah's husband, is otherwise absent from the historical record. The petition for Hannah's release referred to him by first and last name without any indication of a slaveowner, suggesting that he might have been a free man.

25. Record of the Trial of Hannah.

26. Ibid.

27. "Petition for pardon of slave Hannah."

28. Commonwealth of Virginia, Journal of the Council of State, February 19, 1822 (p. 38), LVA; Schwarz, *Twice Condemned*, 27–29; Philip J. Schwarz, *Slave Laws in Virginia* (Athens, Ga., 1996), 97–119.

29. Commonwealth of Virginia, Journal of the Council of State, January 2, 13, 30, June 14, 1823 (pp. 8–9, 17, 32, 135); P. B. Bradley (jailer) to Governor James Pleasants, June 9, 1823, Governor's Office, James Pleasants, Executive Papers, Acc. #42046, LVA; James Pleasants Jr. to Sheriff or Jailor of Fairfax, June 16, 1823, Governor's Office, Executive Letter Books 1823–1830, Acc. #35358, misc. reel 3012, LVA.

30. Commonwealth of Virginia, Journal of the Council of State, August 2, 1823 (p. 180); "Slaves in the Penitentiary reprieved for transportation" and "Proposal of W. C. McAlister to purchase & transport slaves" (both July or August 1823), Governor's Office, James Pleasants, Box 3, Folder 1; Fairfax County Circuit Court Minute Book, June 17, 1823 (p. 268), FxCCA; *Journal of the House of Delegates of the Commonwealth of Virginia* (Richmond, 1823), 47 (December 13, 1823); "The

Penitentiary Burnt!" *Richmond Enquirer*, August 12, 1823; *Alexandria Gazette*, August 16, 1823; Paul W. Keve, *The History of Corrections in Virginia* (Charlottesville, 1986), 46–53.

31. *Alexandria Gazette*, August 9, 16, September 2, 1823.

32. "A List of Slaves and Free persons of color received into the Penitentiary of Virginia for Sale and Transportation," 1816–1842, Auditor of Public Accounts: Condemned Blacks Executed or Transported, Microfilm 2555, LVA.

33. *Alexandria Gazette*, December 20, 1823; *Journal of the House of Delegates*, 47 (December 13, 1823), 129 (January 23, 1824), 206–207 (March 4, 1824). When BW's estate inventory was taken in 1830, none of the slaves matched the age of Hannah's son. Never, in all the documents related to her case, was the child's name mentioned, making it still more difficult to trace him at Mount Vernon. Given the high mortality rate for enslaved children, Hannah's son may well have died by 1830.

34. Dalzell and Dalzell, *George Washington's Mount Vernon*, 155–58; Donald M. Sweig, " 'Dear Master': A Unique Letter from West Ford Discovered," *Fairfax Chronicles* 10 (May–July 1986): 1–5; [Benson J. Lossing], "Mount Vernon as It Is," *Harper's New Monthly Magazine* 18 (March 1859): 443–47; "A Jerseyman in the Old Dominion," *Southern Literary Messenger* 5 (December 1839): 805.

35. John Augustine Washington (I) will, admitted July 31, 1787, Westmoreland County (Va.) Deeds and Wills, Book 18, p. 6; Hannah Bushrod Washington will, admitted April 26, 1801, Westmoreland County (Va.) Deeds and Wills, Book 20, p. 214; both on microfilm, LVA.

36. Thomas D. Morris, *Southern Slavery and the Law, 1619–1860* (Chapel Hill, N.C., 1996), 392–98; Benjamin Joseph Klebaner, "American Manumission Laws and the Responsibility for Supporting Slaves," *Virginia Magazine of History and Biography* 63 (October 1955): 443–53; Ira Berlin, *Slaves Without Masters: The Free Negro in the Antebellum South* (New York, 1974), 46.

37. Recently the historian Henry Wiencek has hypothesized that Venus may have visited Mount Vernon with Hannah in the fall of 1784, when West may have been conceived, but the windows of opportunity were small, and the claim flies in the face of most estimates then and now of Washington's rule-bound character. As the story of Thomas Jefferson and Sally Hemings shows, we should beware of such estimates, and we should beware of beginning sentences with "We shall never know" in an age of DNA evidence. But there are significant differences between the two stories, starting with the fact that Jefferson was a widower and Hemings his wife's half sister who lived at Monticello. Wiencek, *An Imperfect God*, 290–310; for some descendants' accounts, see Linda Allen Bryant, *I Cannot Tell a Lie: The True Story of George Washington's African American Descendants* (New York, 2001).

38. Donald Sweig, ed., *Registrations of Free Negroes: Commencing September Court 1822, Book No. 2, and Register of Free Blacks 1835, Book 3* (Fairfax, Va., 1977), 1–3, 59–60.

39. On Venus, see BW will, admitted December 21, 1829, Fairfax County Will Book P-1, pp. 350–60; BW estate inventory, p. 2; both FxCCA. Simply emancipating

Venus would have been difficult because just twenty-four years after lowering the barriers to manumission, Virginia in 1806 raised them again, requiring that newly freed African Americans leave the state within a year (although the law was enforced only sporadically); see Morris, *Southern Slavery and the Law*, 394. On West Ford's land, see Fairfax County Deed Book A-3, pp. 331–35, FxCCA; Fairfax County Land Tax Books, LVA, reel 93 (1819–1850); Sweig, *Registrations of Free Negroes*, 59–60; Dorothy S. Provine, *Alexandria County, Virginia, Free Negro Registers 1797–1861* (Bowie, Md., 1990), 125. On West Ford's possible ownership of slaves, see Fairfax County Personal Property Tax Books, LVA, reel 108 (1809–1839), 109 (1840–1850).

40. BW will and estate inventory.

41. BW estate division, March 16, 1830, Fairfax County Will Book Q-1, p. 317, FxCCA; BW estate division (manuscript with additional notes), Bushrod Washington Family Papers, Rockefeller Library.

42. For "Jenny (Phil's wife)," see JAW-D, May 21, 1844.

43. BW will and estate division.

44. Tappan Wentworth to John S. Burleigh, March 12, 1833, MVA; *Alexandria Gazette*, August 11, 1831; JCW to JAW and Christian Washington, June 28, 1837, MVA; Marion Stuart Jones, "Personal Recollections of the Last Owner of Mount Vernon," *Southern Literary Messenger* 3 (February 1941): 75. On JCW's substantial role in organizing visitors' experience of Mount Vernon in the 1830s, see Jean B. Lee, "Jane C. Washington, Family, and Nation at Mount Vernon, 1830–1855," in *Women Shaping the South: Creating and Confronting Change*, ed. Angela Boswell and Judith N. McArthur (Columbia, Mo., 2006), 30–49.

45. "Mount Vernon," *Poughkeepsie Casket* 3 (April 26, 1840): 26; Ann S. Stephens, "A Ride to Mount Vernon," *Ladies' Companion* 14 (April 1841): 292–93; "A Visit to Mount Vernon," *New-Yorker* 11 (July 17, 1841): 18, repr. from *New Orleans Bee*; Caroline Healey (Dall) Journals, June 10, 1843 (reel 33), MHS.

46. A. M. Maxwell, *A Run Through the United States, During the Autumn of 1840* (London, 1841), 214–15, 220; Stephens, "Ride to Mount Vernon," 292–93; "Jerseyman in the Old Dominion," 805; William Gilmore Simms, "Washington" (1832?), typescript, ED-MVL.

47. "Great attraction just arrived at Concert Hall. For a short time only. Joice *Heth*, nurse to Gen. George Washington" (Boston, 1835), broadside, American Antiquarian Society, Worcester, Mass. Benjamin Reiss, *The Showman and the Slave: Race, Death, and Memory in Barnum's America* (Cambridge, Mass., 2001), tells the full story, places it in the context of 1830s America, and ingeniously reveals Heth's true history.

48. Obituary for Francis Lee, *Alexandria Gazette and Daily Advertiser*, July 30, 1821; obituary for Samuel (Sambo) Anderson, *Illinois State Journal* (Springfield), April 4, 1845.

49. Alison Goodyear Freehling, *Drift Toward Dissolution: The Virginia Slavery Debate of 1831–1832* (Baton Rouge, La., 1982); June Purcell Guild, *Black Laws of Virginia: A Summary of the Legislative Acts of Virginia Concerning Negroes from Earliest Times to the Present* (Richmond, Va., 1936), 106–108.

50. For contemporaries' image of Mount Vernon as removed from present-day turmoil, see especially Jean B. Lee, "Historical Memory, Sectional Strife, and the American Mecca: Mount Vernon, 1783–1853," *Virginia Magazine of History and Biography* 109 (2001): 255–300. Washington's image was invoked for similarly unifying purposes as slavery increasingly fractured the nation, as François Furstenberg explains in *In the Name of the Father: Washington's Legacy, Slavery, and the Making of a Nation* (New York, 2006).

51. "Young Men's National Republican Convention," *Niles' Weekly Register* 42 (May 19, 1832): 218–19; "Hour at Mount Vernon," 400; "The Tomb of Washington," *Dwight's American Magazine, and Family Newspaper* 3 (May 1, 1847): 273–75.

52. Daniel Mallory, *Short Stories and Reminiscences of the Last Fifty Years* (New York, 1842), 175; *Freedom's Journal*, September 14, 1827; *Liberator* 4 (March 22, 1834): 45; William Jay, *Inquiry into the Character and Tendency of the American Colonization, and American Anti-Slavery Societies* (New York, 1838), 78–79.

53. "Tour at the South," 186.

54. BW, "List of My Negroes, July 24, 1815"; BW estate inventory; JAW list of slaves, 1842, MVA; BW estate division. For Bushrod Corbin Washington's payments for the upkeep of "Old Hannah," see JAW-D, March 27, 1843, November 12, 1844, November 14, 1845, March 2, 1848, December 17, 1849.

55. William Wells Brown, *The Narrative of William W. Brown, a Fugitive Slave* (Boston, 1847; Gutenberg eBook #15132 [2003]), 18.

56. "Tour at the South," 186.

TWO: HANNAH PARKER'S KIN

1. JAW, "Account of work done at Mount Vernon," 1842, Mount Vernon Farm Book, MVA.

2. For midwife fees, see JAW-D, December 3, 1844, October 6, 1848, January 10, 1850; African Americans' ages are based on birth dates listed in those diaries. On childbirth in slave communities, see Marie Jenkins Schwartz, *Born in Bondage: Growing Up Enslaved in the Antebellum South* (Cambridge, Mass., 2000), 19–20, 34–42. On enslaved women's life cycles and plantation networks, see Deborah Gray White, *Ar'n't I a Woman?: Female Slaves in the Plantation South* (New York, 1985, 1999), 91–141; Paul Finkelman, ed., *Women and the Family in a Slave Society* (New York, 1989); and Patricia Morton, ed., *Discovering the Women in Slavery: Emancipating Perspectives on the American Past* (Athens, Ga., 1996).

3. JAW, "Account of work"; JAW-D, September 12, September 15, 1842.

4. JAW, "Account of work"; JAW-D, December 31, 1842, March 24, 1844.

5. John Augustine Washington (II) estate inventory, 1832–33, Jefferson County (W.Va.) Will Book 7, p. 148, JCCA.

6. Hannah Lee Washington estate inventory and division, 1810, pp. 258–59, Fx-CCA; John Augustine Washington (II) estate inventory, 1832–33, p. 148; JAW list of slaves, 1842; Maxwell, *Run Through the United States*, 218–19.

7. Jones, "Personal Recollections of the Last Owner of Mount Vernon," 74–75; JAW list of slaves, 1842.

8. In the 1850s and after, Sarah's sons Joe, West, and Andrew took the surname Ford. Years later West and Andrew each identified himself as either the son or the grandson of old West Ford. Young West was most likely fathered by William Ford, old West's eldest son. Andrew Ford's paternity is murkier and more difficult to determine. In a pension application decades later Andrew Ford listed his father as "John West Ford," possibly the full name of old West himself. Old West Ford's wife, Priscilla Bell, last appeared in the written record on May 10, 1830. When West took their children to reregister as free Negroes on October 17, 1831, Priscilla was not with them; never again did she reregister. She may have died between those dates, and old West may have married or fathered children with the enslaved Sarah at Mount Vernon. Fairfax County Deed Book E-3, pp. 249–52, FxCCA; Arlington Marriage Bonds, 1830–1834, APL-SC, reel 350:6, item 32–21; "End of the Line," *Cedar Rapids Gazette*, c. May 13, 1953.

9. Harriet Martineau, *Retrospect of Western Travel* (London, 1838), 187; "An Hour at Mount Vernon," 399; JAW list of slaves, 1842. Evidence that William studied with Phil comes from JAW's diary and lease agreements with his mother.

10. JAW-D, April 6, 1842.

11. JCW to JAW, December 29, 1840, VHS; Anne E. Saltonstall diary, May 15, 1840, in Saltonstall Papers, box 3, MHS; *Alexandria Gazette*, January 27, May 12, 1842.

12. Penelope M. Osburn, "Exeter Plantation: Its History and Architecture," *Bulletin of the Historical Society of Loudoun County, Virginia, 1957–1976* (1960; repr., Leesburg and Middleburg, Va., 1997), 233–36; JAW-D, April 6, 1843. Beginning in 1844, JAW's diary indicates that garden money went to Nelly; see, for example, April 29, April 30, June 4, 1844.

13. JAW-D, December 17, 18, 22, 1842, May 1, May 26, 1843, July 25, December 7, 1844, January 28, 29, March 6, 1845; JAW to JCW, February 18, 1845, MVA. Walter Johnson, *Soul by Soul: Inside the Antebellum Slave Market* (Cambridge, Mass., 1999), emphasizes how slaves' actions shaped masters' self-images.

14. On Augustine as justice of the peace, see JAW-D, February 14, 1845, October 1, 1847. On slave hiring and Augustine's early practices, see John Joseph Zaborney, "Slaves for Rent: Slave Hiring in Virginia" (Ph.D. diss., University of Maine, 1997); John E. Stealey III, *The Antebellum Kanawha Salt Business and Western Markets* (Lexington, Ky., 1993), 133–57; Jonathan D. Martin, *Divided Mastery: Slave Hiring in the Antebellum South* (Cambridge, Mass., 2004); JAW-D, March 15, December 31, 1842.

15. JAW to Mrs. E. L. Selden, November 26, 1844, MVA; JAW-D, January 1, 5, 1844.

16. JAW-D, May 30, 1845; "Fairfax Agricultural Society," *Southern Planter* 9 (October 1849): 309; John A. Washington, "Use of Guano," *Prairie Farmer* 12 (October 1852): 464–65.

17. For JAW's acreage, see JAW Farm Books for 1842 and 1847–1848, MVA, as well as U.S. census, 1850, Fairfax County, Va., agriculture schedules, pp. 179–80; on wool production and cloth purchases, see JAW-D, September 13, 1842, and JAW

to ESW, July 13, 1848, MVA; for profit margin, see JAW Farm Book, December 4, 1847; for price of Marshall Hall, see JAW-D, October 4, 1851.

18. Washington, "Use of Guano," 464; Patricia Hickin, "1840–1870," in *Fairfax County, Virginia: A History,* 252–60, 270; "Virginia Lands," *American Agriculturist* 2 (September 1843): 176; "Virginia Lands," *American Agriculturist* 3 (January 1844): 8–9; "Farm Lands of Virginia," *Cultivator,* n.s. 1 (February 1844): 63; [Samuel S. Randall], "Emigration to Virginia—Fairfax County Lands—by an Emigrant," *Cultivator,* n.s. 4 (March 1847): 77–78; Richard H. Abbott, "Yankee Farmers in Northern Virginia, 1840–1860," *Virginia Magazine of History and Biography* 76 (January 1968): 56–63; Dorothy Troth Muir, *Potomac Interlude: The Story of Woodlawn Mansion and the Mount Vernon Neighborhood, 1846–1943* (Washington, D.C., 1943), 34–37, 50–69.

19. JAW-D, August 31, 1845, September 8, 12, 23, 1849; JAW to ESW, September 1, 1845, December 10, 1846, September 24, 1849, all MVA.

20. John Griggs estate appraisement, February 18, 1836, Jefferson County Will Book 9, pp. 144–45, JCCA; JAW to ESW, January 20, 1846, MVA; JAW-D, September 24, 1844, March 7, 1842; slave lists in JAW diaries.

21. On Ben and Sally, see JAW-D, September 16, 1847; on "jail fever," see JAW-D, August 31, September 2, 1845, as well as JAW to ESW, September 1, 1845, MVA; on Joe Ford's running off, see JAW-D, April 16, 1849; on the sale of Julia, see JAW to JCW, July 1, 1844, MVA, and JAW-D, July 6, 1844.

22. Caroline Healey (Dall) Journals, June 10, 1843 (reel 33), MHS.

23. "Mount Vernon a Human Stock Farm!" *Liberator* 22 (October 22, 1852): 169; Mrs. Morgan L. Martin diary, February 28, 1847, typescript, MVA; JAW Farm Book, 1847–1848, MVA; James M. Woods, "In the Eye of the Beholder: Slavery in the Travel Accounts of the Old South, 1790–1860," *Southern Studies* 1 (1990): 33–59.

24. JAW-D, September 30, December 3, 1844; U.S. census, 1850, Fairfax County, Va., slave schedules, p. 641; U.S. census, 1860, Fauquier County, Va., slave schedules, p. 64.

25. William H. Snowden, *Some Old Historic Landmarks of Virginia and Maryland* (Washington, D.C., 1904), 29; Fairfax County Personal Property Tax Books, reel 109 (1840–1850), LVA.

26. Christ Church, Alexandria, Va., Parish Register 1828–1847, APL-SC, reel 291.

27. This description of Sarah's possible work is drawn from accounts of enslaved children's labor in Schwartz, *Born in Bondage,* 91–92, 108–109, 131–38, and Wilma King, *Stolen Childhood: Slave Youth in Nineteenth-Century America* (Bloomington, Ind., 1995), 21–41.

28. Description of field work in this and the following paragraph is derived from JAW Farm Book, 1847–1848, MVA; Damian Alan Pargas, "Work and Slave Family Life in Antebellum Northern Virginia," *Journal of Family History* 31 (2006): 335–57, provides useful local context for Augustine Washington's labor practices.

29. JAW to JCW, December 27, 1845; JAW to ESW, July 13, 1848; JAW to ESW, August 9, 1852; ESW to JAW, August 12, 1852; all MVA.

30. JAW to ESW, October 10, 1844; JAW to ESW, September 14, 1845; JAW to ESW, September 4, 1854; JAW to ESW, September 17, 1846; all MVA. For strains of malaria and particularly *Plasmodium vivax* in Virginia, see Todd L. Savitt, *Medicine and Slavery: The Diseases and Health Care of Blacks in Antebellum Virginia* (Urbana, Ill., 1978), 25–27.

31. JAW-D, June 14, 15, 1851, January 20, February 14, 1857; slave lists in JAW diaries; "Visit to Mount Vernon," *Western Literary Messenger* 6 (May 2, 1846): 201.

32. Horace Mann to Mary Peabody Mann, June 3, 1848, Horace Mann Papers (reel 11), MHS; "Bushrod Washington's Greenhouse," *Mount Vernon Ladies' Association of the Union Annual Report 1962* (Mount Vernon, Va., 1963), 28–30; Benajah Ticknor Journal VI, May 24, 1848, Benajah Ticknor Papers, Manuscripts and Archives, Yale University Library; William Ferguson, *America by River and Rail; or, Notes by the Way on the New World and Its People* (London, 1856), 171; insurance policy between JAW and Washington County Mutual Insurance Company, New York, April 28, 1851, MVA; JAW-D, April 28, 1851. The buildings on JAW's "far" property appear on W. Gillingham, "Map of J. A. Washington's Estate at Mt. Vernon," 1869, MVL, and are described in "Auction Sales," *Alexandria Gazette*, May 6, 1869. On "out-door kitchens" and slave quarter design, see John Michael Vlach, *Back of the Big House: The Architecture of Plantation Slavery* (Chapel Hill, N.C., 1993), 43–62, 153–82.

33. JAW Farm Book, May 10, July 19, 1847; JAW-D, December 12, 1848. References to paying slaves for grubbing appear throughout JAW's diaries, for instance, on March 28, April 22, and May 24, 1850; references to buying chickens appear, among other dates, on December 2, 1850, June 16, 1851; the successful judgment of the lawsuit is at January 12, 1850. Dylan Penningroth, *The Claims of Kinfolk: African American Property and Community in the Nineteenth-Century South* (Chapel Hill, N.C., 2003), describes how these informal economies of property ownership persisted among black people from slavery to freedom.

34. JAW Farm Book, 1847–1848; Charlotte Alexander to JAW, December 27, 1854, Ranson-Alexander-Washington Family Papers, acc. #29436, Archives Division, LVA; JAW-D, March 4, 26, 1842.

35. JAW-D, November 18, 1843; JAW to ESW, October 10, 1844, MVA.

36. JAW-D, January 1, July 30, August 2, 1849; Steven Deyle, *Carry Me Back: The Domestic Slave Trade in American Life* (Oxford, U.K., 2005), 42–45.

37. "Emancipation: Jane C. Washington to Charles & Lewis," Jefferson County (W.Va.) Deed Book 30, p. 197, JCCA; "List of Emigrants, by the Liberia Packet, which sailed from Baltimore, February 24, 1849, for Liberia," *African Repository* 25 (April 1849): 122; "From Liberia," *African Repository* 35 (June 1859): 169.

38. JAW-D, December 17, 24, 31, 1849, January 11, 1850; JAW to JCW, December 28, 1849, Adelia Henry Collection, Washington Family Manuscripts 1831–1861, MVA. On the contrast between JCW and JAW, see Lee, "Jane C. Washington, Family, and Nation at Mount Vernon," 43–49.

39. JAW to JCW, December 28, 1849; JAW-D, January 5, 10, 1850.

THREE: WEST FORD'S TRIPLE LIFE

1. Rambler, "A Trip to the Episcopal Convention at Alexandria—Mount Vernon, &c.," *Alexandria Gazette*, June 19, 1850.

2. West Ford's financial and managerial role at Mount Vernon runs throughout JAW's diaries; see, for example, May 17, 1845, January 20, 1846, October 6, 1848, December 14, 1848, January 11, 1850.

3. U.S. census, 1850, Fairfax County, Va., p. 12; U.S. census, 1850, Fairfax County, Va., agriculture schedules, p. 179.

4. Guild, *Black Laws of Virginia*, 106–108, 112, 114; U.S. census, 1850, Fairfax County, Va., slave schedules, p. 3.

5. "Memorial of certain Justices of the Peace of Fairfax County," January 14, 1851, Virginia General Assembly Legislative Petitions, reel 50 (Fairfax County, 1831–1860), LVA; JAW to William Norvell Ward, October 26, 1853, William Norvell Ward Papers, MSS 4423, Special Collections, University of Virginia Library. The burning of Augustine Washington's overseer's house (on his "far" property, away from the mansion house grounds) is documented only by correspondence about his insurance policy: a letter to a New York attorney (JAW to the Hon. Mr. Hughes of N.Y., March 2, 1855, acc. #22795, LVA), along with an affidavit from two neighbors, who saw the fire from a distance and reached the property as it was burning out. Washington's diary for 1854 has not survived, nor have any letters revealing his explanation of the blaze.

6. JAW-D, February 6, 13, 20, 1852; Frances M. Willis estate appraisement, January 27, 1852, Jefferson County Will Book 13, pp. 252–54, JCCA; Frances M. Willis estate sale, February 6, 1852, Jefferson County Will Book 13, p. 266, JCCA; ESW to JAW, February 18, 1853, MVA; ESW to JAW, July 26, 1852, MVA.

7. JAW to ESW, July 22, 1852; ESW to JAW, August 12, 1852; JAW to ESW, August 24, 1852; JAW to ESW, August 9, 1852; ESW to Mary S. Page, September 2, 1853 (typescript); JAW to ESW, September 5, 1853; all MVA.

8. JAW-D, August 7, 8, December 29, 1856, MVA; [Lossing], "Mount Vernon as It Is," 438–39.

9. Information about Sarah's family members is drawn from the slave lists in JAW's diaries; for Milly's remarriage, see Charlotte Alexander to JAW, December 27, 1854, Ranson-Alexander-Washington Family Papers, acc. #29436, LVA.

10. *Alexandria Gazette*, December 23, 1856; JAW-D, January 1, 7, 1857.

11. *Alexandria Gazette*, December 18, 21, 23, 25, 29, 1857.

12. JAW to ESW, March 10, 1858, MVA; Harold W. Hurst, "Decline and Renewal: Alexandria Before the Civil War," *Virginia Cavalcade* 31 (Summer 1981): 32–37; Harold W. Hurst, "The Merchants of Pre–Civil War Alexandria: A Dynamic Elite in a Progressive City," *Records of the Columbia Historical Society of Washington, D.C.* 52 (1989): 327–43.

13. "A Glimpse at Mount Vernon," *Rural Repository* 13 (October 8, 1836): 69–70; "A visit to MV Friday April 13, 1849," ED-MVL; Mrs. Morgan L. Martin diary, February 27, 1847, typescript, MVA; "A Visit to Mount Vernon," *Harper's Weekly*,

July 3, 1858, 420–21; "New York Literary Correspondence: The Drama of Humbug," *Ladies' Repository* 19 (April 1859): 253.

14. JAW-D, August 15, 1850; *National Era* 5 (January 16, 1851): 11; JAW to ESW, [September] 18, 1850, MVA; ESW to Mary S. Page, September 26, 1850 (typescript), MVA.

15. ESW to Mary S. Page, August 31, 1853 (typescript), MVA.

16. John Sears, *Sacred Places: American Tourist Attractions in the Nineteenth Century* (New York, 1989); Dona Brown, *Inventing New England: Regional Tourism in the Nineteenth Century* (Washington, D.C., 1995).

17. G.H.C., "Two Visits: or Blenheim Palace and Mt. Vernon," *Yale Literary Magazine* 24 (October 1858): 20–21; John S. Adams, *Town and Country; or, Life at Home and Abroad* (Boston, 1856), 97; Charles Hale to his mother, December 22, 1850 (typescript), ED-MVL.

18. E. Kennedy, "Mount Vernon—A Pilgrimage," *Southern Literary Messenger* 18 (January 1852): 53, 56–57; "A Visit to Mount Vernon," *Harper's Weekly,* July 3, 1858, 421.

19. Robert R. Hershman, "Gas in Washington," *Records of the Columbia Historical Society of Washington, D.C.,* vol. 50, *1948–1950* (Washington, D.C., 1952), 141–42; Joseph H. Bradley to JAW, June 23, 1854, JAW Papers, VHS; JAW-D, February 1, 2, 1856; [Lossing], "Mount Vernon as It Is," 434; Charles H. Wiggin diary, June 14, 1859, Manuscripts and Archives, American Antiquarian Society.

20. *Saturday Evening Post,* January 24, 1857, 3; "Editor's Easy Talk," *Graham's American Monthly Magazine* 50 (March 1857): 263; "Small Change," *National Magazine* 10 (April 1857): 376; G.H.C., "Two Visits," 22; "A Visit to Mount Vernon," *Harper's Weekly,* July 3, 1858, 420–21.

21. "The Tomb of Washington," *National Era* 7 (December 29, 1853): 206; Lee, "Historical Memory, Sectional Strife, and the American Mecca," 269–78.

22. Erastus Brooks, "Meditation Among the Tombs: Congressional Burying Ground," *Southern Literary Messenger* 8 (January 1842): 83–84; "Congressional Burying-Ground," *National Era* 4 (September 19, 1850): 149; "Use for Mount Vernon," *Littell's Living Age* 16 (February 28, 1857): 538; Thomas P. Rossiter, "Mount Vernon, Past and Present: What Shall Be Its Future?" *Crayon* 5 (September 1858): 252; Charles Lyell, *A Second Visit to the United States of North America* (New York and London, 1849), 1:202; "Department of the Interior," *Valley Farmer* 2 (December 1850): 387; "Washington Agricultural Institute," *Genesee Farmer* 14 (October 1853): 302–303; "Government Aid to Agriculture," *Cultivator* 2 (January 1854): 10; "United States Ag. Society," *Cultivator* 2 (April 1854): 117; "Editor's Table: Mount Vernon for an Agricultural College," *Genesee Farmer* 15 (April 1854): 126; "United States Agricultural Society," *The Plough, the Loom, and the Anvil* 9 (March 1857): 554.

23. Judith Anne Mitchell, "Ann Pamela Cunningham: 'A Southern Matron's' Legacy" (master's thesis, Middle Tennessee State University, 1993), 47–71.

24. APC to SCT, May 26, 1866, ER-MVLA. On the connections between the MVLA campaign and Virginia Democratic politics, see Patricia West, *Domesticating History: The Political Origins of America's Historic House Museums* (Washington, D.C., 1999), 11–25.

25. A Southern Matron [Ann Pamela Cunningham], "Appeal to the Ladies of the South," *Charleston Mercury*, December 2, 1853. For an example of the nationwide appeal, see "The Ladies' Mount Vernon Association," *Godey's Lady's Book* 51 (August 1855): 177–78; on the MVLA as an example of women's use of domesticity in the name of Union, see Elizabeth R. Varon, *We Mean to Be Counted: White Women and Politics in Antebellum Virginia* (Chapel Hill, N.C., 1998), 124–36, and Steven Conn, "Rescuing the Homestead of the Nation: The Mount Vernon Ladies' Association and the Preservation of Mount Vernon," *Nineteenth-Century Studies* 11 (1997): 71–93. On the MVLA and slavery, see West, *Domesticating History*, 26–29.

26. Mary Morris Hamilton, "Mount Vernon and the Ladies," *Horticulturist and Journal of Rural Art and Rural Taste* 8 (September 1858): 400–402; the MVLA's efforts at the local level, in one Maine county, can be traced in Mount Vernon Ladies' Association of the Union, Maine Women Writers Collection, University of New England Library, Portland, Maine. The fullest history of the MVLA's fund-raising efforts is Elswyth Thane, *Mount Vernon Is Ours: The Story of the Preservation and Restoration of Washington's Home* (New York, 1966), 3–130. The conversion to 2003 dollars is based on the consumer price index and calculated using Economic History Services, "What Is Its Relative Value in US Dollars?" http://eh.net/hmit/compare/.

27. *Wisconsin Free Democrat*, reprinted in *Liberator* 28 (October 15, 1858): 168; for Stanton's and Chase's letters, see "Purchase of Mount Vernon," *Liberator* 28 (December 31, 1858): 212.

28. *Alexandria Gazette*, December 25, 28, 1858; "Playing on the Bones," *New York Tribune*, January 1859, repr. in *Liberator* 29 (January 14, 1859): 1.

29. "The Mount Vernon Estate," *New Bedford Republican Standard*, repr. in *Liberator* 29 (January 14, 1859): 8; "The Mount Vernon Excitement," *Boston Olive Branch*, repr. in *Liberator* 29 (January 21, 1859): 9; "Mount Vernonism," *New York Saturday Evening Press*, repr. in *Liberator* 29 (March 4, 1859): 36.

30. Cheryl H. Shepherd, "Waveland, Fauquier County, Virginia" (National Register of Historic Places Registration Form, July 17, 2003), 1–4, 13–15.

31. JAW slave list in JAW-D 1856–58.

32. JAW to Lewis W. Washington, September 18, 1859, VHS; Oswald Garrison Villard, *John Brown, 1800–1859: A Biography Fifty Years After* (Boston, 1910), 438–39.

33. For children born to Betty and Susan, see JAW slave list in JAW-D 1856–58; U.S. census, 1860, Fauquier County, Va., slave schedules, pp. 63–64. On Marietta's illness and death, see JAW to ESW, August 31, 1859, MVA; JAW to ESW, September 24, 1859, MVA; Upton Herbert account, "John A. Washington Esqr. to the Ladies Mount Vernon Ass.," c. 1859–60, ER-MVLA, box 2.

34. E. B. Otis to "My Dear Wife," December 4, 1859, William B. Taliaferro Papers, Earl Gregg Swem Library, College of William and Mary, Williamsburg, Va.; John Beauchamp Jones, *Border War: A Tale of Disunion* (New York, 1859), 356–60, 370–75.

35. [Lossing], "Mount Vernon as It Is," 443–45; JAW to ESW, February 25, 1859, MVA; U.S. census, Fairfax County, Va., 1860.

36. John Terry Chase, *Gum Springs: The Triumph of a Black Community* (Fairfax, Va., 1990), 13.

37. On ESW's death and JAW's religious awakening, see Mary Anna Randolph Lee to Annie Custis Lee, October 21, 1860, Lee Family Papers, VHS; Cassius F. Lee to JAW, October 11, 1860, VF Correspondence, box 240, APL-SC; Joseph Packard funeral sermon for John Augustine Washington, September 21, 1861, transcribed in Anne Lee Peyton Commonplace Book, Peyton Family Papers, VHS. For West Ford's presence at Waveland in July and at Mount Vernon in November, see the Fauquier County and Fairfax County censuses for 1860. The enumeration at Waveland occurred on October 23, but this census taker appears to have listed people present on the census date, because he included Nelly Washington (who died on October 9). The enumeration at Mount Vernon occurred on November 29, and I believe that the Fairfax census taker listed people there at that time, rather than in July.

38. JAW to ESW, November 1858, MVA; SCT to APC, April 30, May 3, 1861, ER-MVLA; [Raconteur], "On the Potomac," *The States and Union* (Washington, D.C.), July 10, 1860; "Repairs at Mt. Vernon. The Work Begun," *Mount Vernon Record* 2 (July 1859): 19; Thane, *Mount Vernon Is Ours*, 128–30, 146–62; Dorothy Troth Muir, *Mount Vernon: The Civil War Years* (Mount Vernon, Va., 1993), 25–27, 63–64; *Excursion of the Putnam Phalanx to Mount Vernon, December, 1860* (Hartford, Conn., 1861), 20–27; SCT to APC, December 1, 1860, April 30, 1861, ER-MVLA.

39. U.S. census, 1860, Fairfax County, Va., slave schedules, p. 9. Tentative conclusions about who was at Mount Vernon in November 1860 are drawn from the Fairfax slave schedules, although the listed ages are approximations. My conclusions are based also on which people do not appear in the Fauquier slave census.

FOUR: ANDREW FORD'S AMERICA

1. JAW to Gustavus A. Myers, August 12, 1861, Gustavus Augustus Myers Papers, Earl Gregg Swem Library, College of William and Mary; Robert E. Lee to Mary Custis Lee, August 9, 1861, in *The Wartime Papers of R. E. Lee*, ed. Clifford Dowdey (New York, 1961), 63; JAW to Anna Maria Washington, August 7, 1861, Beverley Dandridge Tucker Papers, MSS 7959, Special Collections, University of Virginia Library; Andrew Ford pension application, April 8, 1889, case #370689, NARA; JAW estate inventory, recorded December 2, 1861, Fauquier County (Va.) Will Book 29, pp. 243–53, FqCCA; Roll of Colored Voters Registered at Gum Spring Precinct in Mt. Vernon Magisterial District, Fairfax County, Va., General Register 1902–1903, FxCCA.

2. Muir, *Mount Vernon: The Civil War Years*; Mary V. Thompson, " 'A Sacred Duty': Mount Vernon During the Years of the Civil War" (2003), typescript in possession of author.

3. For the 1860 election and the secession debate in Virginia, see William A. Link, *Roots of Secession: Slavery and Politics in Antebellum Virginia* (Chapel Hill, N.C., 2003), 195–244.

4. Jonathan Roberts, "The Quaker Scout: Life in the Old Dominion Before and During the War," *National Tribune* (Washington, D.C.), pt. 1, November 19, 1891; Thomas F. Chapman, Jr., "The Secession Election in Fairfax County—May 23, 1861," *Historical Society of Fairfax County Yearbook* 4 (1955): 49–51.

5. George Mason to Robert E. Lee, May 5, 1861, MVA, in *War of the Rebellion: Official Records of the Union and Confederate Armies* (Washington, D.C., 1880–1901), ser. 1, 51:66–67; John A. Washington to George Mason, May 8, 1861, in *War of the Rebellion*, ser. 1, 2:815; Noel Harrison, "Atop an Anvil: The Civilians' War in Fairfax and Alexandria Counties, April 1861–April 1862," *Virginia Magazine of History and Biography* 106 (Spring 1998): 139; *Evening Post*, May 25, 1861, ED-MVL.

6. Harrison, "Atop an Anvil," 135, 147; Roberts, "Quaker Scout"; Mary H. and Dallas M. Lancaster, eds., *The Civil War Diary of Anne S. Frobel, Wilton Hill in Virginia* (1986; repr. McLean, Va., 1992), 24.

7. U.S. census, 1860, Laurens County, S.C., p. 36; U.S. census, 1860, Laurens County, S.C., slave schedules, pp. 35–37; Muir, *Mount Vernon: The Civil War Years*, 25–27, 63–64.

8. APC to Lucy Pickens, March 23, 1862, Pickens and Dugas Family Papers (collection #1492), Manuscripts Department, Southern Historical Collection, University of North Carolina, Chapel Hill; "Mount Vernon to Be Confiscated," *New York Times*, September 28, 1861; "A Grave Charge," *New York Times*, August 29, 1861; Thane, *Mount Vernon Is Ours*, 238, 243, 253.

9. Joseph P. Reidy, " 'Coming from the Shadow of the Past': The Transition from Slavery to Freedom at Freedmen's Village, 1863–1900," *Virginia Magazine of History and Biography* 95 (October 1987): 403–28; APC to Pickens, March 23, 1862.

10. SCT to APC, May 2, 1861, ER-MVLA; Mount Vernon Subscription Book, 1860–1865, MVA; SCT to MAC, November 30, 1861, ER-MVLA; Robert Knox Sneden diary and sketchbook, December 23, 1861, VHS; George C. Round, "Thanksgiving Day at Mount Vernon," *Ladies' Repository* 24 (April 1864): 217–20.

11. *Alexandria Gazette*, July 11, 1862; Record Book, 1860–1882, MVA, pp. 74–75, 90.

12. Thane, *Mount Vernon Is Ours*, 246, 261, 264; SCT to MAC, November 30, 1861, March 16, 1864, ER-MVLA; *Alexandria Gazette*, May 14, 1862; "Letter from Washington," *Burlington (Vt.) Weekly Times*, May 10, 1862.

13. SCT to APC, December 1, 1860, April 30, May 3, June 1, June 17, 1861, ER-MVLA; Mollie [McMakin] to Caroline L. Rees, October 21, [1861?], Letters to the Kirby and Rees Families, MSS 7786-w, Special Collections, University of Virginia Library. I have identified McMakin as the author of the letter to Rees on the basis of internal evidence: Mary McMakin was the third resident of the MVLA's "parlor circle" (i.e., white resident of the mansion) for most of the war.

14. Passes for MVLA employees are in ER-MVLA, box 9.

15. SCT to MAC, August 14, 1861, ER-MVLA.

16. Muir, *Mount Vernon: The Civil War Years*, 58; Thane, *Mount Vernon Is Ours*, 226.

17. SCT to APC, June 17, 1861, ER-MVLA.

18. Report of Col. Thomas A. Davies, Sixteenth New York Infantry, July 14, 1861, in *War of the Rebellion*, ser. 1, 2:299.

19. D. S. Miles, instructions to Col. Davies, July 15, 1861, ibid., 299–300.

20. Edward Carter Turner Account Book, 1839–1868, Turner Family Papers, VHS; JAW to Edward Carter Turner, August 5, 1861, MVA; JAW to Eliza (Lily) Washington, August 26, 1861, typescript, MVA; JAW to Louisa Clemson Washington, August 31, 1861, VHS.

21. Robert E. Lee to Mary Custis Lee, September 17, 1861, in *The Wartime Papers of R. E. Lee*, 74; Fanny Scott to Robert Taylor Scott, September 20, 1861, Keith Family Papers, VHS; Anne Lee Peyton Commonplace Book, September 21, 1861, Peyton Family Papers, VHS.

22. Peyton Commonplace Book, September 21, 1861; *Burlington (Vt.) Weekly Times*, May 10, 1862.

23. Peyton Commonplace Book, September 24, 25, 1861; Executor's and Trustee's Account for John Augustine Washington Estate, October 12, 13, November 6, 1861, Fauquier County Will Book 30, p. 262, FqCCA; JAW estate inventory.

24. Andrew Ford pension application; Edward [*sic*] Parker vs. Jonathan Roberts, August 18, 1865, Joe and West Ford vs. Jonathan Roberts [September 2, 1865], in BFRAL, Miscellaneous Records 1865–1868, entry 3878.

25. Executor's and Trustee's Account, November 13, 1861, February 24, 1862, December 10, 1862; Turner Account Book, November 7, 1861; Account "Sales of Property" made by R. B. Washington Executor of Col. Jno. A. Washington Dec'd, January 15, 1862, Fauquier County Will Book 29, pp. 344–59, FqCCA; Shepherd, "Waveland, Fauquier County, Virginia," 16; U.S. census, 1860, Jefferson County, Va., slave schedules, p. 44.

26. Turner Account Book, November 12, 14, 17, 1861; Executor's and Trustee's Account, October 30, November 20, December 1, 1861.

27. Executor's and Trustee's Account, November–December 1861; Hector Davis & Company account book, 1857–1864, Chicago Historical Society; Hector Davis & Company ledger, February 6, 1862, New York Public Library. On the Richmond slave trade, see Deyle, *Carry Me Back*, 115–18.

28. The discussion of wartime Richmond is drawn from Midori Takagi, *"Rearing Wolves to Our Own Destruction": Slavery in Richmond, Virginia, 1782–1865* (Charlottesville, Va., 1999), 126–42.

29. *Alexandria Gazette*, June 20, 1862; Parker vs. Roberts; Ford and Ford vs. Roberts; statement of Gabriel Johnson and James Starks, September 9, 1865, also in BFRAL, Miscellaneous Records 1865–1868, entry 3878; Andrew Ford pension application.

30. Parker vs. Roberts; Ford and Ford vs. Roberts; Harrison, "Atop an Anvil," 163.

31. Material in this and the next paragraph is from Jonathan Roberts's curator's report on the estate of John A. Washington, 1863–1864, Fairfax County Will Book Z-1, pp. 314–17, FxCCA.

32. SCT to MAC, June 29, 1863, ER-MVLA; *Alexandria Gazette*, July 31, 1863.

33. George A. Armes to Capt. James J. Ferree, August 1, 1865, in BFRAL, Letters Sent, 2nd Division (Fairfax County), 10th Sub-District Virginia, item 3965; Ferree to Armes, August 3, 1865, in BFRAL, Letters Received (No. 2), 2nd and 3rd Divisions, 10th Sub-District Virginia, Endorsement Book, item 3966; *Alexandria Gazette*, September 30, October 4, 1865.

34. Parker vs. Roberts; Ford and Ford vs. Roberts; statement of Gabriel Johnson and James Starks.

35. Parker vs. Roberts; Memorandum #54, September 21, 1865, Weekly Memorandums, in BFRAL, Miscellaneous Records 1865–1868, entry 3878.

36. Complaint of Selena [*sic*] Parker (Col'd) vs. Chatman Ranow, July 17, 1865, in BFRAL, Miscellaneous Records 1865–1868, entry 3878. For the identification of "Chatman Ranow" as Chapman Renoe, see U.S. census, Prince William County, Va., 1860, p. 39. Michelle Ann Krowl, "Dixie's Other Daughters: African American Women in Virginia, 1861–1868" (Ph.D. diss., University of California, Berkeley, 1998), examines numerous instances of freedwomen's appeals to the Freedmen's Bureau.

37. Details in this and the following paragraphs about Andrew Ford's Civil War and postwar experience come from his pension application (see note 1, above).

38. APC to SCT, October 9–13, November 17, 1865, ER-MVLA.

39. Ibid.

40. For United States Colored Troops, see 102nd Regiment, United States Colored Infantry, Civil War Soldiers & Sailors System, National Park Service (www .itd.nps.gov/cwss/regiments.htm).

41. John Townsend Trowbridge diary (Ms.qAm 1069, vol. 3), September 4, 1865, Boston Public Library; J. T. Trowbridge, "A Visit to Mount Vernon," *Our Young Folks* 2 (February 1866): 91.

42. *Alexandria Gazette*, May 13, May 19, June 7, 1865; Mount Vernon Subscription Book, 1860–1865, MVA; Record Book, 1860–1882, MVA; SCT to Philoclea Edgeworth Eve, August 22, 1865, ER-MVLA; SCT to MAC, August 11, 1865, ER-MVLA; SCT to APC, September 9, 1865, ER-MVLA.

43. *Alexandria Gazette*, June 12, 1865; SCT to Abby Wheaton Chace, November 7, 1865, ER-MVLA; *Flag of Our Union* 20 (July 22, 1865): 463; "A Visit to Mount Vernon," from *Evening Post* (c. October 26, 1865), ED-MVL; "Mount Vernon," *Davenport* (Iowa) *Daily Gazette*, June 16, 1865 (repr. from *Washington Chronicle*).

44. *Alexandria Gazette*, July 24, 1865.

45. John Townsend Trowbridge, *My Own Story, with Recollections of Noted Persons* (Boston, 1903), 271–73; Trowbridge, *The South: A Tour of Its Battlefields and Ruined Cities* (Hartford, Conn., 1866); Michael R. Little, "John Townsend Trowbridge," *American National Biography*, ed. John A. Garraty and Mark C. Carnes (New York, 1999), 21:849–51.

46. Trowbridge, "A Visit to Mount Vernon," 91; Trowbridge diary, September 4, 1865. Sarah's clause "tho, sir, I don't think twas altogether right" appeared in Trowbridge's diary but not his published article or book.

47. Trowbridge, "A Visit to Mount Vernon," 91; Record Book, 1860–1882, MVA.

48. Trowbridge, "A Visit to Mount Vernon," 91.

5: THE JOHNSONS' NEIGHBORHOOD

1. Walter M. Macomber, "Butler's House: Report on Construction Research," June 23, 1947, and Macomber to Mrs. Harold Lee Berry, June 28 and November 9, 1947, both in "Butler's House" file, MVA; "Store House" file, MVA; "Storehouse in Circle: Photographs, 1935, 1947, 1990," MVA. The description in this paragraph and the next is also drawn from an inspection of the interior of the house, conducted in November 2005 with Gretchen Goodell (assistant curator), Justin Gunther (manager of restoration), and Phil Mark (restoration specialist), MVLA. The description of the gardener's house, where the Johnsons may have lived earlier, is drawn from inspection and discussion with Dennis Pogue (associate director for preservation) and Jordan Poole (manager of restoration) in June 2007.

2. SCT to APC, October 22, 1867, ER-MVLA.

3. Ella B. Washington, "A Day and Night at Mount Vernon," *Appleton's Journal of Literature, Science and Art* 5 (April 29, 1871): 488.

4. List of Colored Voters of the Third Magisterial District of Fairfax County, Virginia, October 22, 1867, State Board of Election General Election Results, RG 14, box 49, LVA; U.S. Post Office Department, Report of Site Locations, 1837–1850: Virginia, Mss. 10, no. 389, reel 8, VHS; Brian A. Conley, comp., *Return to Union: Fairfax County's Role in the Adoption of the Virginia Constitution of 1870* (Fairfax, Va., 2001), 38–41.

5. W. Fitzhugh Brundage, *The Southern Past: A Clash of Race and Memory* (Cambridge, Mass., 2005), 12–54; Catherine W. Bishir, " 'A Strong Force of Ladies': Women, Politics, and Confederate Memorial Associations in Nineteenth-Century Raleigh," in *Monuments to the Lost Cause: Women, Art, and the Landscapes of Southern Memory*, ed. Cynthia Mills and Pamela H. Simpson (Knoxville, Tenn., 2003), 3–26; John M. Coski and Amy R. Feely, "A Monument to Southern Womanhood: The Founding Generation of the Confederate Museum," in *A Woman's War: Southern Women, Civil War, and the Confederate Legacy* (Richmond, Va., 1996), 131–63.

6. APC to Lucy Pickens, November 25, 1867, Pickens and Dugas Family Papers (collection #1492), Manuscripts Department, Southern Historical Collection, University of North Carolina, Chapel Hill; SCT to Abby Wheaton Chace, February 1, 1868, and APC to NMH, December 18, 1868, both in ER-MVLA.

7. APC to MAC, May 5, 1868, and APC to NMH, November 30, 1868, both in ER-MVLA.

8. MAC to John Anthony Nicholson, July 15, 1868, ER-MVLA.

9. "A Visit to Mount Vernon," newspaper clipping dated October 23, 1865, MVA; "Mount Vernon," *Alexandria Gazette*, August 23, 1869; APC to NMH, November 25, 1868, and Sarah W. Tiffey to APC, July 1, 1869, both in ER-MVLA.

10. Receipts, September 21, 1868–April 13, 1869; Bill of Articles for Mt. Vernon, January 1869; both in Nancy Marsh Halsted Papers, RG 248, box 1, folder 4, NJHS. Biographical information is derived from the NJHS's finding aid for the Halsted collection.

11. APC to NMH, June 9, November 25, November 30, December 9, 1868, ER-MVLA; *MOC*, 1868, p. 7; Washington, "Day and Night at Mount Vernon," 489.

12. Tiffey to APC, August 30, 1869, and APC to NMH, September 3, 16, 1869, all ER-MVLA.

13. APC to NMH, April 2, 1869, and NMH to Joseph Henry, April 28, 1869, both in ER-MVLA; Washington, "Day and Night at Mount Vernon," 489; HHD to SEJH, October 14, 1886, HHD-L.

14. "Miss Grundy's Gossip. The Week's Record of Social Affairs at the Capital," undated newspaper clipping, 1879 or 1880, LMLP, box 6.

15. Maria Diedrich, *Love Across Color Lines: Ottilie Assing and Frederick Douglass* (New York, 1999), 283–84.

16. "Travel Stains," *Zion's Herald* 46 (March 18, 1869): 11.

17. APC to NMH, March 15, May 11, 1869, ER-MVLA; "Nathan's Bill," April 6, 1869, Halsted Papers. This section builds on numerous scholars' work on freedpeople's labor and family lives soon after the Civil War, notably Roger L. Ransom and Richard Sutch, *One Kind of Freedom: The Economic Consequences of Emancipation* (Cambridge, U.K., 1977); Nancy Bercaw, *Gendered Freedoms: Race, Rights, and the Politics of Household in the Delta, 1861–1875* (Gainesville, Fla., 2003); Noralee Frankel, *Freedom's Women: Black Women and Families in Civil War Era Mississippi* (Bloomington, Ind., 1999); Jacqueline Jones, *Labor of Love, Labor of Sorrow: Black Women, Work, and the Family from Slavery to the Present* (New York, 1985); and Leslie A. Schwalm, *A Hard Fight for We: Women's Transition from Slavery to Freedom in South Carolina* (Urbana, Ill., 1997).

18. Tiffey to APC, June 7, 10, July 3, 15, 1869, ER-MVLA.

19. Philoclea Edgeworth Eve to NMH, February 5, 1869, and Tiffey to APC, December 7, 1869, both in ER-MVLA.

20. U.S. census, 1870, Alexandria, Va., Ward 4, p. 64. Warner May's household also included a fifty-year-old woman named Maria, perhaps a second wife.

21. Poll List, Accotink Precinct, Third Magisterial District, Fairfax County, July 6, 1869, State Board of Election General Election Results, RG 14, box 49, LVA; Conley, *Return to Union*, 9–11, 76–78. The black Republican's candidacy for the state's second-highest office had been a Conservative (Democratic) political ploy. Democrats encouraged his selection for the Republican ticket, figuring that many white Republicans would not vote for a black man. A Republican split resulted when "Moderates" nominated a separate slate of candidates, who bested Radicals for every statewide office. Conservatives won Fairfax County's two seats in the state senate.

22. Wallace, *I Once Was Young*, 63–64.

23. "Auction Sales," *Alexandria Gazette*, June 1, 1869; John A. Washington, by Commissioner, to E. C. Gibbs, Fairfax County Deed Book O-4, p. 64, FxCCA; W.

Gillingham, "Map of J. A. Washington's Estate at Mt. Vernon," 1869, MVL; U.S. census, 1870, Fairfax County, Va., Mount Vernon District, pp. 34–35.

24. "Freedmen's Schools in Virginia," *Alexandria Gazette*, October 16, 1867; Jane Dailey, *Before Jim Crow: The Politics of Race in Postemancipation Virginia* (Chapel Hill, N.C., 2000), 21–25; Judith Saunders-Burton, "A History of Gum Springs, Virginia: A Report of a Case Study of Leadership in a Black Enclave" (Ed.D. diss., Vanderbilt University, 1986), 40–46; Helen A. Hurley, Teacher's Monthly School Report, March 1869, for Gum Spring [*sic*] School, Fairfax County, Records of the Superintendent of Education for the State of Virginia, BRFAL, National Archives Microfilm Publication M1053 (Washington, D.C., 1977), reel 15. Sources disagree on whether newly built Gum Springs School and newly built Bethlehem Baptist Church were two structures or one.

25. Josephine Baker, Teacher's Monthly School Reports, October–December 1869, for Gum Spring School, Fairfax County, Records of the Superintendent of Education for the State of Virginia, BRFAL, reel 17.

26. Information on the students who attended school in 1869–70 is drawn from the U.S. census, 1870, Fairfax County, Va., Mount Vernon District. On the creation of Virginia's segregated public school system, see Dailey, *Before Jim Crow*, 21–25.

27. Mount Vernon Visitors' Register, July 7, 1869–April 20, 1871, MVA; U.S. census, 1870, District of Columbia, Ward 1, p. 14; *Washington Evening Star*, August 13, 18, 19, 1869; *Alexandria Gazette*, August 10, 1869.

28. APC to NMH, August 25, 1869, ER-MVLA; [Samuel I. Prime], "Washington's Home Going to Ruin," *New-York Observer and Chronicle* 47 (January 28, 1869): 4; *New-York Observer and Chronicle* 47 (February 18, 1869): 7.

29. APC to NMH, December 9, 31, 1868, January 7, 1869 (misdated 1868), all ER-MVLA.

30. Mrs. C. A. Hopkinson to APC, c. 1867–69, ER-MVLA; M.C.A. (Mary Clemmer Ames), "A Woman's Letters from Washington," *Independent* 21 (April 29, 1869): 1065.

31. Margaretta S. Morse to NMH, May 7, 1868, APC to MJMS, January 28–29, 1868, APC to NMH, January 7, 1869, Tiffey to APC, June 22, July 3, 1869, all ER-MVLA; *MOC*, 1868, p. 8.

32. SCT to APC, September 11, 1867, APC to MJMS, January 28–29, 1868, MAC to Nicholson, July 15, 1868, all ER-MVLA; U.S. census, 1870, Fairfax County, Va., Mount Vernon District, agriculture schedules, p. 7.

33. Trowbridge, "A Visit to Mount Vernon," 91; [Prime], "Washington's Home Going to Ruin," 4.

34. APC to NMH, December 18, 27, 1868, MAC to Hannah Blake Farnsworth, c. 1868, Tiffey to APC, August 26, 1869, APC to NMH, September 22, 1870, all ER-MVLA.

35. APC to MAC, September 12, 1870, APC to NMH, September 22, October 10, 1870, APC to JMcHH, September 23, 1872, all ER-MVLA.

36. Fairfax County (Va.) personal property tax records, 1869, microfilm reel 502, LVA; U.S. census, 1870, Fairfax County, Va., Mount Vernon District, p. 34; Ledger, July 1872–June 1874, MVA.

37. U.S. census, 1870, Alexandria, Va., Ward 4, p. 64; "Minutes of the Proceedings of Grand Council of MVLA" (manuscript), June 1870, ER-MVLA, box 8.

38. Margaret J. M. Sweat, "History of the Maine Vice-Regency," pp. 107–108, ER-MVLA, box 15.

39. Ibid., pp. 131–36; SEJH to MJMS, July 25, 1872, ER-MVLA.

40. Sweat, "History of the Maine Vice-Regency," p. 143.

41. Ledger, July 1872–June 1874; *Report of the Mount Vernon Ladies' Association of the Union 1872* (New Haven, Conn., 1893), 8.

42. On postwar labor systems and on freedpeople's sporadic response to constricting choice, see Eric Foner, *Reconstruction: America's Unfinished Revolution, 1863–1877* (New York, 1988), 170–75, 404–409, 573.

SIX: NATHAN JOHNSON'S ENTERPRISE

1. The daily routine is reconstructed from Elizabeth L. Broadwell, "Nathan's Instructions," July 16, 1879, in Ledger, July 1872–April 1880, ER-MVLA; for Nathan's willingness to run the lunchroom entrepreneurially, see JMcHH to MJMS, February 3, 1879, ER-MVLA.

2. This paragraph and the next are drawn from NMH to Abby Wheaton Chace, June 25, 1878, ER-MVLA; *Diary and Letters of Rutherford Birchard Hayes, Nineteenth President of the United States*, ed. Charles Richard Williams (Columbus, Ohio, 1924), 3:488.

3. "Mount Vernon and Photography" (typescript research essay, 1992, MVL), pp. 4–5; SCT to APC, May 18, 1866, and Sarah W. Tiffey to APC, July 1, 1869, both in ER-MVLA.

4. R. E. Cowan, "The Stevenson Regiment," and H. R. Wagner, "John McHenry Hollingsworth," both in "Journal of John McHenry Hollingsworth, a Lieutenant in Stevenson's Regiment in California," *California Historical Society Quarterly* 1 (January 1923): 207–209; J. M'H. Hollingsworth Muster Roll, 1st Battalion D.C. Militia Infantry, RG 94, NARA; U.S. census, 1870, Georgetown, D.C., p. 132.

5. William McLeod, "A Visit to Mount Vernon" (manuscript description), c. 1877–1879, William McLeod Papers (MS 325), Historical Society of Washington, D.C.; on Hollingsworth's agricultural production, see *MOC*, 1874–1884; SEJH to JMcHH, July 24, 1872, ER-MVLA; Philoclea E. Eve and SEJH to JMcHH, November 8, 1872, ER-MVLA.

6. Betsey C. Mason to JMcHH, c. September 1872, SEJH to JMcHH, March 20, 1874, both in ER-MVLA.

7. SEJH to JMcHH, September 25, 1872, ER-MVLA; "Our Southern Trip. Mount Vernon," *Grand Traverse Herald* (Traverse City, Mich.), March 26, 1874; *MOC*, 1877, p. 15.

8. For the lunchroom food and suppliers, as well as for payroll employees, see entries for the 1870s in Ledger: Cash Account, June 1874–April 1893, MVA. Suppliers in Georgetown and Washington were identified by using the U.S. census: John L. Owens, grocer (1870, Georgetown, D.C., p. 13); M. H. Homiller, butcher (1870,

D.C., Ward 6, p. 150); Benjamin Charlton, baker (1880, Washington City, D.C., p. 34).

9. Muir, *Potomac Interlude*, 144–49; *MOC*, 1874, p. 2; JMcHH to NMH, October 7, 1874, ER-MVLA; NMH to JMcHH, September 22, 1874, ER-MVLA; NMH to Benson J. Lossing, September 30, 1874, ER-MVLA; Benson J. Lossing, "Mount Vernon," *American Historical Record* 3 (December 1874): 37–38.

10. *The Mount Vernon Ladies' Association of the Union vs. Howland and others*, complaint and decree, Fairfax County Chancery Causes 1877-016, FxCCA; *MOC*, 1877, p. 16.

11. *MVLA vs. Howland*, complaint, p. 4; NMH to Lossing, September 30, 1874.

12. *MOC*, 1877, p. 15; Ledger: Cash Account, June 1874–April 1893, pp. 116–17; JMcHH to MJMS, November 20, 1877, ER-MVLA.

13. NMH to Abby Wheaton Chace, March 1, 1875, Hannah Blake Farnsworth to NMH, March 1, 1875, NMH to LML, April 13, 1875, all ER-MVLA.

14. MAC to JMcHH, March 3, 9, 16, April 18, May 8, 1876, SEJH to JMcHH, October 5, 1875, all ER-MVLA.

15. Descriptions of Mount Vernon excursions of the 1870s include McLeod, "A Visit to Mount Vernon"; Lucy Scott West journal, March 10, 1878, Rutherford B. Hayes Presidential Center, Fremont, Ohio; "Alice in Washington, Letter X," *Godey's Lady's Book and Magazine* 92 (June 1876): 554–55; "A Day at Mt. Vernon," *Friends' Intelligencer* 36 (May 3, 1879): 11–14; George Alfred Townsend, *Washington, Outside and Inside* (Hartford, Conn., 1874), 722–32; "Journal of Ten Days Travel on board Steamer Frances, Left Bridgeport Sep. 7 1873," manuscript diary, VHS. [Doughty], *Days at Mount Vernon*, is a humorous compilation of visitors' experiences and mishaps.

16. Jim Weeks, *Gettysburg: Memory, Market, and an American Shrine* (Princeton, N.J., 2003), 13–111; Rutherford B. Hayes to Samuel Birchard and to Lucy Webb Hayes, both April 15, 1866, in *Diary and Letters of Hayes*, 3:23–24; a similar sentiment appeared in Caroline H. Dall, *On the Way; or, Patty at Mount Vernon* (Boston, 1870), 39–42. On Lincoln's entering the national pantheon beside or even above Washington, see Merrill D. Peterson, *Lincoln in American Memory* (New York, 1994), 25–27, 135.

17. Versions of JMcHH's story appeared in McLeod, "A Visit to Mount Vernon"; "Journal of Ten Days Travel"; and numerous other descriptions of visits. For a skeptical response to the story, see Charles T. Jerome, "The Church, Home, and Tomb of Washington," *Potter's American Monthly* 12 (June 1879): 91–92.

18. Cunningham's farewell address is reprinted every year in the MVLA's *Annual Report*; for the final paragraphs (quoted here), see also Thane, *Mount Vernon Is Ours*, 443–44. Martha Washington Tea Parties are described in Karal Ann Marling, *George Washington Slept Here: Colonial Revivals and American Culture, 1876–1986* (Cambridge, Mass., 1988), 44–51. The colonial revival has often been analyzed as a fundamentally conservative response to the social upheavals of immigration, urbanization, and industrialization, although recent studies discuss particular aspects with more contextual nuance; see Michael Kammen, *Mystic*

Chords of Memory: The Transformation of Tradition in American Culture (New York, 1991), and Richard Guy Wilson, ed., *Re-creating the American Past: Essays on the Colonial Revival* (Charlottesville, Va., 2006).

19. Elizabeth B. Johnston, *Visitors' Guide to Mount Vernon*, 3rd ed. (Washington, D.C., 1879), 38; William Dean Howells, "A Sennight of the Centennial," *Atlantic Monthly* 38 (July 1876): 106; Homer Gage, *A Boy in Washington in 1878* (Worcester, Mass., 1938), 23–24; on northern tourists' image of African Americans at 1870s southern resorts, see Nina Silber, *The Romance of Reunion: Northerners and the South, 1865–1900* (Chapel Hill, N.C., 1993), 66–84.

20. "Visiting Mount Vernon," *Frederick (Md.) Daily News*, September 13, 1884; "The Tomb of Washington," *New York Times*, June 20, 1885; [Doughty], *Days at Mount Vernon*, 14–15; undated newspaper clipping, c. 1880, in Margaret J. M. Sweat, comp., "Mount Vernon Items" (scrapbook), MVL, p. 42.

21. Undated newspaper article, c. June 1881, LMLP, box 6; Cunningham, farewell address.

22. This composite of the MVLA council meetings is derived from the *MOC* for 1870–1890.

23. U.S. census, 1880, Stratford, Fairfield County, Conn., p. 25; U.S. census, 1880, Summerville, Richmond County, Ga., p. 29; "The Mount Vernon Regents," *Forney's Sunday Chronicle* (Washington, D.C.), June 12, 1881, in LMLP, box 6.

24. NMH to JMcHH, October 24, 1874, July 16, 1877, ER-MVLA; "Contents of Box sent to Col. Hollingsworth July 25th/77," ER-MVLA; SEJH to JMcHH, June 11, 1877, ER-MVLA.

25. SEJH to JMcHH, July 11, 12, 15, 1877, NMH to JMcHH, July 16, 1877, JMcHH to MJMS, July 9, 1878, all ER-MVLA. On paying employees' doctor bills, see LML to JMcHH, October 11, 1873; Ledger: Cash Account, June 1874–April 1893, pp. 85–87 (for 1876); *MOC*, 1882, p. 27.

26. Broadwell, "Nathan's Instructions"; *MOC*, 1879, p. 20; *MOC*, 1880, pp. 6–7.

27. Philoclea Edgeworth Eve to JMcHH, June 25, 1874, ER-MVLA.

28. MAC to LML, May 26, 1876, ER-MVLA.

29. SEJH to JMcHH, December 17, 1877, JMcHH to MJMS, November 20, 1877, January 3, 1878, MJMS to JMcHH, December 16, 31, 1877, July 9, 1878, all ER-MVLA; Margaret J. M. Sweat Diary, September 27, 1877, Margaret Jane Mussey Sweat Papers, box 1, Maine Women Writers Collection, University of New England, Portland.

30. Connie Burns, "Private Sphere/Public Sphere: Rethinking Paradigms of Victorian Womanhood Through the Life and Writings of Margaret Jane Mussey Sweat, 1823–1908" (master's thesis, University of Southern Maine, 1993), 93; Annals of the Cobweb Club, Washington, March 3, 1890, in Sweat Papers, box 1. Poll lists for Fairfax County (FxCCA) show Mount Vernon's employees voting throughout the late 1870s; Dailey, *Before Jim Crow*, is an excellent history of Readjuster politics.

31. JMcHH to LML, December 9, 1880, ER-MVLA; JMcHH to LML, September 15, 1881, LMLP.

32. *MOC*, 1881, pp. 8–9; Ledger: Cash Account, June 1874–April 1893, pp. 263–64, 269.

33. *MOC*, 1883, pp. 6–8, 11–12, 15–16.

34. Sybil, "A Day at Mount Vernon: The Plea of a Visitor for Restoration of the Lunch Table," *Washington Post*, September 30, 1883.

35. "The Mount Vernon Regency," undated newspaper article, c. May 26, 1883, in LMLP, box 6; JMcHH to Philoclea Edgeworth Eve, August 15, 1883, ER-MVLA.

36. JMcHH to Eve, August 15, 1883; JMcHH to the Regent and Vice Regents of the MVLA, May 25, 1884, LMLP; for JMcHH's failure to meet the payroll, see entries for 1883–1884 in Ledger: Cash Account, June 1874–April 1893.

37. Martha Mitchell to SEJH, June 18, 1884, ER-MVLA; JMcHH to the Regent and Vice Regents of the MVLA, May 25, 1884; Tera W. Hunter, *To 'Joy My Freedom: Southern Black Women's Lives and Labors After the Civil War* (Cambridge, Mass., 1997), 60–61.

38. JMcHH to SEJH, April 3, 1885, ER-MVLA; Norris N. Halsted to NMH, May 27, 1882, JVRT to NMH, May 11, 1884, both in Halsted Papers, box 1, folder 3.

39. *MOC*, 1884, pp. 14–16; *Washington Post*, May 23, 1884; *Alexandria Gazette*, May 23, 1884; JMcHH to SEJH, November 13, 1884, ER-MVLA.

40. *MOC*, 1884, p. 17. The MVLA's questions to JMcHH do not survive, but it is possible to reconstruct most of them from his answers (JMcHH to the Regent and Vice Regents of the MVLA, May 25, 1884).

41. *MOC*, 1884, pp. 19–20.

42. Ibid., p. 21; JMcHH to the Regent and Vice Regents of the MVLA, May 25, 1884.

43. *MOC*, 1884, pp. 22–24.

44. Ibid., pp. 27–29.

45. *Washington Sunday Gazette*, June 8, 1884, in Sweat, "Mount Vernon Items"; Mitchell to SEJH, June 18, 25, 1884, ER-MVLA.

46. Mitchell to SEJH, July 2, 1884, JMcHH to SEJH, November 13, 1884, April 3, 1885, all ER-MVLA.

47. JMcHH to SEJH, April 3, 1885; *MOC*, 1885, pp. 39–46; JMcHH to LML, May 30, 1885, ER-MVLA.

48. *Trade, Traveler and Excursionists' Guide*, May 30, 1885, clippings in Sweat, "Mount Vernon Items."

49. "Local Brevities," *Alexandria Gazette*, May 9, 1885.

SEVEN: SARAH JOHNSON'S PAPERS

1. HHD-D, July 15, 1885; HHD, "To the Employees of Mount Vernon," July 15, 1885, MVA; HHD to LML, July 16, 1885, HHD-L.

2. HHD to LML, June 9, 1885, Ben. Perley Poore to LML, June 5, 1885, Martha Mitchell to NMH, July 31, 1885, all ER-MVLA. On Dodge's demeanor and habits, see Elswyth Thane, *Mount Vernon: The Legacy* (Philadelphia, 1967), 1–12.

3. HHD-D, July 17, 1885; HHD to LML, July 20, 1885, HHD-L.

4. "In the Old Mansion. The Ladies of the Mount Vernon Association in Session," *Washington Evening Star*, May 16, 1891; "Supply and Demand," *Youth's Compan-*

ion, January 24, 1895, p. 41; HHD-D, June 15–16, 1885; HHD to LML, July 20, 1885, HHD-L.

5. Harrison Howell Dodge, *Mount Vernon: Its Owner and Its Story* (Philadelphia, 1932), 92–94; Elliott J. Gorn, "Black Spirits: The Ghostlore of Afro-American Slaves," *American Quarterly* 36 (1984): 549–65.

6. HHD-D, August 3, December 26, 1885, December 18, 22, 25, 1886.

7. HHD to Emma R. Ball, December 24, 1885, HHD to JVRT, June 2, 1888, HHD to Ada L. Egerton, May 20, 1886, HHD to LML, May 24, 1886, all HHD-L; LML to NMH, April 20, 1886, ER-MVLA; *MOC,* 1886, pp. 32–33, 39.

8. HHD to LML, July 24, 28, August 11, September 9, 1885, HHD-L.

9. Ledger: Cash Account, June 1874–April 1893, p. 444; U.S. census, 1880, Fairfax County, Va., Mount Vernon District; Fairfax County personal property tax records, 1891, FxCCA; G. M. Hopkins, "Mt. Vernon Dist. No. 3," map (Washington, D.C., 1878); Lovelace Brown and Sarah Brown to Thomas R. Keith, trustee, and John M. Johnson and R. W. Moore, January 26, 1898, Fairfax County Deed Book A-6, pp. 232–33, FxCCA.

10. Thane, *Mount Vernon: The Legacy,* 144, 188–89; HHD to Rebecca B. Flandrau, December 15 and 28, 1891, HHD-L; "The Letter-Box," *St. Nicholas* 19 (March 1892): 397–98.

11. Caroline Healey Dall Journals, December 7, 1883 (reel 38), February 19, 1887 (reel 39), MHS; Sophie Bledsoe Herrick, "Mount Vernon as It Is," *Century Magazine* 35 (November 1887): 26.

12. "The Jolly Landlords," *New York Times,* May 12, 1887; HHD-D, March 5–8, 1889. Biographical information on Dall and Herrick is drawn from Anne C. Rose, "Caroline Wells Healey Dall," *American National Biography,* ed. John A. Garraty and Mark C. Carnes (New York, 1999), 6:26–27; Aaron M. Lisec, "Sophia McIlvaine Bledsoe Herrick," ibid., 10:667–68.

13. Dall Journals, February 19, 1889 (reel 39); Herrick, "Mount Vernon as It Is," 25. Herrick's article appeared in *Century* magazine, in which a popular series, "Battles and Leaders of the Civil War," played a pivotal role in redefining the recent conflict as a war between valiant white Yankees and Confederates, now reunited; see David W. Blight, *Race and Reunion: The Civil War in American Memory* (Cambridge, Mass., 2001), 173–81.

14. Herrick, "Mount Vernon as It Is," 26; Ledger: "Monthly account, Sarah Johnson, milk, butter, ice and eggs," 1885–1889, MVA; Ledger: "Milk et cetera," 1889–1895, MVA.

15. Herrick, "Mount Vernon as It Is," 25–27.

16. HHD-D, December 12, 1888; Dodge, *Mount Vernon: Its Owner and Its Story,* 187–91.

17. Dodge, *Mount Vernon: Its Owner and Its Story,* 91.

18. William Ford, eldest son of old West, died at age sixty-two in September 1874, five years after his wife, Henrietta; see Elizabeth R. Frain, *Fairfax County Death Register, 1853–1896* (Westminster, Md., 2002), 68.

19. Bryant, *I Cannot Tell a Lie,* 206–22, 241–50; U.S. census, 1880, Beaufort County, S.C., Beaufort township, p. 43; George Ford and Hattie Ford to West Ford, May

24, 1881, Deed Book A-5, pp. 332–33, FxCCA. Several sources (including Dodge's memoir) describe West Ford as the grandson of his namesake and as the third generation of Fords to work in Mount Vernon's garden. The likeliest possibility is that young West Ford was William's son and George's half brother.

20. Fairfax County Court Order Book, 1888–1892, p. 232 (West Ford licensed as marriage celebrant), FxCCA; HHD-D, January 1, 1887; J. West and Martha E. Ford to Trustees of Mount Vernon School District, November 24, 1888, Fairfax County Deed Book H-5, p. 294, FxCCA; U.S. census, 1880, Fairfax County, Va., Mount Vernon District, p. 51 (literacy of West Ford's family).

21. Paula Elsey, "The 'Willing Workers': A Black Community on Mason Neck," *Yearbook: The Historical Society of Fairfax County, Virginia* 26 (1997–98): 93–122; Sallie E. Mason to William Robertson [*sic*], January 28, 1880, Deed Book Z-4, pp. 107–108, and Sallie E. Mason to William Robinson and Elizabeth Williams, February 26, 1887, Deed Book H-5, pp. 236–37, both FxCCA; Patrick Reed, "1870–1925," in *Fairfax County, Virginia: A History*, 444–58; U.S. census, 1880, Fairfax County, Va., Mount Vernon District. My summary of black landholding in the Mount Vernon District is drawn from the 1891 Fairfax County land tax registers, FxCCA. On black landholding in Virginia, see Dianne Swann-Wright, *A Way out of No Way: Claiming Family and Freedom in the New South* (Charlottesville, Va., 2002), 69–89; Loren Schweninger, *Black Property Owners in the South, 1790–1915* (Urbana, Ill., 1997), 173–76. By the early 1900s, Schweninger writes, landowners constituted the "large majority" of the Old Dominion's black farmers (173).

22. HHD to LML, July 5, August 12, September 23, 1886, HHD-L; SEJH to LML, September 2, 1886, ER-MVLA; HHD to SEJH, September 24, 1886, HHD-L; *MOC*, 1887, p. 17; HHD-D, August 13, 16, October 16, 1888.

23. HHD-D, November 29, December 16, 22, 29, 1887, April 28, 1888; HHD to LML, January 6, 1888, HHD-L; *MOC*, 1888, pp. 24–25; Dodge, *Mount Vernon: Its Owner and Its Story*, 60–61.

24. HHD-D, May 26, 28, 1888; Dodge, *Mount Vernon: Its Owner and Its Story*, 62; HHD to JVRT, June 2, 1888, HHD-L; HHD to NMH, June 11, 1888, HHD-L.

25. On the Newby family, see Philip J. Schwarz, *Migrants Against Slavery: Virginians and the Nation* (Charlottesville, Va., 2001), 149–68. William Robinson's birthplace is named on his and Sarah Johnson's marriage license, October 25, 1888, FxCCA. On William and Harriet Robinson's family, see U.S. census, 1870, Fairfax County, Va., Falls Church District, p. 62; 1880, Mount Vernon District, p. 31. For William's land purchases: Sallie E. Mason to William Robertson [*sic*], January 28, 1880, Deed Book Z-4, pp. 107–108, and Sallie E. Mason to William Robinson and Elizabeth Williams [Robinson's daughter], February 26, 1887, Deed Book H-5, pp. 236–37, both FxCCA.

26. HHD to Emily L. Harper, June 23, 1888, HHD to MJMS, August 31, September 8, 1888, HHD to Mary T. Leiter, September 8, October 23, 1888, all HHD-L.

27. Wedding invitation of Sarah Johnson and William Robinson, 1888, in Sweat, "Mount Vernon Items."

28. Marriage license of Sarah Johnson and William Robinson, October 25, 1888, FxCCA.

29. Marriage license of Sarah Johnson and William Robinson; HHD to LML, October 26, November 3, 1888, HHD-L; HHD to Ella B. Washington, October 26, 1888, HHD-L; HHD-D, October 25, 1888.

30. HHD to SEJH, January 5, 1889, HHD-L; HHD to LML, April 5, 1889, HHD-L; *MOC*, 1889, pp. 58–59; marriage license, Louisa Robinson and Ulysses Brown, February 13, 1889, FxCCA. Unlike Sarah and William's marriage license, Ulysses and Louisa's identified the bride's and groom's fathers, testimony to their parents' legal unions after emancipation.

31. Lloyd Washington to Sarah Johnston [*sic*], April 16, 1889, Deed Book I-5, p. 128, FxCCA.

32. This analysis is based on a survey of all "colored" landowners in the Mount Vernon District of Fairfax County in 1891, from that year's Fairfax County land tax registers, FxCCA.

33. HHD to LML, August 3, 1888, January 4, 1890, HHD-L; HHD to SEJH, January 29, 1890, HHD-L; HHD-D, October 14–23, 1888, November 4, December 31, 1889; *MOC*, 1890, p. 79; Frain, *Fairfax County Death Register*, 68; Chase, *Gum Springs*, 31.

34. *MOC*, 1890, p. 79; Ledger: Cash Account, June 1874–April 1893, pp. 538–663 (for William Robinson's pay for day labor, recorded monthly); HHD, Receipts and Expenditures ledgers, 1886–1892 and 1892–1895 (for Sarah's lamp oil), MVA.

35. "In the Old Mansion."

36. HHD-D, February 26, April 21–22, May 4, 1891; HHD to Harden ("Star") Hand Grenade Fire Extinguishing Co., Chicago, December 15, 1885, HHD-L; HHD to LML, May 28, 1886, HHD-L; Thane, *Mount Vernon: The Legacy*, 128–30; *MOC*, 1892, p. 71.

37. "The Next Chief-Justice . . . A Proposed Virginia Land Speculation," *New York Times*, May 2, 1888; "A Grand Avenue to Mount Vernon," *Phrenological Journal and Science of Health* 84 (November 1887): 279; HHD to Emma R. Ball, April 16, 1889, HHD-L; John E. Merriken, *Old Dominion Trolley Too: A History of the Mount Vernon Line* (Dallas, Texas, 1987), 3; LML to Frank Thomson, July 18, 1888, ER-MVLA.

38. LML to Frank Thomson, July 18, 1888; *MOC*, 1892, 75–77, 90–91.

39. Warrenton Gillingham plan of proposed turnpike, May 16, 1892; G. A. Fowle, Thomas H. Haislip, and J. E. Merchant to Fairfax County Court, c. May 1892; John P. Agnew et al. (fifty signers) to Fairfax County Court, c. May 1892; J. Owen Kirby et al. (thirty-nine signers) to Fairfax County Court, c. May 1892; Warrenton Gillingham to F. W. Richardson (clerk of Fairfax County Court), May 31, 1892: all in Gum Springs Folder, FxCCA. See also Chase, *Gum Springs*, 39–40. Information about petitioners' race and residence is drawn from the 1880 and 1900 U.S. censuses for the Mount Vernon District of Fairfax County.

40. T. F. Burroughs et al. (fifty-two signers) to the Honorable Judge of the Court of Fairfax County, "Petition to establish precinct with Gum Spring School House,

1882," in box "Voting" (election districts, petitions), FxCCA; HHD-D, November 6, 1888, November 5, 1889.

41. HHD-D, September 5, 1892; HHD to JVRT, September 6, 16, 1892, HHD-L; *MOC*, 1893, p. 29.

42. HHD-D, September 16–24, 1892; HHD to JVRT, September 21, 1892, HHD-L.

43. HHD-D, September 20–23, 1892; HHD to JVRT, October 7, 1892, HHD-L.

44. Bureau of Vital Statistics: Marriages, Alexandria City, Virginia, 1870–1924 (August 23, 1915), reel 55, LVA; World War I Draft Registration Card, "Nathaniel Thomas Johnson," film in APL-SC; Lloyd Washington to Smith Johnson, March 21, 1891, Deed Book W-5, pp. 527–29, FxCCA. Details of Smith Johnson's marriage are elusive. He married sometime in the late 1880s, but his wife, Mary, had died by 1900, when the census listed him as a widower. (The 1890 manuscript census was destroyed by fire in the early twentieth century.)

45. "In the Old Mansion"; *MOC*, 1892, p. 71. Studies of African American women and family life in the late nineteenth century have influenced this portrayal of Sarah's self-image, notably Hunter, *To 'Joy My Freedom*; Sharon Ann Holt, *Making Freedom Pay: North Carolina Freedpeople Working for Themselves, 1865–1900* (Athens, Ga., 2000); and Swann-Wright, *A Way out of No Way*.

46. HHD-D, October 1, 1892; HHD to JVRT, October 11, 1892, HHD-L; HHD to Mr. Forbes, December 18, 1892, HHD-L.

47. *MOC*, 1893, pp. 13, 28–29.

48. MVLA manuscript minutes of council, 1893, MVA; *MOC*, 1893, p. 43.

EIGHT: EDMUND PARKER'S PERFORMANCES

1. Description of Parker's appearance and activity at the tomb, in this paragraph and the next, is drawn from "Guardian of the Dead. Watchman for Half a Century at the Tomb of Washington," *Washington Post*, November 18, 1894; "The National Capital. Old and New Guard of the Tomb of Washington," *Mansfield (Ohio) News*, February 22, 1899; Mrs. O. W. Scott, "Little Folks. Where Washington Lived," *Zion's Herald* 73 (February 13, 1895): 103; J. S. Patterson to John Young, May 9, 1896, J. S. Patterson Letters, Special Collections, University of Arkansas Libraries, Fayetteville; "At Mount Vernon," *Harper's Bazaar* 26 (May 13, 1893): 378; "Guardian of the Tomb. Edmund Parker, Watchman of Mount Vernon, Dying," *Washington Post*, August 14, 1898; "Sketches of Mount Vernon as It Is Today," *Chicago Daily Tribune*, February 22, 1900.

2. The quotation is from "Guardian of the Dead."

3. Patterson to Young, May 9, 1896.

4. Bushrod C. Washington, "Mt. Vernon, the Mecca of America," *Peterson Magazine*, n.s., 8 (January 1898): 1–3. Lamenting the loss of true reverence was nothing new in the 1890s. However, with increasing access to leisure among the working classes, including immigrants and African Americans, even places like Mount Vernon were no longer sanctuaries from the common folk, if they ever had been.

5. For Parker's commute, see "Guardian of the Tomb." Information on the Parkers' residence and on the occupations of Edmund's children is drawn primarily from

the U.S. census: 1870, Alexandria, Va., Ward 1, p. 73; 1880, Chambersburg, Franklin County, Pa., pp. 21–22; 1900, Washington City, D.C., enumeration district 44, sheet 19 (Caroline Turner and Mildred Parker); 1900, Washington City, D.C., enumeration district 57, sheet 1 (Esau Parker); 1900, Washington City, D.C., enumeration district 50, sheet 20 (Harry Parker). For Parker's return to Mount Vernon in 1882, see Ledger: Cash Account, June 1874–April 1893.

6. Benjamin Cummings Truman, *History of the World's Fair, Being a Complete and Authentic Description of the Columbian Exposition from Its Inception* (Chicago, 1893), 474. For descriptions of the Virginia Building and its preparation, see John Samuel Apperson, *Communication from the Governor Inclosing the Report of the World's Fair Commissioners* (Richmond, Va., 1893); "For a Mount Vernon. A Virginia Woman Intends to Duplicate the House," *Chicago Daily Tribune*, June 13, 1892; "The Great Fair. Colonial Architecture Among the State Buildings," *Cambridge (Ohio) Jeffersonian*, August 24, 1893; and Lydia Mattice Brandt, "Variations on Mount Vernon: Replicas of an Icon as Vehicles for American Memory" (master's thesis, University of Virginia, 2006).

7. "Virginia's Exhibit. The Mother of Civilization," *Oshkosh (Wis.) Daily Northwestern*, October 14, 1893; "Tell of Early Days. Interesting Furnishings for the Fair's Mount Vernon," *Chicago Daily Tribune*, May 14, 1893; "For a Mount Vernon."

8. Sarah's work for council, each year from 1894 to 1906 except 1898, appears in Ledger: Cash Account, May 1893–April 1909, MVA. For Aunt Jemima at the World's Columbian Exposition, see M. M. Manring, *Slave in a Box: The Strange Career of Aunt Jemima* (Charlottesville, Va., 1998), 75–78; African American workers and visitors are discussed in Christopher Robert Reed, *"All the World Is Here!": The Black Presence at White City* (Bloomington, Ind., 2000); for the controversy over black participation and stereotypes, see Ida B. Wells, Frederick Douglass, Irvine Garland Penn, and Ferdinand L. Barnett, *The Reason Why the Colored American Is Not in the World's Columbian Exposition: The Afro-American's Contribution to Columbian Literature* (1893), ed. and intro. by Robert W. Rydell (Urbana, Ill., 1999).

9. "Ghost of Washington Haunts Mount Vernon: Ladies of the Mount Vernon Association Sleep in the Room in Which the General Died," (New York) *World*, c. May 28, [1897], in Sweat, "Mount Vernon Items" (dated based upon *MOC*). On the cultural functions of mammy images, see Grace Elizabeth Hale, *Making Whiteness: The Culture of Segregation in the South, 1890–1940* (New York, 1998), 98–104, as well as Manring, *Slave in a Box*.

10. U.S. census, 1900, Fairfax County, Va., Mount Vernon District, pp. 3, 8; HHD to Mrs. Van Rensselaer, May 30, 1901, HHD-L; Fairfax County (Va.) Personal Property Tax Records, 1892–1908, FxCCA; Reed, "1870–1925," in *Fairfax County, Virginia: A History*, 480–81; William Roberson [sic] will, December 31, 1901, Will Book 4, FxCCA.

11. U.S. census, 1900, Alexandria, Va., Ward 1, p. 14; "Killed His Son," *Alexandria Gazette*, January 20, 1898; HHD to Mrs. Van Rensselaer, May 30, 1901, HHD-L; R. H. Lancaster Lodge No. 1370, Grand United Order of Odd Fellows of the State of Virginia, Records, 1890–1910 (box 76, folders 2, 3, 8), APL-SC; "Eman-

cipation Anniversary," *Washington Post*, September 8, 1894; "The Negro's Day of Jubilee," *Washington Post*, September 15, 1896. On African Americans' rituals of memory, see Mitchell A. Kachun, *Festivals of Freedom: Memory and Meaning in African American Emancipation Celebrations, 1808–1915* (Amherst, Mass., 2003).

12. Ledger: Cash Account, May 1893–April 1909; HHD to JVRT, May 29, June 18, 1894, June 13, 1895, April 9, 1901, HHD-L; HHD, letter of reference for Louisa Brown, October 18, 1898, HHD-L; *MOC*, 1894, pp. 45, 85; HHD to Mrs. Van Rensselaer, May 30, 1901.

13. HHD to Upton Herbert, April 13, 1896 (quotation), HHD to Lawrence Washington, April 8, 1896, both in HHD-L.

14. For the visitors' hours, see HHD to Emma R. Ball, August 10, 1893, HHD to Mary Polk Yeatman, March 19, 1896, HHD to Captain Blake, February 23, 1901, all HHD-L. For regular employees' difficulty of attending to maintenance during visitors' hours, see HHD to MJMS, April 19, 1895, HHD-L.

15. Lists of permanent employees and their positions appeared in the *MOC* through the 1890s; see, for example, 1895, p. 74; 1896, p. 83; 1899, p. 75. Dodge described Vickers's work to Elna Waln Harrison, April 14, 1903, and Stout's to Emma R. Ball, May 28, 1895, both in HHD-L. For the frequent changes of cook, see HHD-D, June 5, 1897, October 1 and 31, 1898, January 30, 1899, December 14, 1901, and July 13, 1904. Dodge regularly sought and received passes for employees to ride the streetcars and steamboat; see, for example, HHD to G. E. Abbott (president and general manager of the Washington, Alexandria & Mount Vernon Railway), October 12, 1897, HHD-L; HHD to Mt. Vernon & Marshall Hall Steamboat Co., January 3, 1903, HHD-L.

16. HHD to Christine Blair Graham, April 10, 1910, HHD-L.

17. *MOC*, 1903, p. 8; *MOC*, 1906, p. 9; Washington, Alexandria & Mt. Vernon Railway Company, Time-Table in Effect May 1, 1902; Caroline Healey Dall Journals, April 3, 1893, May 12, 1894 (reel 39), MHS; Minnie Kendall-Lowther, *Marshall Hall and Other Potomac Points in Story and Picture* (n.p., 1925), 22–23.

18. HHD to JVRT, July 4, 1895, HHD to Mary Yeatman Webb, April 23, 1903, both in HHD-L.

19. HHD to JVRT, October 7, 1892, HHD-L.

20. *Report of the Mount Vernon Ladies' Association of the Union for 1894* (New Haven, Conn., 1894), 36; *Report of the Mount Vernon Ladies' Association of the Union for 1895* (New Haven, Conn., 1895), 43; *Annual Report of the Mount Vernon Ladies' Association of the Union for 1896* (New Haven, Conn., 1896), 45–46; James M. Lindgren, *Preserving the Old Dominion: Historic Preservation and Virginia Traditionalism* (Charlottesville, Va., 1993).

21. "Guardian of the Tomb"; HHD-D, June 27, 28, July 6, 1898; HHD to JVRT, July 7, 1898, HHD-L.

22. "Guardian of the Tomb"; HHD-D, August 2, 1898; HHD to JVRT, January 6, 1899, HHD-L.

23. Edmund Parker death certificate, December 30, 1898, Vital Records Division,

District of Columbia Department of Health; HHD to JVRT, January 6, February 6, 1899, HHD-L.

24. "Guarded Mt. Vernon Tomb. Death of Edward [sic] Parker, Watchman There for Half a Century," *Washington Post*, December 31, 1899; "A Faithful Guardian of Washington's Tomb," *New York Sun*, January 15, 1899; "The National Capital. Old and New Guard of the Tomb of Washington," *Mansfield (Ohio) News*, February 22, 1899; *Stevens Point (Wis.) Journal*, March 18, 1899; *Daily Iowa State Press*, April 8, 1899; "Washington's Tomb. Mount Vernon Now Guarded by a New Watchman," *Reno (Nev.) Evening Gazette*, April 14, 1899.

25. HHD to JVRT, August 5, 1898, HHD-L.

26. Ibid.; HHD-D, October 4, 5, 1898.

27. "Mt. Vernon's Keeper. Thomas Bushrod, of the Fitzhughs and the Lees. Successor of Edmund Parker," *Washington Post*, February 26, 1899; "Washington's Tomb Has a New Guardian," *Atlanta Constitution*, March 27, 1899; "Sketches of Mount Vernon as It Is Today"; V. M. Herbert, "Mount Vernon: A Pathetic Glimpse," *Anglo-American Magazine* 8 (September 1902): 24.

28. "Mt. Vernon's Keeper"; "At Mount Vernon"; Bertha Gerneaux Davis, "Mount Vernon, the Home of Washington," *Christian Advocate* 73 (February 17, 1898): 264; Lindgren, *Preserving the Old Dominion*, 110; "Draws Many a Visitor. 'The Hermitage' an Attraction to Strangers in Nashville," *Chicago Daily Tribune*, May 23, 1897; Brundage, *The Southern Past*, 32–35.

29. J. Douglas Smith, *Managing White Supremacy: Race, Politics, and Citizenship in Jim Crow Virginia* (Chapel Hill, N.C., 2002), 28; Guild, *Black Laws of Virginia*, 146–47; Roll of Colored Voters Registered at Gum Spring Precinct in Mt. Vernon Magisterial District, Fairfax County, Virginia, Fairfax County General Register, 1902–1903, FxCCA; Howard N. Rabinowitz, *Race Relations in the Urban South, 1865–1890* (New York, 1978), 191; *Acts and Joint Resolutions Passed by the General Assembly of the State of Virginia During the Session of 1899–1900* (Richmond, 1900), 236–37, 340; *Acts and Joint Resolutions Passed by the General Assembly of the State of Virginia During the Extra Session of 1901* (Richmond, 1901), 329–30; "Alexandria News in Brief," *Washington Post*, June 12, 1901; *Acts and Joint Resolutions Passed by the General Assembly of the State of Virginia, During the Session of 1901–1902* (Richmond, 1902), 639–40; Charles E. Wynes, *Race Relations in Virginia 1870–1902* (Charlottesville, Va., 1961), 51–83.

30. "First Case," *Alexandria Gazette*, May 3, 1902; "Arrest of Miss Lee," *Alexandria Gazette*, June 14, 1902; "Sequel to an Episode: Soldiers of South Want Jim Crow Measure Repealed," *Washington Post*, June 16, 1902; "Alexandria's 'Jim Crow' Law," *Washington Post*, February 21, 1904; August Meier and Elliott Rudwick, "Negro Boycotts of Segregated Streetcars in Virginia, 1904–1907," *Virginia Magazine of History and Biography* 81 (October 1973): 479–87.

31. Snowden, *Some Old Historic Landmarks of Virginia and Maryland*, 5–29 (quotations at 10 and 29); Washington, Alexandria & Mt. Vernon Railway Company, Time-Table in Effect May 1, 1902.

32. HHD to JVRT, December 28, 1897, January 11, 1900, HHD-L; HHD to Amy

Townsend, May 28, 1910, HHD-L; H. L. Mencken, "The Plague of Books," *Smart Set* 52 (June 1917): 143.

33. For Whelan's reprise of West Ford's old story, see "Rose of Romance," *Washington Post*, October 17, 1910. Discussions of souvenir sales appear in HHD to JVRT, July 11, 1894, and HHD to HCC, July 3, 1910, both in HHD-L. On the acquisition of old-fashioned equipment to make the old kitchen more authentic, see HHD to Amy Townsend, January 31, 1900, HHD-L. Turn-of-the-century visitors' accounts include Arthur Giles, *Across Western Waves and Home in a Royal Capital* (London, 1898), 74–75; Rufus Rockwell Wilson, *Rambles in Colonial Byways* (Philadelphia, 1901), 228–32; "Daughter to Father Letter," July 11, 1912, MS 202, Kiplinger Library, District of Columbia Historical Society.

34. HHD to JVRT, January 6, 1902, HHD to JVRT, March 7, 1904, HHD to Jennie Meeker Ward, March 9, 1904, HHD to JVRT, April 6, 1904, all HHD-L; Dodge, *Mount Vernon: Its Owner and Its Story*, 95–96; [Edon Hammond], "Mount Vernon," unpublished pamphlet, c. 1905, MVA.

35. [Hammond], "Mount Vernon," 4–6.

36. Washington, Alexandria & Mt. Vernon Railway Company, Time-Table in Effect May 1, 1902; Frederick Tilp, *This Was Potomac River*, 3rd ed. (Alexandria, Va., 1987), 161–62; *Washington Bee*, June 16, 1888; receipt for excursion on the *River Queen*, July 13, 1905, R. H. Lancaster Lodge No. 1370 Records, 1890–1910 (box 76, folder 13), APL-SC. For the development of African American leisure, and particularly Potomac resorts and steamboats, I am indebted to Andrew W. Kahrl of Indiana University, currently writing a dissertation on the subject, for sharing his research and insights.

37. HHD to JVRT, December 17, 1904, May 24, 1905, June 5, August 7, 1906, HHD-L; for the proceedings of the National Negro Young People's Christian and Educational Congress, see *Washington Post*, August 1–6, 1906, especially "Congo Cruelties up at Colored Congress," August 5, 1906, which discusses the delegates' excursions on the *River Queen*.

38. HHD-D, December 9, 1905; HHD to JVRT, January 4, July 7, 1906, HHD-L; Dodge, *Mount Vernon: Its Owner and Its Story*, 95–96; HHD to HCC, February 4, 1913, HHD-L.

39. Ledger: Cash Account, May 1893–April 1909; Thane, *Mount Vernon: The Legacy*, 227–32; HHD to Phoebe Apperson Hearst, June 18, 1909, April 29, 1913, box 48:17–18, George and Phoebe Apperson Hearst Papers, Bancroft Library, University of California, Berkeley; Financial Records, February–December 1908, R. H. Lancaster Lodge No. 1370 Records (box 76, folder 3), APL-SC; Fairfax County Land Tax Records, 1908 and 1909, FxCCA; U.S. census, 1910, Fairfax County, Va., Mount Vernon District, p. 18. Because Virginia did not collect death certificates between 1896 and 1912, the dates of William Robinson's and Smith Johnson's deaths are estimated from the Odd Fellows' payment to Sarah and notations in the Fairfax County tax lists.

40. See the following letters from HHD, all HHD-L: to JVRT, September 9, 1894; to Emma R. Ball, May 28, 1895; to George G. Bain, March 3, 1898; to JVRT,

May 22, 1901; to HCC, June 19, 1910, March 3, April 27, 1911; to Joshua Sherwood, Supt. of Alms House, Alexandria, Va., November 4, 1911.

41. For Hearst's Christmas gifts, see HHD to Hearst, December 26, 1908, December 27, 1911, box 48:17, George and Phoebe Apperson Hearst Papers. The MVLA's provision for Cassie Thomas's tuberculosis is found in HHD to HCC, April 23, 1914, January 1, 6, 19, 1915, HHD-L. For the employment of the next generation of white workers, see HHD to HCC, March 1, 1918, HHD-L.

42. HHD to JVRT, July 7, November 4, 1907, HHD to Ida Richardson, December 23, 1907, HHD to HCC, September 4, 1914, July 1, 1915, February 21, 1918, James Young to HHD, August 28, 1912, all HHD-L. For the employees' housing arrangements, see U.S. census, 1910, Fairfax County, Va., Mount Vernon District, p. 41.

43. "Requisition of Expenses at Mount Vernon," August 23, 1887, HHD-L; HHD to JVRT, August 6, 1903, HHD-L; HHD-D, June 1, 1907; HHD to JVRT, July 5, 1907, HHD-L.

44. HHD to HCC, October 28, 1916, HHD-L; HCC to Ella Waln Harrison, October 30, 1916, Regent's Correspondence files, MVA; Time and Payroll Book, May 1912–March 1917 (showing day laborers' raise to twenty cents an hour, November 1916), MVA.

45. HHD to HCC, October 28, November 5, 16, 23, 1916, HHD-L; HCC to Ella Waln Harrison, November 20, 1916, Regent's Correspondence files, MVA.

46. HHD to HCC, March 10, 1917, HHD-L; World War I draft registration cards, Gum Springs Precinct, Fairfax County, Va., 1917 and 1918 (microfilm in APL-SC); Fairfax County Muster Roll in the War with Germany, FxCCA; HHD to HCC, October 18, 29, 1917, January 21, 26, 31, February 21, 25, 26, March 1, 5, April 8, 11, 1918, HHD-L; Time and Payroll Book, April 1917–January 1922 (showing regular employees' overtime, beginning April 1918), MVA.

47. HHD to HCC, November 4, 1917, HHD-L; Harold Keats, District of Columbia War-Camp Community Service Division, to HCC, April 24, 30, 1918, Regent's Correspondence files, MVA; Commanding Officer, Camp A. A. Humphreys, to HCC, May 13, 1918, Regent's Correspondence files, MVA; HHD to HCC, May 21, June 2, 1918, HHD-L.

48. "Peace by Sword Only . . . Vast Throng at Mount Vernon," *Washington Post*, July 5, 1918; "War Cannot End with Compromise, Wilson Declares," *New York Times*, July 5, 1918; Woodrow Wilson to various ethnic societies, [May 23, 1918], in *The Papers of Woodrow Wilson*, ed. Arthur S. Link (Princeton, N.J., 1985), 48:117; HHD to HCC, August 1, 1918, HHD-L.

49. "War Cannot End with Compromise."

50. "Peace by Sword Only"; Woodrow Wilson, "An Address at Mount Vernon," July 4, 1918, in *Papers of Wilson*, 48:514–17.

51. "A Foolish Boast," *Fort Wayne (Ind.) News and Sentinel*, July 10, 1918; Woodrow Wilson to George Creel, June 18, 1918, in *Papers of Wilson*, 48:346; J. Milton Waldron and John MacMurray to Woodrow Wilson, May 25, 1916, in *Papers of Wilson*, 48:155–61; "German Propaganda among Negroes," *Washington Bee*, July 27, 1918; "Are They German Propagandists?" *Washington Bee*, August 10,

1918; Anne L. Mercer, "Tinner Hill and the Segregation Ordinance of 1915" (unpublished seminar paper, George Washington University, 2000), VHS; E. B. Henderson, "History of the Fairfax County Branch of the NAACP" (Falls Church, Va., 1965).

52. Dodge, *Mount Vernon: Its Owner and Its Story*, 97; Mary Talbert Burnett, "Concerning the Frederick Douglass Memorial," *Crisis* 14 (August 1917): 167; "A Pilgrimage," *Washington Bee*, July 6, 1918; "Pilgrimage to the Home of Frederick Douglass," *Washington Bee*, July 13, 1918; "An Effort to Save the Douglass Home," *Southwestern Christian Advocate* (New Orleans), October 16, 1913.

CONCLUSION: OLD NEGROES, NEW MEMORIALS

1. HHD to HCC, January 8, 1920, HHD-L.

2. Nathan Johnson and Frances Washington, Virginia Bureau of Vital Statistics: Marriages, Alexandria City, 1870–1924 (microfilm reel 55), LVA; Sarah Robinson to County of Fairfax, October 18, 1915, Fairfax County Deed Book Y-7, pp. 326–27, FxCCA; Sarah Robinson to Ernest R. Boyer, September 5, 1918, Fairfax County Deed Book I-8, pp. 118–19, FxCCA; "E. R. Boyer, Contractor," business card, VF Businesses, Box 240, APL-SC; Sarah Robinson, Louisa Bailey, John M. Bailey, Wilbert P. Brown, and Sadie M. Brown to Charles H. Williams, June 7, 1919, Fairfax County Deed Book L-8, pp. 99–100, FxCCA.

3. For Sarah's residence in the Home for the Aged and Infirm, see U.S. census, 1920, Washington, D.C., enumeration district 364, sheet 4B. The only other census listings for "Sarah Robinson" in Fairfax County, Alexandria, or Washington are clearly different people, and Sarah's residence in the home fits with her friends' depiction of her slide into indigence. On the institution, its facilities, and its segregation, see Eighth Annual Report of the Home for the Aged and Infirm, in *Annual Report of the Commissioners of the District of Columbia, Year Ended June 30, 1914* (Washington, D.C., 1914), 793–802 (quotation at 802). On Freedmen's Hospital, see Kevin Boyle, *Arc of Justice: A Saga of Race, Civil Rights, and Murder in the Jazz Age* (New York, 2004), 91–93, 99–100.

4. *Alexandria Gazette*, January 26, 1920; HHD-D, January 27, 28, 29, 1920; HHD to HCC, January 29, 1920, HHD-L; "L. Washington Dies of Pneumonia," *Alexandria Gazette*, January 28, 1920; "Great-nephew of Washington Dead," *Washington Post*, January 29, 1920.

5. "Deaths Reported," *Washington Post*, January 27, 1920; *Alexandria Gazette*, January 26, 1920; HHD-D, January 28, 1920; *Fairfax County, Virginia Gravestones*, vol. 5 (Merrifield, Va., 1998), SA-127–40; visit to Snowden & Bethlehem Cemetery, July 2004.

6. Micki McElya, "Commemorating the Color Line: The National Mammy Monument Controversy of the 1920s," in *Monuments to the Lost Cause*, 203–18; Brundage, *The Southern Past*, 190–99. Early expositions of the New Negro include William Pickens, *The New Negro: His Political, Civil and Mental Status and Related Essays* (New York, 1916), 224–39; Alain Locke, "Enter the New Negro," *Survey Graphic* 6 (March 1925): 631–34.

7. *MOC*, 1928, p. 75; J. F. Manning Company to HHD, January 18 (letter), March 28 (receipt), 1929, Slave Memorial file, MVLA Historic Structures Reports, MVA; *MOC*, 1929, pp. 14–15, 26, 46, 62; Dodge, *Mount Vernon: Its Owner and Its Story*, 97.

8. W.E.B. Du Bois, "George Washington and Black Folk: A Pageant for the Bicentenary, 1732–1932," *Crisis* 39 (April 1932): 121–24; Roumiana Velikova, "Replacing the Father: W.E.B. Du Bois's Reflections on George Washington's Birthday," *Callaloo* 29 (2006): 658–79; Marling, *George Washington Slept Here*, 325–31; Dodge, *Mount Vernon: Its Owner and Its Story*, 60–63, 90–98.

9. Julie Des Jardins, *Women and the Historical Enterprise in America: Gender, Race, and the Politics of Memory, 1880–1945* (Chapel Hill, N.C., 2003), 122–26.

10. "Tomb Watcher: Negro Guards Famous Vault," *Ebony* 10 (October 1955): 135–38; *MOC*, 1936, p. 20; *MOC*, 1965, pp. 5–6, 69. Unlike Sarah Johnson and her compatriots, Holland may really have been the descendant of slaves freed by George Washington's will; see Medford, "Beyond Mount Vernon," 151–52.

11. Dorothy Gilliam, "Remembrance," *Washington Post*, February 6, 1982, p. B1; Jube Shiver, Jr., "A Memorial to Slaves: Mount Vernon Burial Site Officially Opened," *Washington Post*, February 23, 1982, pp. C1, C4.

12. Mike Sager, "30 Teams Vied for Design of Slave Memorial at Mt. Vernon," *Washington Post*, November 3, 1982, p. VA11; Carla Hall, "Renewed Memorial," *Washington Post*, September 5, 1983, p. E7; Phil McCombs, "Repaying a Debt at Mount Vernon: National Memorial Honors Washington's Slaves," *Washington Post*, September 22, 1983, pp. E1–2; Brundage, *The Southern Past*, 162–77, 313–15; Fath Davis Ruffins, "Mythos, Memory, and History: African American Preservation Efforts, 1820–1990," in *Museums and Communities: The Politics of Public Culture*, ed. Ivan Karp, Christine Mullen Kreamer, and Steven D. Lavine (Washington, D.C., 1992), 506–611.

13. McCombs, "Repaying a Debt at Mount Vernon," pp. E1, E4.

14. Programs for annual slave memorial wreath-laying celebrations, "Slave Memorial" vertical file, MVL; "The 2006 Slave Memorial Wreathlaying Ceremony" (program), September 23, 2006; personal observation, September 23, 2006.

15. Information about Mount Vernon's recent interpretation is based on firsthand observation and participation in teacher institutes between 2003 and 2006, as well as conversations with research specialist Mary V. Thompson about Gladys Quander Tancil. Discussions of Mount Vernon's work in recovering African American life include Philip Burnham, *How the Other Half Lived: A People's Guide to American Historic Sites* (Boston, 1995), 43–53; Dennis J. Pogue, "Slave Lifeways at Mount Vernon: An Archaeological Perspective," in *Slavery at the Home of George Washington*, 111–35. Staff publications include Mary V. Thompson, "And Procure for Themselves a Few Amenities: The Private Life of George Washington's Slaves," *Virginia Cavalcade* 48 (1999): 178–90; and Dennis J. Pogue, "The Domestic Architecture of Slavery at George Washington's Mount Vernon," *Winterthur Portfolio* 37 (2002): 3–22.

16. Jennifer L. Eichstedt and Stephen Small, *Representations of Slavery: Race and Ideology in Southern Plantation Museums* (Washington, D.C., 2002), 172–79, classifies

Mount Vernon among plantation sites in the mid-1990s with "segregated knowl-edges" (black history on the grounds, white history in the big house); see also Kee-ley Aurelia McGill, "The Presentation of Slavery at Mount Vernon: Power, Priviledge [sic], and Historical Truth" (master's thesis, University of Maryland, College Park, 2005). The example of enslaved women mentioned by name in the mansion tour is from personal observation, October 7 and November 4, 2006.

17. Roger Wilkins, *Jefferson's Pillow: The Founding Fathers and the Dilemma of Black Patriotism* (Boston, 2001), offers an important meditation on how African Ameri-cans might reconcile their revulsion at the founders' slaveholding with a desire to celebrate American ideals.

18. Conversation with Pamela Nosek, curator, African American Historical Museum and Cultural Center of Iowa, November 1, 2006. Recent examples of the por-trayal of nineteenth-century African American history on America's monumental landscape include the African American Civil War Memorial in Washington, D.C. (1997), the African-American Monument in Columbia, South Carolina (2001), and the National Underground Railroad Freedom Center in Cincinnati (2004).

19. Recognizing slavery on the American historic landscape has been a hard battle, as the essays in James Oliver Horton and Lois E. Horton, eds., *Slavery and Public History: The Tough Stuff of American Memory* (New York, 2006), make clear. But that recognition increasingly occurs, partly because emancipation and the civil rights movement allow many Americans, white as well as black, to cast slavery as a shameful but finished chapter in American history. It is much more difficult to notice, much less commemorate, landscapes of everyday working-class history, a story that continues to this day. This challenge is described in Dolores Hayden, *The Power of Place: Urban Landscapes as Public History.*(Cambridge, Mass., 1995), and Cathy Stanton, *The Lowell Experiment: Public History in a Postindustrial City* (Amherst, Mass., 2006).

ACKNOWLEDGMENTS

The very existence of this book attests to the commitment among the scholarly staff of the Mount Vernon Ladies' Association to telling stories besides George Washington's. From the time I realized that there were resources enough to write a book about Sarah Johnson and her community, members of Mount Vernon's collections, preservation and archaeology, and education divisions have given advice, assistance, and answers to questions of all sorts. Their enthusiasm for this project unfailingly stoked my own, and I cherish their friendship. Research Specialist Mary V. Thompson, who knows more about George Washington and his slaves than anyone else alive, is also the model of scholarly generosity and humor. Mary shared more than two decades of her own research, read the entire manuscript, and saved me from numerous errors large and small. Librarian Barbara McMillan allowed me extraordinary access to archival collections, including uncataloged material. Curator Carol Borchert Cadou, who completed her own book as I was writing this one, provided camaraderie and insight into Mount Vernon's material culture past and present. Dawn Bonner, coordinator of photographic services, helped locate most of the visual images in this book, many published here for the first time. Numerous others currently or formerly on Mount Vernon's staff have aided my research in diverse ways, from sources and anecdotes to behind-the-scenes tours of places that Sarah once knew: Linda Ayres, Ann Bay, Nathan Campbell, Gretchen Goodell, Justin Gunther, Nancy Hayward, Sue Keeler, Jennifer Kittlaus, Phil Mark, Melissa Naulin, Lisa Odum, Dennis Pogue, Jordan Poole, Kimberly Riley, John Rudder, and Esther White.

Along the way I have learned much about Virginia history, the Washington family, and the local African American community from scholars and descendants. Philip Schwarz and Jean B. Lee read the entire manuscript and offered important suggestions and correctives. Frank Grizzard offered support in more ways than I can count. Marie Tyler-McGraw shared her work in progress and introduced me to sites and resources in Jefferson County. Sherrie Carter and Ashton Robinson, descendants of Harriet Newby Robinson, put me on to the early life of Sarah's second husband and shared their painstaking genealogical research. Judith Saunders Burton and Ruby Saunders, descendants of West Ford, shared their scholarship on that family's history. John Washington, the keeper of family history, solved numerous genealogical puzzles. He and Walter Washington of Charles Town, West Virginia, welcomed me into their homes with great hospitality. Conversations with Ron Chase of the Gum Springs Historical Society were always illuminating. Many other scholars have shared their findings and provided assistance great and small: Brigitte Burkett, Helen Deese, Maria Diedrich, Cathy Hellier, Reiko Hillyer, Richard John, Andrew W. Kahrl, Gregg Kimball, Michelle Krowl, Brian Lang, Carolyn Lawes, Lauranett Lee, Kristin Miller, Pamela Nosek, Christine Patrick, Rebecca Starr, Michael Tadman, Craig Tuminaro, Jack Warren, Alton S. Wallace, and Henry Wiencek.

Numerous archives and archivists besides Mount Vernon's contributed pieces to this story. At the Library of Virginia, Brent Tarter has been a friend to this project since the beginning, providing countless research tips and reading most of the manuscript. At the Virginia Historical Society, Greg Stoner and Frances Pollard welcomed my queries, and an unparalleled catalog enabled me to trace connections far beyond the Washington family. At the Fairfax County Courthouse Archives, Sandra Rathbun helped access its range of public documents. Other collections and archivists included the Alexandria Public Library (Special Collections, George Combs); the Maine Women Writers' Collection at the University of Southern Maine (Cally Gurley); the Boston Public Library (Roberta Zonghi); the Rockefeller Library, Colonial Williamsburg (Gail Greve); the New Jersey Historical Society; the New York Public Library; the West Virginia State Archives; the Southern Historical Collection at the University of North Carolina, Chapel Hill; the District of Columbia Historical Society; the National Archives; the Massachusetts Historical Society; and the courthouse archives of Fauquier County and Alexandria, Virginia, and Jefferson County, West Virginia.

I was fortunate to receive financial support from several institutions. A National Endowment for the Humanities Fellowship at the Winterthur Museum, Gardens, and Library and a Peterson Fellowship at the American Antiquarian Society supported initial research that ultimately led to this project. At the Virginia Historical Society, a Mellon Fellowship assisted my research. I owe a particular debt to Ann Fabian, Chris Grasso, Robert Gross, and Stephen Nissenbaum, who wrote letters of support for the fellowships that allowed me to write this book in 2005 and 2006.

At the National Humanities Center, I enjoyed the intellectual, social, and culinary support of an extraordinary community of fellows and staff. Notably, Eliza Robertson, Betsy Dain, and Jean Houston tracked down hundreds of books, articles, and microfilms from libraries across the United States. Karen Carroll copyedited most of the manuscript; Marie Brubaker photocopied more pages than I can count; Lois Whittington saw to daily arrangements from housing to auto mechanics; and Kent Mullikin managed everything with grace and wit. Jane and Martin Rody offered much more than an apartment: friendship, local knowledge, even chicken soup. It is difficult not to mention every fellow and staff member, for all offered advice and camaraderie throughout the year. In particular, Mark Fiege—astute reader, brilliant historian, great friend—helped me untangle many writing knots; he and Phyllis Whitman Hunter, an exemplary reading group, both commented on nearly the entire manuscript. Peter Mallios read the introduction at a critical juncture, and Theresa Braunschneider, Linda Colley, Gary Macy, Christopher Matthews, Janet Ore, Phil Rupprecht, Paul Saint-Amour, Brenda Schildgen, Ben Vinson, Deborah Wong, and Madeline Zilfi provided key insights at opportune moments. Cara Robertson shared (but never overshared) super advice about telling a good story, not to mention cheese sticks, 1930s movies, and great humor.

At the Virginia Foundation for the Humanities, I completed the manuscript amid another superb cohort of fellows. Grace Hale and Bill Freehling each read a portion of the manuscript and offered sharp, smart advice about writing and argument. Katherine McNamara and Ken Bilby followed up my seminar with thoughtful comments. Roberta Culbertson and Ann White Spencer, who coordinate the fellowship program, made a semester in Charlottesville most pleasant. I was also fortunate to present my work to an excellent collective of University of Virginia graduate students, and at Washington and Lee University, thanks to Ted DeLaney, Marc Conner, and a wonderful undergraduate class on African American history.

Eighteen months in the East only deepened my love for home in the West, at the University of Nevada, Reno. A UNR sabbatical and the support of Provost John Frederick, Vice Provost Jannet Vreeland, and Interim Dean Eric Herzik made possible the time necessary to write the book. In the Department of History, the John and Marie Noble Endowment for Historical Research underwrote much of the archival research. A Scholarly and Creative Activities Grant from the College of Liberal Arts defrayed illustration and production costs.

Nobody has done more for this book than Elizabeth Raymond. Elizabeth read all the chapters (often multiple drafts), exchanged countless e-mails with me about argument and evidence, and always reminded me of the power of ordinary people's lives and stories. Ann Ronald read everything with her pitch-perfect ear for purposeful storytelling. Lois Snedden and Greta de Jong each read portions of the manuscript, and Dennis Dworkin asked exactly the right questions about why this story mattered. Other Nevada colleagues, notably Alicia Barber, Stacy Burton, Linda Curcio, Richard Davies, Jane Detweiler, Martha Hildreth, Jen Huntleysmith, Michelle Moran, Andrew Nolan, Bill Rowley, Hugh Shapiro, and Barbara Walker, listened, advised, and suggested readings. In the Northern Nevada Teaching American History Project's 2006 summer seminar, two dozen teachers offered insights into the attempted murder case in chapter 1. Jeffrey Groves, a lifelong westerner, if not a Nevadan, offered immeasurable support and read the first half in an earlier incarnation. Jennifer Johnson provided administrative assistance in myriad ways.

When Eric Rauchway introduced me to Thomas LeBien at a conference many years ago, I had no inkling that working with Hill and Wang would transform how I think about writing. It has done so, thanks to Thomas, to Liz Maples, and especially to June Kim, and I'm profoundly appreciative.

My greatest support has always come from my family. Writing this book has afforded the fringe benefit of time on the East Coast with them. My mother, Frances Casper, lets me pitch base camp in the room where I grew up, tell too many new stories about old history, and coax her into marathon Scrabble sessions—all to my eternal delight. Muriel Gutman, my grandmother and biggest fan, doesn't buy green bananas anymore and has wanted this book to come out yesterday for longer than I can recall. My brother, Andrew Casper, sister, Tracy Casper Lang, and brother-in-law, Eric Lang, the consummate New York hosts, all offered important advice early in this project. And the best reasons to visit New York are Audrey, Emily, and Oliver Lang.

INDEX

First Michigan Colored Infantry,
  98–99
fish, 37, 43, 50, 85, 88
Florida, 21, 145
folk beliefs, 161
Ford, Almira, 100
Ford, Andrew, 40, 59, 79–80, 91, 93, 94,
  98–101, 144, 169, 213, 225, 238n8;
  in army, 98–100, 105–106
Ford, Barney, 122
Ford, Ellen, 93, 148
Ford, Fanny, 93, 120
Ford, George, 158, 170, 175–76, 180,
  218, 220
Ford, George W., 168–69, 259n19
Ford, Henrietta, 76, 168, 255n18
Ford, Joe, 40, 46, 59, 61, 91, 93, 94, 96,
  97, 98, 109, 119, 120, 238n8
Ford, Priscilla, 26–27, 238n8
Ford, West (old), 24–27, 38, 40, 46, 50,
  56, 58–60, 64, 75–78, 85, 86, 95,
  109, 115, 120, 134, 162, 168, 175,
  179, 180, 185, 191, 219, 221,
  235n37, 238n8, 244n37, 256n19;
  death of, 95
Ford, West (young), 37, 40, 59, 91, 93,
  94, 96, 97, 98, 109, 119, 128, 130,
  134, 143, 148–49, 158, 165, 168–70,
  175–76, 180, 185, 194, 218, 219,
  238n8, 256n19
Ford, William, 27, 76, 77, 85, 88, 120,
  168, 238n8, 255n18, 256n19
Fort Sumter, 81
Fourteenth Amendment, 119
Fraser, 87
Frazier, George, 29, 37
free blacks, 13–15, 25–27, 32, 40, 42,
  55, 59–60; registered, 27
Freedmen's Bureau, 95–98
Freedmen's Hospital, 215, 216
Freedmen's Village, 83, 201
Freedom's Journal, 33
freedpeople, 6, 93–106, 110; education,
  121–22; labor, 93–106, 107–31, 148;
  legal rights, 97–98, 138; postwar life

and work, 107–31; *see also* employees,
  black
free labor ideology, 46, 94–95, 96, 104,
  105, 148
Freese, Jacob, 94
Frémont, John C., 89
Frobel, Anne, 82
Fugitive Slave Law, 60
furnishings, 12, 64, 90, 110, 112–15,
  139–41, 159, 161, 164, 188;
  authenticity issue, 113–15

Gabriel, *see* Johnson, Gabriel
Gabriel's Rebellion, 13
Gage, Homer, 143
gardens, 25, 28, 30, 39, 41, 53, 102,
  108n, 125–26, 134, 168–70, 203,
  210; slave, 53–54, 170; Wishing Rose
  tale, 168, 202
Gardner, Alexander, 134
Garrison, William Lloyd, 32, 34
George II, King of England, 25
Georgia, 8, 34, 69, 117, 144, 145, 156
Gettysburg, 103, 140, 186, 187, 212
Gibbs, Edward C., 120, 136, 152
Gibbs, Joseph, 179
Gibbs restaurant, 179, 190, 202
Gilliam, Dorothy, 221
Glymont, 204
Gone with the Wind (Mitchell), 218
Grand Army of the Republic, 100;
  convention (1892), 180–81
Grant, Ulysses S., 116, 120, 124; tomb
  of, 186
graveyards, *see* tombs and graveyards
Great Britain, 35, 203
Greeley, Horace, 72
Green, Nancy, 189
guano, 44, 45, 50
guidebook, 65, 138, 142, 166, 201–202,
  219
Gum Springs, 53, 60, 76, 120, 137, 163,
  168, 169, 175, 176, 179–80, 190,
  200, 215, 221